
VOLUME XVIII/2

New Institutions for Human Rights Protection

The Collected Courses of the Academy of European Law
Edited by Professor Marise Cremona,
Professor Bruno de Witte, and Professor Franceso Francioni
Assistant Editor: Anny Bremner

This series brings together the Collected Courses of the Academy of European Law in Florence. The Academy's mission is to produce scholarly analyses which are at the cutting edge of the two fields in which it works: European Union law and human rights law. A 'general course' is given each year in each field, by a distinguished scholar and/or practitioner, who either examines the field as a whole through a particular thematic, conceptual, or philosophical lens, or who looks at a particular theme in the context of the overall body of law in the field. The Academy also publishes each year a volume of collected essays with a specific theme in each of the two fields.

New Institutions for Human Rights Protection

Edited by
KEVIN BOYLE
Professor of Law at the University of Essex

OXFORD
UNIVERSITY PRESS

OXFORD
UNIVERSITY PRESS

Great Clarendon Street, Oxford OX2 6DP

Oxford University Press is a department of the University of Oxford.
It furthers the University's objective of excellence in research, scholarship,
and education by publishing worldwide in

Oxford New York

Auckland Cape Town Dar es Salaam Hong Kong Karachi
Kuala Lumpur Madrid Melbourne Mexico City Nairobi
New Delhi Shanghai Taipei Toronto
With offices in
Argentina Austria Brazil Chile Czech Republic France Greece
Guatemala Hungary Italy Japan South Korea Poland Portugal
Singapore Switzerland Thailand Turkey Ukraine Vietnam

Oxford is a registered trade mark of Oxford University Press
in the UK and in certain other countries

Published in the United States
by Oxford University Press Inc., New York

Reprinted 2010

ISBN 978-0-19-957054-6

Printed in the United Kingdom by
Lightning Source UK Ltd., Milton Keynes

Summary Contents

Contents

List of Contributors

Gudmundur Alfredsson was Professor of International Law at the University of Lund until 2008 and a former director of the Raoul Wallenberg Institute. He is now Professor at the Faculty of Social Sciences at the University of Akureyri and Invited Professor at the Law Faculty at the Robert Schuman University, Strasbourg. He was a member of the UN Sub-Commission on the Promotion and Protection of Human Rights (2004–6) and Chairman of the UN Working Group on Minorities (2006). He is Editor-in-Chief of the *International Journal on Minority and Group Rights.*

Nadia Bernaz is a lecturer in law at the University of Middlesex. She previously held a lectureship in human rights law at the Irish Centre for Human Rights, National University of Ireland, Galway. She holds a PhD in public international law from the University Paul Cézanne, Aix-Marseille. Her monograph, *Le droit international et la peine de mort,* was published in 2008.

Kevin Boyle is Professor of Law, University of Essex and was the director of the Human Rights Centre until 2007. He was senior adviser to Mary Robinson then UN High Commissioner for Human Rights, 2001–2. He is Chair of the International Council of Minority Rights Group. His publications include Mary Robinson, *A Voice for Human Rights* (2006).

Olivier De Schutter is Professor at the University of Louvain and at the College of Europe (Natolin), and a member of the Global Law School Faculty at New York University. He chaired the EU Network of Independent Experts on Fundamental Rights (2002–6) and is currently the Senior International Expert for the Network of legal experts of the EU Fundamental Rights Agency (FRALEX). In 2008 he was appointed UN Special Rapporteur on the Right to Food.

Sir Nigel Rodley is Professor of Law and Chair of the Human Rights Centre, University of Essex. He has been a Member of the Human Rights Committee since 2001 and served as UN Special Rapporteur on Torture of the UN Commission on Human Rights (1993–2001). He is the author of *The Treatment of Prisoners in International Law* (2nd edn, 1999, 3rd edn, 2009 forthcoming).

Isabelle Rorive is Professor in Comparative Law, Anti-discrimination Law and Methodology of Law at the University of Brussels (Université Libre de Bruxelles). She is an active member of the European Network of Legal Experts in the Non-discrimination Field and lectures on equality law in various fora, including the French High Authority against Discrimination and for Equality.

Table of Cases

Table of Legislation

CHARTERS

CONVENTIONS

COVENANTS

DECLARATIONS

DIRECTIVES

PROTOCOLS

REGULATIONS

STATUTES

Belgium

Ireland

Sweden

UK

Treaties

Introduction

Kevin Boyle

From the outset of the international human rights movement with the proclamation of the Universal Declaration of Human Rights, an abiding theme has been that of implementation. How might the human rights commitments made by states be translated into protection for individuals in practice? Sixty years after the Declaration was proclaimed it remains the central challenge. Human rights institutions, international, regional, and national, provide an indispensable means to meet that challenge and hence their importance for study.

It is a characteristic of sovereignty that it is for the state alone to secure its international commitments within its jurisdiction. But the entitlement of the international community to monitor or hold the state to account for its human rights failings has emerged as an accepted fact in international relations, even if remains an uneasily established principle and one which still provokes claims of interference in internal affairs. More accepted, and perhaps more productive, is the willingness of states to request international assistance in the implementation of human rights commitments including with the creation of effective institutions or with institutional reform.

Nevertheless, with the agreement of states, institutions, and mechanisms have been created at global and regional levels which have given substance to the idea of international protection. States in turn have been influenced to establish at national level a range of institutions for human rights protection. The totality of these institutional arrangements within and beyond the state can be thought of as constituting, however imperfectly, a highly connected if not yet a single system of human rights protection. The constant exchange of ideas and information including judicial precedents, vertically and horizontally between institutions, which has accelerated enormously with new communications technology, and the entitlement of different actors including Non-Governmental Organizations (NGOs) and National Human Rights Institutions (NIHRIs) to participate at all levels, represent hopeful developments. Alfredsson's account of the normative and institutional advances of minority rights through the Council of Europe and the Organisation for Security and Co-Operation in Europe (OSCE) as well as within the UN, demonstrates well this interconnectedness of protection efforts.

The problem, however, is that these developments have had but limited impact on effective implementation. One cause for celebration of the Universal Declaration is the global recognition of its enduring values and aspirations. But the credibility of human rights remains highly vulnerable when measured against the reality of violation and the failure of states to respect the corpus of international law obligations that has been so painstakingly established.

A little acknowledged but powerful diagnosis of the conditions which human rights institutions, national and international, exist to remedy was produced in 2005 by the UN High Commissioner for Human Rights.[1] Prepared as part of the process of UN institutional reform launched by the former Secretary General, Kofi Annan, its analysis provides a sobering context for the challenges that face both old and new human rights institutions. The Plan identifies the 'implementation gap' between the agreed human rights principles and norms and the experience of perhaps the majority of humankind who are denied their protection. It recites a number of challenges that account for the gap including, above all, poverty which affects a billion people and undermines the universality of human rights. Poverty, the Report notes, is a reflection of global inequalities as well as the persistence of discrimination practiced or tolerated on all the grounds prohibited in international law. A connected challenge is that of the suffering and human rights abuse that arises from armed conflict and violence including terrorism. Civilians are the predominant victims of conflicts and are subject to indiscriminate killings, disappearances, massacres, ethnic cleansing, and forced displacement. The repressive responses by states result in a further challenge, that of impunity. While there has been positive progress in establishing accountability for the worst atrocities through international criminal prosecutions, impunity for torture, rape, and arbitrary killings at national level represents the depressing norm. To this catalogue the Report adds the challenges of the weakness of democratic systems in many countries alongside the absence of the Rule of Law. Effective governmental institutions including executive authorities, parliaments, judicial, and policing systems are needed if human rights are to be realized. But too often, the High Commissioner notes, such institutions are weak, corrupt, and inefficient. Against this backdrop of global human rights and development realities, the challenges for human rights institutions whether at UN, regional, or national levels are formidable.

The High Commissioner's analysis of implementation challenges acknowledged the influence of Kofi Annan's central thesis on UN reform, that progress on human rights protection was directly linked to the pursuit of the other purposes for which the United Nations was established; development, peace, and security. Changing the world's human rights record requires deep change in the global economic and political order. Change is not a matter of institutional reform alone but requires the full commitment of states to the cooperation which the UN Charter requires if global peace and social justice is to be achieved. In concrete terms this should mean, for example, a determination to achieve the Millennium Development Goals (MDGs) by 2015. While all states endorsed the MDGs in

[1] *The OHCHR Plan of Action: Protection and Empowerment* (Geneva, 2005).

the Millennium Summit and its follow up in 2005, their full realization in that time scale remains a remote prospect.

A fresh opportunity at the global level for leadership and a new impetus for human rights implementation has arisen from the establishment of the United Nations Human Rights Council in 2006. This new intergovernmental institution replaced the former Commission on Human Rights that had been in existence for the previous 60 years. As Boyle notes the agreement on creating a new Human Rights Council at the 2005 UN Summit, seen against the failure of larger institutional reform goals that were in prospect in particular in respect of the Security Council, was a relatively minor achievement. The case for expansion of permanent membership of the Security Council is acknowledged by the international community. But disagreements over which states from the South should have permanent seats and over deeper reforms of the Council left the issue unresolved. Continued failure to achieve an expanded Council, to reflect the new geopolitical and economic conditions of the 21st century, must diminish the capacity of the United Nations to be the effective multilateral forum it needs to be if its interconnected goals of global security and peace, development, and universal human rights are to be achieved.

The pressure for the abolition of the Commission on Human Rights on the claim that it had become increasingly politicized and ineffective was generated by Western states led by the United States. However the decision to replace it was not resisted by other states. A consensus does appear to have emerged that the Commission's authority and standing had much diminished and that the new Council offered a fresh opportunity to assert a higher priority for UN human rights work.

Those who promoted the new Human Rights Council hoped it might be constituted with equal status to the other Councils, the Security Council, and the Economic and Social Council giving an institutional reflection of the equal and connected nature of UN purposes. That was agreed to be a possible option for the future when the institution falls for review in 2011. For now, the Council is established as a subsidiary body of the General Assembly whereas its predecessor the Commission was answerable to the Economic and Social Council. The elevated status of the new Council, along with the greater frequency of its meetings as compared with the Commission, are key differences distinguishing it from its predecessor.

General Assembly Resolution 60/251 establishing the Human Rights Council enjoined it 'to preserve and build on the achievements [of the Commission] and to redress its shortcomings'. The Commission's standard setting achievements as the body that drafted the Universal Declaration of Human Rights and its later contributions, including through its Sub-Commission, to much of the corpus of international law of human rights built on the Declaration, are well known. Its role over the decades in the development of the system of special procedures which have come to represent an indispensable vehicle of international scrutiny and protection as well as for the development of international human rights norms is a further achievement. That system has been reviewed by the new Human Rights Council and has been preserved. In the review process, however, the pressure from some states to constrain the freedom of action of the special procedures was starkly evident and is unlikely to abate in the years ahead. The competence of the former Commission to receive, assess, and respond to complaints of gross and reliably attested violations of human rights has also been preserved, albeit it is too early to determine what use NGOs and victims will make of this confidential complaint procedure and whether Council members will cooperate across the regional groups to develop its potential.

The shortcomings of the former Commission on Human Rights relate to the intrusion of the political divisions between states and their regional groups and political blocs into its meetings. Its downfall arose from these tensions and the new Council was formally directed to ensure that it was guided by the principles of 'universality, impartiality, objectivity and non selectivity' in its work. These principles are much invoked by states in the Council's sessions to date, but they have hardly been successful in suppressing political differences from emerging. Scepticism over the possibility of the Council transcending the faults of the Commission remains. The United States, the chief critic of the former Commission, has already withdrawn from the Council as an observer state (it has not stood for election), citing in particular the excessive targeting of Israel. A key issue is how the new Administration in Washington after the November 2008 presidential elections will behave. As Boyle notes, the largely negative posture of the current US Administration towards the council from its inception dishonours that country's proud history as the progenitor of the Commission on Human Rights. It is not a constructive position to write off this central pillar of the United Nations human rights system and is not one followed by the European Union. The majority of the state members elected to the Human Rights Council are from the Asian and African regional groups and many are members of cross-regional blocs such as the Organisation of the Islamic Conference (OIC) and the Non-Aligned Movement (NAM). That was also the case in the last decades of the former Commission but in the somewhat reduced size of the Council their dominance is more pronounced. It is therefore the human rights priorities and policies of the developing world which dominate and will continue to dominate the Council, not those of developed states. Hence the need for the other principle which the Council is enjoined to uphold, 'constructive international dialogue and co-operation'. Nevertheless the Human Rights Council will face considerable challenges if the most powerful state in the world persists in its boycott of the new body.

Much of the work of the Council in its first and 'institution building year' 2006–7 has been codification and simplification of the inherited practices and mechanisms of the former Commission. Alfredsson expresses concern that the process in the case of minorities, which has seen the replacement of the former

Working Group on Minorities with a Minorities Forum, will diminish not enhance the Council's engagement with minority rights. But there has been innovation also, in particular the new mechanism of universal periodic review (UPR). Under this mechanism all UN member states will submit to a periodic review of their human rights performance to be conducted by their peers on the Human Rights Council over a cycle of four years. The idea was born in response to the most persistent complaint that had undermined the legitimacy of the Commission on Human Rights, namely that the powerful could avoid being the target of international attention or action over their human rights problems and violations but weaker states could not. The intention was to institute UPR as a cooperative mechanism to review the practice of all states as regards their human rights obligations and commitments. UPR it was hoped might help not only to diminish the palpable politicization and the claims of double standards that had dogged the Commission, but might also prove more effective in inducing states to strengthen human rights protection at home. Boyle notes the positive features of the first reviews which began in 2008 in terms of the constructive atmosphere of the process, the degree of self-criticism, and the relative openness of at least some of the states under review to address issues raised on their performance by other states. Bernaz, while acknowledging the inherently political nature of the United Nations as an intergovernmental body, seeks to study the new UPR mechanism from the standpoint of public international law. One part of her contribution is to examine the sources on which the UPR is to be conducted. In particular she questions the inclusion in the sources of review of both treaty-based commitments of states and soft law sources such as their voluntary commitments and pledges. One value of this contribution is that it documents the arguments in the Council over the potential sources for evaluating human rights performance by states. Whether as practice evolves states will seek to confine their responsibilities to such obligations which arise from treaty commitments alone will be interesting to observe. But Bernaz does note that one positive result of the voluntary commitments, such as those made by states when standing for election to the Council, arises when the commitment made is to become party to human rights treaties. Indeed announcement by states that they intend to ratify treaties has been a feature of a number of UPR sessions to date.

Creating or re-designing institutions, whether global, regional, or national, inevitably raises issues over the impact of change on other bodies and actors that work in the same field. Questions that may appear bureaucratic and technical concerning overlapping functions and duplication often disguise concerns over institutional competition. This theme arises in Rodley's account of the United Nations system, in de Schutter's study of the genesis of the new European Union Fundamental Rights Agency, and equally Rorive's analysis of national level human rights equality bodies in EU countries. Rodley reminds us that the UN human rights protection efforts as they have evolved are bifurcated between a treaty-based system and the intergovernmental institution of the Human Rights

Council. He explores first the question of potential conflict or complementarity between the new Council and the treaty bodies which supervise the implementation of the human rights treaties. The particular focus of interest is the UPR system. In establishing the Council, the General Assembly directed that UPR should 'complement and not duplicate the work of the treaty bodies'. But as Rodley notes, no guidance was given as to how this was to be achieved. The similarities in the UPR mechanism, which is primarily based on the state's own report, and the report prepared by a state for a treaty body are, he concedes, considerable. A fear expressed had been that if a recommendation made to the state under review by a state participating in UPR review consisted of a request to implement a recommendation made in the 'conclusions' of a treaty body and the state rejected this, then the authority of the treaty body would be undermined. Whether this will arise or not, some states conducting the UPR have recommended that the state under review implement treaty body proposals, which suggests a positive and reinforcing use of the work of the treaty bodies in the UPR. A further concern expressed was over the possibility that the Council would itself adopt 'conclusions' under UPR which might be different or even conflict with those of treaty bodies. In the event, the outcome document of UPR does not take this latter approach, listing only the recommendations made to the state and identifying those which the concerned state accepts and those it does not, as well as recording any voluntary commitments it has made. However, UPR is in its earliest phase and it is premature to judge how this new mechanism may ultimately relate to the treaty system.

Bernaz offers the interesting speculation that should the UPR mechanism over time be judged successful and if attention returns to rationalization of the different components of the UN human rights machinery, then UPR might conceivably come to replace the system of reporting to the treaty bodies. Rodley notes that had the former Commission on Human Rights achieved a comprehensive supervisory function over states' human rights commitments at the outset, the later treaty body reporting system might not have been created. There is no doubt that the treaty system which now includes eight core treaties constitutes a significant burden on states in terms of reporting obligations. To that has now been added the UPR report. The former High Commissioner Louise Arbour strongly supported treaty body reform and promoted the option of one standing treaty body receiving a single report from states relating to their multiple human rights treaty commitments. That proposal has not been supported by states and, for now, it seems likely that the two-track system, the treaties, and the Human Rights Council with its new mechanism of UPR, will continue to operate. Apart from the innovation of UPR, the parallel functioning of the Council and treaty bodies raises a further issue namely that of the respective roles of the Council's independent experts, the special procedures, and the treaty bodies. Rodley recalls that once the treaty bodies had come into existence, concern was expressed over duplication and the continued need for the special procedures was even questioned by some states. In the event, the special procedures prospered and represent the most important protection mechanism inherited from the former Commission on Human Rights. Rodley's detailed study finds that the overlap between the system of special procedures and the treaty bodies is minimal in practice and that synergy between both has grown through better communication, such as has been engendered by the now annual meeting of chairs of treaty bodies and the special procedures.

But with the arrival of the Human Rights Council, the plurality of specialist human rights institutions and mechanisms within the United Nations (and to the list should be added the significantly expanded Office of the High Commissioner for Human Rights) will need to address how their common mission is advanced rather than impeded by their separate institutional foundations. One role given by the General Assembly to the new Council is to work for the better coordination as well as mainstreaming of human rights within the United Nations system as a whole. The High Commissioner for Human Rights has a similar mandate. The tensions which have already emerged in the relationship between the High Commissioner and the Council suggest, however, that progress on coordination and rationalization of the UN system will neither be immediate nor dramatic.

The unique density and complexity of the human rights institutions of Europe, as compared to other regions, is well known. One challenge, as in the case of the UN, is how to ensure harmonious co-existence and cooperation rather than duplication and competition between institutions. De Schutter's account of the genesis of the new EU Fundamental Rights Agency (FRA) reviews the extensive consultations between the EU and the Council of Europe over the concerns that the latter might suffer an eclipse in its human rights mission in particular, were the FRA to develop an active monitoring function for EU member states (and accession states), all of which are also members of the Council of Europe and subject to its monitoring mechanisms. He notes that similar concerns were expressed by the Council of Europe during the negotiations over the EU Charter of Fundamental Rights in 1999–2000. All EU member states, in addition to their Council of Europe commitments, are also subject to the monitoring mechanisms of the UN human rights system, including now UPR. De Schutter argues that such duplication as exists with UN and Council of Europe instruments has not proved to be a problem and has not resulted in the reduction of human rights standards.

Nevertheless, while the concerns of the Council of Europe may have been misplaced, the ultimate mandate given the FRA steered away from any explicit monitoring of EU human rights standards such as under the EU Charter. The new institution will undertake thematic studies rather than country-specific studies, in deference to the Council of Europe's country work. FRA builds upon its predecessor body, the European Union Monitoring Centre on Racism and Xenophobia (EMUC), and will offer assistance and expertise to EU bodies and member states on fundamental rights when implementing Community law.

FRA is directed to cooperate closely with the Council of Europe, as well as other organizations including the OSCE and the United Nations. The special relationship of the Council of Europe with the FRA is expressed additionally by its right to appoint an independent person to the FRA's Executive and Management Boards. De Schutter is confident that the FRA, which is now operational, will develop a significant role in enhancing the promotion and protection of fundamental rights within an enlarged and more diverse Union. It should also contribute to the deepening of cooperation on human rights between the EU, the Council of Europe, and the OSCE.

The FRA mandate explicitly continues EMUC's work on racism, xenophobia, and related intolerance. This is consonant with the Union's long established commitment to equality and the elimination of ethnic, racial, and sex discrimination. With respect to sex discrimination, that commitment is reflected in a further new European level institution, the European Gender Equality Institute established by Regulation (EC) No 1922/2006. Based in Vilnius, the Institute is directed to work cooperatively with the FRA. At national level, the two Equality Directives of 2000—the Racial Equality Directive and the Employment Equality Directive—required member states to designate or establish equality bodies to promote equality of treatment. In analysing these specialized bodies Rorive notes the great diversity of their origins and mandates. Some existed prior to the Directives, others were a response to them. A general trend now to be discerned is the creation of comprehensive bodies that work across all discrimination grounds through the merging of existing single discrimination ground bodies. Many national equality bodies are given implementation authority beyond research and advisory work. They can have investigatory powers, initiate litigation on behalf of victims, and can undertake dispute resolution as well as training and promotional campaigns. It is of interest to note, as Rorive brings out, that many equality bodies have been influenced in their attributes, particularly as regards their independence, by the UN Paris Principles 1993 drawn up for specialized human rights bodies or national human rights institutions. Indeed an emerging further stage of reordering of national bodies in Europe could be the amalgamation of equality and human rights bodies such as has occurred in Britain and has been proposed in Ireland.

The focus of the essays in this volume is on recent developments in respect to global and also European human rights institution. But there is ongoing debate, reform, and innovation in respect of human rights institutions involving states in other world regions which should be noted. Thus, in 2006, the General Assembly of the Organization of American States initiated a dialogue between the organs of the Inter-American Convention on Human Rights, the Commission and the Court, and state parties to the Convention, with the aim of agreeing procedural reforms of the Inter American system.

The Arab League, which comprises 22 states, adopted a revised Human Rights Charter in May 2004, to replace a much criticized 1994 text that had never entered into force and which was not consistent with international human rights standards. The revised Charter received its seventh ratification on 15 January 2008, and entered into force on 15 March 2008. The Charter establishes a committee of seven members which will review state reports. Members are required to be expert and will serve for a four-year term in their personal capacity. The Committee, which is yet to be formed, will review state reports. When established it will be the first independent human rights institution to supervise the implementation of a human rights treaty within the League of Arab States.

In June 1998, the states parties to the African Charter on Human and Peoples Rights adopted a Protocol establishing an African Court of Human and Peoples' Rights, alongside the African Commission. This protocol entered into force in January 2004 with the Court coming into existence in 2006. In a decision motivated by financial considerations, African Union leaders then decided that the new African Human Rights Court should merge with the African Court of Justice of the African Union. This will be achieved by a further protocol which has now been agreed by the African Union and has been opened for adoption by member states. However, the limited number of states to date which have ratified the 1998 protocol suggests that an African Union Court with continent-wide human rights jurisdiction will not be achieved easily or soon.

In Asia, the United Nations has over several decades encouraged states to establish both national level human rights institutions and regional human rights protection arrangements. There has been progress in the establishment of national human rights institutions in a number of countries. At regional level, an important step occurred in November 2007 when the Association of South East Asian States (ASEAN) adopted a Charter for this grouping at its 13th Summit in Singapore. The Charter aims to provide ASEAN with a legal personality and to establish more clearly its institutional framework and rules of procedure. Ratification of the Charter by the ten member states of ASEAN is expected by December 2008. The Charter provides for the establishment of a human rights body. Agreement on the latter's creation and its mandate is expected by the end of 2009. Meanwhile, in the Pacific, NGOs continue to promote debate with governments over the need for a regional charter and ultimately a regional human rights commission or other protection mechanism for the 22 Pacific islands and territories.

The creation of new human rights institutions or the reform of existing human rights bodies properly induces a degree of optimism about the strengthening of human rights protection and the continued commitment of states to that goal. The essays collected here address primarily the institutional features of such initiatives. But the added value of such institutions must ultimately be measured by what improvement is registered in the implementation of human rights norms for the benefit of individuals and communities. The gap between aspiration and achievement in the field of human rights remains the challenge for the entire international community.

1

The United Nations Human Rights Council: Origins, Antecedents, and Prospects

Kevin Boyle

The human rights business at the United Nations is very much one of seeking to advance idealism in the midst of hard nosed politics. Idealism without political understanding amounts to amateurism[1]

1. Introduction

This chapter will provide an account of a new human rights institution, the United Nations Human Rights Council. Its emphasis will be on its institutional history; how and why in 2006 the Council came to be established and the composition, functions, and powers bestowed upon it by the General Assembly. It will also give an account of the institution which the Council replaced, the United Nations Commission on Human Rights, and will conclude with some reflections on the likely prospects for the Council based on two years experience of its functioning to date.

A. Chronology

The chronology of the transition from Commission on Human Rights to Human Rights Council is straightforward to record and important to bear in mind. From 14–16 September 2005, the United Nations Secretary General convened in New York what became the largest ever gathering of the world's heads of state and government in a follow up to the Millennium Summit of 2000.[2] The Millennium +5 Summit was convened both to review progress made on the Millennium Development Goals and to agree on a package of reforms for the

[1] B Ramcharan, 'Norms and Machinery' in TG Weiss & S Daws (eds), *The Oxford Handbook of the United Nations* (2007) 450.

[2] United Nations Millennium Declaration, A/Res/55/2, 18 September 2000.

United Nations on the 60th anniversary of its creation. The Summit did not achieve agreement on the most pressing issue of institutional reform, that of the Security Council, but did approve in principle the creation of a Human Rights Council to replace the Commission on Human Rights.[3] On 15 March 2006, after months of difficult negotiations, the General Assembly adopted Resolution 60/251 establishing the Human Rights Council.[4] On 22 March, the Economic and Social Council (ECOSOC) voted to dissolve the Commission on Human Rights.[5] On 27 March the Commission concluded its 62nd brief and final session in Geneva.[6] The new Human Rights Council held its inaugural session in Geneva from 9–30 June 2006.[7] By the end of its fifth session in June 2007 it had agreed upon a major document on its institutional architecture, including a formal agenda and programme of work, meeting the deadline for these goals set by Resolution 60/251.[8] The Council concluded its eighth regular session on 18 June 2008, with no less than seven special sessions being held since its inception in June 2006.[9]

B. Overview: Council Compared to Commission

Like its predecessor, the Human Rights Council is an intergovernmental body and is comprised of representatives of 47 member states. At its abolition the Commission had 53 members. The differences between the two bodies will be discussed in more detail later, but at the outset a number of features of the Council should be mentioned which, taken together, may give rise to some optimism for its prospect of strengthening international human rights protection. First, the new Council is established as a subsidiary organ of the General Assembly, whereas the former Commission was one of a number of subsidiary bodies of ECOSOC. This enhanced status for the Council is intended to, and should have, the effect of making its deliberations more authoritative, visible, and influential within the United Nations as well as outside it. Within five years, the General Assembly will review the status of the Council and the original hopes of reformers that it might become a full Council in its own right alongside the existing Security Council and the Economic and Social Council will be an option.[10] Secondly,

[3] 2005 World Summit Outcome, UN Doc A/60/l (2005) paras 157–9.

[4] GA/Res/60/251, 15 March 2006.

[5] ECOSOC Res 2006/2, 22 March 2006.

[6] Commission on Human Rights Report on the Sixty-Second Session, E/CN.4/2006/122, 13–27 March 2006.

[7] First Report of the Human Rights Council, A/61/53 (2006).

[8] Institution-building of the United Nations Human Rights Council, A/HRC/Res/5/1, 18 June 2007.

[9] Information and comprehensive documentation on the Human Rights Council and its sessions to date are available on the Office of the High Commissioner for Human Rights website, <http://www.ohchr.org>.

[10] GA/Res/60/251, para 1. The Council in turn is directed to undertake a review of its work and function after five years (or by 2011) and report to the General Assembly, para 16.

the Council is virtually a standing body; it is required to meet for 10 weeks per year over at least three sessions with the option of holding special sessions at the request of a third of its membership.[11] In contrast, the Commission on Human Rights met for a single six-week session each year.[12] Thirdly, the Council has been given a new task of immense potential, that of establishing and conducting for all states a peer review system, the Universal Periodic Review (UPR), in respect of their human rights obligations and commitments.[13] The modalities of UPR were agreed by the Council in June 2007 and in September 2007 a calendar for the review of all 192 UN member states over a four-year cycle was adopted.[14] The first session of UPR involving 16 states was held in April 2008 and a second session also involving 16 states was held in May 2008.[15]

An important difference between the former Commission and the Council lies in the system of election of its members and the standards to be met by candidate states. Members of the Council are to be elected for the allocated regional distribution of seats 'directly and individually' by secret ballot and by a simple majority of the General Assembly's 192 members.[16] The Commission's membership had been elected by the smaller electorate of ECOSOC with its 54 members and was often agreed upon without election from previously agreed regional 'clean slates' of candidates. Where this resulted in the presence on the Commission of states with questionable human rights records, controversy flared.[17]

When electing members of the Council, states are directed to weigh candidate states' human rights records and voluntary pledges that they have made on improving national human rights protection.[18] No such standards existed for election to the Commission. All elected Council members will be considered under the UPR process during their tenure on the Council. Where a state elected to the Council is responsible for gross and systematic violations of human rights, the General Assembly could suspend that state from the Council.[19] To encourage rotation of its members no state can be elected for more that two terms without

[11] Ibid, para 10.

[12] Including the meetings of its subsidiary body, the Advisory Committee on Human Rights, and intra-sessional working groups the Human Rights Council will likely hold meetings for 25 weeks a year.

[13] UPR is not entirely without precedent. During the 1950s a system of annual human rights reports to the Commission on Human Rights from all states had been approved at the initiative of the United States. See H Tolley Jr, *The U.N. Commission on Human Rights* (1987), 36–40 and Alston 'Reconceiving the UN Human Rights Regime: Challenges Confronting the New UN Human Rights Council', 7 Melbourne Journal of International Law 2006, 185–224 at 201.

[14] The Council's year runs from the commencement of its first session (ie from 19 June).

[15] Full documentation for these cycles of UPR can be accessed on the Human Rights Council web page, n 9 above.

[16] Thus a state would have to obtain at least 96 votes of support in the secret ballot to be elected.

[17] See below, Commission on Human Rights.

[18] GA/Res/60/251, para 8.

[19] Ibid, para 8. A two-thirds majority vote of members present and voting is required.

leaving the Council.[20] One effect of the latter rule is to put an end to a convention or practice that had operated intermittently under the Commission on Human Rights, whereby the Permanent Five on the Security Council would be assured of a seat.[21] At present all five are elected members of the new Council with the significant exception of the United States. The United States voted against Resolution 60/251 creating the Council in the General Assembly on the grounds that the Council was flawed.[22] It decided not to stand for election but promised to participate in the Council's meetings and to work constructively with it.[23] The United States did not stand for election in 2007 and in June 2008 it announced an effective withdrawal from the Council.[24] A question of great importance for the future of the new Council is whether the United States will maintain this position. The role of the United States, the world's most powerful state, in the demise of the Commission and the creation of the Council is considered further below.

C. Contexts

The Human Rights Council's origins, and to some extent its design, need to be seen within several contexts. The most immediate is that of the process of United Nations reform of which it is a by-product. In turn the wider geo-political environment within which the UN has functioned in the post Cold War era, particularly after the 9/11 attacks on the United States, had a direct bearing on the creation of the Council and will equally shape its future development. But first it is necessary to recall the legal foundations on which international efforts to establish universal human rights standards and secure their implementation are based.

[20] Ibid, para 7. However it seems that absence from the Council need be for no more than one year after serving a second term. A term is for a period of three years.

[21] The United States supported an unsuccessful proposal for permanent seats on the Council for the permanent members of the Security Council, Burci, 'The United Nations Human Rights Council', *The Italian Yearbook of International Law* (vol xv, 2005) 32.

[22] Explanation of Vote by Ambassador John R. Bolton, US Permanent Representative to the United Nations on the Human Rights Council Draft Resolution, in the General Assembly, 15 March 2006, <http://www.state.gov/p/io/rls/rm/63143.htm>.

[23] US Department of State, *The United States Will Not Seek Election to the UN Human Rights Council* (Press Release, 6 April 2006) <http://www.state.gov/r/pa/prs/ps/2006>. For the political background to the decision see Lauren 'To Preserve and Build on its Achievements and to Redress its Shortcomings: The Journey from the Commission on Human Rights to the Human Rights Council' 29 HRQ (2007) 307–47 at 338–40.

[24] A UN embassy spokesperson offered the following comment on the decision to an NGO, reported on its website: 'The US remains deeply dedicated to human rights around the world but unfortunately the UN Human Rights Council has repeatedly demonstrated an unwillingness to serve that purpose. Instead it continues to refuse to address grave and ongoing human rights violations including Zimbabwe, Iran and taken only weak and ineffective action on Sudan while passing 20 unbalanced resolutions against a single country: Israel.' Human Rights Tribune, 11 June 2008 <http://www.humanrights-geneva.info>.

1. *International Accountability Versus State Sovereignty*

An enduring issue that has faced the United Nations from its inception has been how to reconcile its authority and the obligations of its members to address matters of human rights at the international level with the sovereignty of the same member states. The United Nations and particularly its human rights institutions have been and continue to be shaped by the tension between provisions in its Charter which address the issue.[25] Article 1 sets out as one purpose of the body the achievement of international cooperation, 'in promoting and encouraging respect for human rights and for fundamental freedoms for all without distinction as to race, sex language or religion'. By virtue of Article 55(c) the United Nations is directed to promote 'universal respect for, and observance of, human rights and fundamental freedom for all without distinction as to race, sex, language or religion'. In turn Article 56 provides that all member states 'pledge themselves to take joint and separate action in cooperation with the Organisation' to achieve this purpose.

Article 2 of the Charter enshrines the principle of the sovereign equality of member states and includes the stricture in Article 2(7) denying the UN authority, 'to intervene in matters essentially within the domestic jurisdiction of any state or [to require members] to submit such matters to settlement under the present Charter.'[26]

Throughout its history member states have proved extraordinarily effective at negotiating, drafting, and agreeing norms on human rights and freedoms. The former Commission on Human Rights played a central role in these achievements. It is equally impressive to note how these diplomatic achievements have been embraced by states through the ratification of multilateral treaties that have given us the substantial corpus of international human rights law. The process of standard setting is ongoing under the new Council. In its first session in June 2006, it approved two new instruments, the International Convention for the Protection of All Persons from Enforced Disappearance, as well as the United Nations Declaration on the Rights of Indigenous Peoples.[27] In its eighth session it approved an Optional Protocol to the International Covenant on Economic, Social and Cultural Rights establishing a complaint mechanism.[28]

However, seeking to address violations of international human rights standards within member states has been an altogether different experience. The original idea was to permit human rights issues to be addressed at the level of

[25] United Nations Charter, UNCIO XV, 335; amendments by General Assembly Resolution in UNTS 557, 143/638, 308/892, 119.

[26] Art 2(7) adds the important proviso that 'this principle shall not prejudice the application of enforcement measures under Chapter VII'.

[27] These texts of course had been long under consideration by the former Commission on Human Rights. The International Convention for the Protection of All Persons from Enforced Disappearances was adopted by the General Assembly by consensus on 20 December 2007. The Declaration on the Rights of Indigenous Peoples was approved by the General Assembly on 13 September 2007, GA/Res/61/295.

[28] Human Rights Council Res 8/2, 18 June 2008.

principle but not to enable the United Nations to become a forum for inquiry or redress for victims such as would offend the principle of state sovereignty. It had been the Great Powers who had inserted the shield of Article 2(7) of the Charter, fearing that their internal human rights practices might be a target of criticism or 'meddling'.[29] It was the new independent countries in Africa which would first seek to circumvent this restriction in their campaign to challenge South Africa and Apartheid and whose efforts would create the foundations on which the Commission on Human Rights' system of special procedures and its complaint mechanism would be built.[30] Thus the history of international progress on human rights has been built through shifting understanding of the interplay between Articles 1 and 2(7) of the Charter. At a high point of post Cold War consensus in 1993, the World Conference on Human Rights held in Vienna could agree that 'the promotion and protection of all human rights and fundamental freedoms... is a legitimate concern of the international community'.[31] But equally states emphasized that 'the international community must treat human rights globally in a fair and equal manner, on the same footing, and with the same emphasis'.[32]

The process of seeking to apply these principles has proved enormously difficult.[33] Accusations of selectivity in the countries that became the focus of the Commission's attention became a staple feature at its meetings. Powerful countries were able to avoid the attention of the Commission while the least powerful were not. Countries were accused of seeking membership of the Commission to shield themselves or other violators from scrutiny. There was complaint also that economic, social, and cultural rights were given little attention compared with civil and political rights. The resentments which developed over what were experienced as double standards and politicization undermined the credibility, authority, and effectiveness of the Commission.[34] It is salutary to note that states had created through the human rights treaty system an explicitly legal and non-political mechanism by means of which concerns over human rights violations in one state might be raised before a treaty body. Thus under Article 41 of the International Covenant on Civil and Political Rights states have the option of accepting the jurisdiction of the Human Rights Committee to receive complaints over non-fulfilment of human rights obligations. No states have moved to enable

[29] The USSR, the United Kingdom, and the United States insisted upon the language of Art 2(7) of the Charter, A W Brian Simpson, *Human Rights and the End of Empire: Britain and the Genesis of the European Convention* (2001), 264–8, Lauren, n 23 above, at 312–13.

[30] Tolly, n 13 above, at 55–82.

[31] Declaration and Programme of Action, World Conference on Human Rights A/CONF/157/24, para 4.

[32] Ibid, para 5.

[33] For a detailed account of the early efforts to address human rights violations see Alston, 'The Commission on Human Rights' in P Alston (ed), *The United Nations and Human Rights: A Critical Appraisal* (1992) 126–210.

[34] Lauren, n 23 above, at 325.

the activation of this inter-state mechanism. It remains a dead letter despite the exhortation of the Human Rights Committee, emphasizing the collective duty of states parties to assert interest in potential violations in another state should not be seen as an unfriendly act.[35] When states are unwilling to invoke formal treaty-based mechanisms against another state over human rights violations, the tensions and hostility over public accusations of violations in an essentially political forum, the Commission on Human Rights is unsurprising.

However, the Human Rights Council, just as the former Commission, has the responsibility to address human rights violations including gross and systematic violations and to make recommendations.[36] With this mandate in mind the founding texts adopted by the General Assembly and by the new Council are replete with references to objectivity, transparency, non-selectivity, genuine dialogue, and the elimination of politicization in the work of the Council. The language expresses high expectations that there can be a new beginning in building international cooperation afresh based on shared commitments of all states to advance the protection of universal human rights. Hopes for that goal rest above all on the system of universal periodic review of states, but achieving consensus on urgent action over human rights crises in particular states has already proved to be unattainable.[37] Meanwhile the 2005 Millennium Summit, which approved the creation of the Human Rights Council, accepted a new doctrine of responsibility to protect, whereby the international community has responsibility to help protect people from genocide, war crimes, ethnic cleansing, and crimes against humanity.[38] How this reconfiguration of international jurisdiction and state sovereignty will itself develop and what influence it may have in the long term on the approach of the Human Rights Council towards its protection mandate remains to be seen.[39]

2. *The Role of Regional and Political Groupings*

(a) Regional groups

The United Nations Charter enshrines the principle of the sovereign equality of all its members.[40] This principle is reflected in the rule that each member state has the right to one vote only in decision-making. But the United Nation's 192 members do not act only as individual states; rather they operate through

[35] 'To draw attention to possible breaches of Covenant obligations by other States Parties and to call on them to comply with their Covenant obligations should, far from being regarded as an unfriendly act, be considered as a reflection of legitimate community interest.' General Comment No 31 [80] Nature of the General Legal Obligation Imposed on States Parties to the Covenant, CCPR/C/21/Rev1/Add13, 26 May 2004.

[36] GA/Res/60/251, para 4.3. [37] See Special Sessions below.

[38] 2005 World Summit Outcome UN Doc A/60/1 (2005) paras 138–40.

[39] See lecture by Louise Arbour, United Nations High Commissioner for Human Rights, 'The Responsibility to Protect as a Duty of Care in International Law and Practice', Trinity College Dublin, 23 November 2007.

[40] UN Charter, Art 21.

a variety of groupings and alliances, in particular regional and political interest groups or blocs.[41] As a universal body the United Nations is based on the principle of full participation in its work by all its members. Arrangements to ensure such participation in decision-making within the organization are built around the requirement of the 'equitable geographical distribution' of membership of committees and positions for all regions of the world organized through elections or rotation.[42] 'Equitable geographical distribution' is equally a criterion for staff appointments.[43] Equitable representation reflects weighting based on the number of states in each region. The five geographical groupings: Africa, Asia, East European, Latin American and Caribbean, and the Group 'Western European and Others', were established in 1963.[44] Since then these groupings have been used throughout the United Nations system for the purpose of the election to seats including in the Security Council, General Assembly, ECOSOC, the former Commission on Human Rights, and now the Human Rights Council.[45]

The most evident impact that regional groupings have had over the history of the United Nations has resulted from increased membership mainly from the developing world. Whereas at its creation in 1945, when there were 51 states, the United Nations was predominantly a body of European and Latin American states, there has been a gradual emergence of a new political majority in its 192 members from Asia and Africa. This majority has been able to reflect its concerns and influence across the entire field of United Nations activities and will dominate the new Human Rights Council. In the distribution of seats in the new Council this dominance has been even strengthened when compared to the former Commission. The majority of seats, 26 out of 47, are held by Africa and Asia. The Western group share decreased from 10 to seven seats. As the United Nations has become fully representative of the world's peoples, the historical pre-eminence of the Western group in its politics has significantly diminished. The implications for the international protection of human rights will emerge not least through the actions of the Human Rights Council in the years to come.

(b) Political groupings

The 'other' states in the Western group (WEOG) (Australia, New Zealand, and Canada), signal clearly that there is more than objective geographical criteria

[41] For an account of the operation of all manner of groups in the United Nations, see C B Smith, *Politics and Process and the United Nations: The Global Dance* (2006) at 53–78.

[42] The term 'equitable geographical distribution' is used in Art 23(1) of the UN Charter with respect to elections to the Security Council.

[43] UN Charter, Art 101.

[44] GA Res 1991 (XVIII) (1963), S Daws, 'The Origins and Development of UN Electoral Groups' in R. Thakur (ed) *What is Equitable Geographical Distribution in the 21st Century,* (United Nations University, 1999) 11–29.

[45] The Groupings and their allocation of seats on the Human Rights Council are: Group of African States, (13); Group of Asian States, (13); Group of Eastern European States, (6); Group of Latin American and Caribbean States, (8); and Group of Western European and other States (7).

involved in the composition of such groupings.[46] States are linked by political and other interests and affinities which in some cases, such as Africa, coincide with geography but in others, such as Eastern Europe, equally reflect geo-political realities, for example the former Soviet Union. There are multiple overlapping blocs and political caucuses of states both large and small, inside and outside the United Nations. These include for example, the United States created Community of Democracies (CCD), organizations such as the Association of South East Nations (ASEAN), the Arab League, the European Union, African Union, and groupings such as the Non-Aligned Movement (NAM) and the Organisation of the Islamic Conference (IOC).[47] It is the interaction and negotiation between groupings, regional and political, that have largely shaped the global human rights agenda of the past and will continue to do so for the future.

In the former Commission the influence or indeed control of its membership by regional groups manifesting themselves in block voting on resolutions and initiatives was much criticized as restricting and frustrating its work. In effect, states did not have freedom to act as individual members of the Commission; solidarity with the positions of regional and political groupings determined votes especially where a resolution or decision involved another state which was also a member of the group. One result was that groups were controlled by the more extreme members 'who effectively dictate[d] the policy of the whole Group and then, because of group solidarity, every member or almost every member of the Group vote[d] as part of that block'.[48]

It is the policy of the African Group that it alone may table a resolution on an African state and the Group's rules require that the state in question should be consulted over any resolution.[49] In the European Union case voting behaviour is coordinated by the member states as a group and as part of common foreign and security policy. The visibility of regional and political groupings as members of the Council present collective rather than individual positions is as evident in the Human Rights Council sessions to date as it was in the former Commission.

3. United Nations Reform

The mission of ongoing reform of the United Nations including its human rights machinery was a commitment of Kofi Annan's tenure as Secretary General which began in 1997.[50] This culminated in his second term of office with the

[46] The United States does not formally belong to any Group but participates in the WEOG for election purposes. Israel is a 'guest' member of the WEOG.

[47] For details of these groupings see Smith, n 41 above, at 53–78 and for listing of state membership the website, <http://www.eyeontheun.org/view.asp?l=11&p=55>.

[48] M Abraham, 'A New Chapter for Human Rights: A handbook on issues of transition from the Commission on Human Rights to the Human Rights Council', International Service for Human Rights and Friedrich Ebert Stiftung (Geneva, 2006) at 28.

[49] Ibid at 28.

[50] Report of the Secretary General to the General Assembly, 'Renewing the United Nations: A Programme for Reform' UN Doc A/51/950, 14 July 1997.

publication of his powerful report 'In Larger Freedom' prepared for the 2005 World Summit.[51] The push for comprehensive reform of the organization, but also a greater commitment to multilateralism, was in part a reaction to increasingly fierce political criticism of the organization from the United States Congress, stemming from the Security Council's failure to endorse the invasion of Iraq.[52] The starting point was the appointment by the Secretary General of an independent High Level Panel, charged with reviewing new global security threats in the 21st century and the challenges they presented to the world community and the United Nations.[53] The report was in part a response to the new radical doctrine on national security adopted by the United States after 9/11, which asserted that country's right of pre-emption in the use of force. The Panel rebuffed the doctrine and declared that the UN Charter rules on use of force did not require revision. The Panel's main contribution however was to promote an enlarged view of security that went beyond the traditional state-centred concept of military security. In a post-9/11 era the proliferation of weapons of mass destruction, international terrorism, and organized crime were identified as major concerns for the future. But the High Level Panel also highlights poverty, food insecurity, infectious disease, civil wars and conflicts, environmental degradation, and climate change, as neglected and connected sources of threat and insecurity affecting the human rights of millions on the planet. The international community should urgently recognize these threats and above all their interconnectedness.[54]

'In Larger Freedom' built on this theme of interconnectedness through restating the goals of the United Nations as global security, development, and human rights and insisting on their interdependence.[55] Kofi Annan made a series of institutional reform proposals in respect of each of these goals including as regards the Security Council and the Economic and Social Council, adding the proposal for a Human Rights Council to replace the Commission on Human Rights and to stand alongside the existing Councils. These proposals would be decided upon at the 2005 Summit. Although proposals for reform of the Security Council failed, two new intergovernmental institutions were endorsed at the 2005 Summit, a Human Rights Council and a Peace-building Commission.[56] The negotiations over the Human Rights Council are discussed below.

[51] Report of the Secretary General, 'In Larger Freedom: Towards Development Security and Human Rights For All' UN Doc A/59/2005, 23 May 2005.

[52] J Traub, *The Best Intentions: Kofi Annan and the UN in the Era of American Power* (2006), at 168–87.

[53] Report of the High Level Panel on 'Threats, Challenges and Change, A More Secure World: Our Shared Responsibility', UN Doc A/59/565 (2004).

[54] Ibid, especially at para 111, 'Security, infectious disease and environmental degradation'.

[55] 'Accordingly, we will not enjoy development without security, we will not enjoy security without development, and we will not enjoy either without respect for human rights. Unless all these causes are advanced, none will succeed.' 'In Larger Freedom', n 51 above, at para 17.

[56] 2005 World Summit Outcome UN Doc A/60/1(2005), para 97; Human Rights Council, Peacebuilding, paras 157–59. On the Peacebuilding Commission see, 'In Larger Freedom', n 51 above, Addendum 2.

2. The Commission on Human Rights (1946–2006)

With its short and rather forlorn 62nd and final session in Geneva on 27 March 2006, the Commission on Human Rights ended six decades of existence. The Commission had first met in 1946 under the chairmanship of Eleanor Roosevelt and had thus been in existence for 60 years. Despite the criticism it attracted, the pre-eminence that the Commission achieved as well as the advance of world concern over human rights can be measured by the statistics of involvement in its 61st session in 2005, its last substantive session Three thousand attended, including representatives of 153 states, 30 international organizations and agencies, 56 national human rights institutions, and some 262 NGOs.[57] By the time of its demise the Commission had been aptly described as having become, 'an annual convention of the whole international human rights movement, in all its governmental, quasi-governmental, intergovernmental and nongovernmental expressions'.[58]

The United States, the principal architect of the United Nations as a whole, was equally the source of the idea for a Commission on Human Rights. The Commission has the distinction of being the only such specific body mandated by the Charter.[59] John Foster Dulles worked for this achievement at the San Francisco Conference establishing the United Nations. He dubbed the Commission the 'soul' of the Charter.[60] The abolition of the Commission and the launch of the Human Rights Council have attracted a considerable volume of writings both academic and journalistic over the last three years.[61] This stands in stark contrast to the dearth of scholarly interest over the years in the Commission.[62]

A. Status, Membership, and Subordinate Bodies of the Commission

The Commission was a functional body of the United Nations Economic Social Council (ECOSC) reporting to ECOSOC and in turn to the General Assembly

57 P Prove, 'Re-commissioning the Commission on Human Rights: UN Reform and UN Human Rights Architecture' at 9. Available online at, <http://www.lutheranworld.org/What_We_Do/OIahr/Issues_Events/UN_Reform-Human_Rights.pdf>.

58 Ibid at 9.

59 Art 68: The Economic and Social Council shall set up commissions in economic and social fields and for the promotion of human rights, and such other commissions as may be required for the performance of its functions.

60 J S Nurser, *For All Peoples and All Nations* (2005) at 7; Lauren, n 23 above, at 310.

61 For a sample of that literature see in this volume, N Bernaz, 'Reforming the UN Human rights Protection Procedures: A Legal Perspective on the Establishment of the Universal Periodic Review' ch 3, n 2.

62 Three books have been published on the Commission, J B Marie, *La Commission des droits de l'homme de l'Onu*, (1975); H Tolley Jr, *The U.N. Commission on Human Rights* (1987); M Lempinen, *The United Nations Commission on Human Rights and the Different Treatment of Governments: An Inseparable Part of Promoting and Encouraging Respect for Human Rights?* (2005). See also, Alston, 'The Commission on Human Rights' in P Alston (ed), *The United Nations and Human Rights: A critical appraisal* (1992) 126–210; G Oberleitner, *Global Human Rights Institutions* (2007) 41–54.

(3rd Committee). At the outset the question was raised whether the Commission on Human Rights ought to be comprised of individuals with expertise on human rights sitting independently of governments. The initial Commission established in 'nuclear form' and chaired by Eleanor Roosevelt proposed this model on the argument that since states' representatives sat in the parent body ECOSOC and in the General Assembly to which ECOSOC reported, there was the need for an independent and expert perspective which could be provided through the Commission.[63] This option however was not acceptable to governments (particularly the Soviet Union) which opted for their representatives to comprise the membership of the Commission. Subject to all the limitations of hindsight this result was surely for the best.[64] The drafting of the International Bill of Human Rights, the Universal Declaration of Human Rights, and the subsequent Covenants, required states to be directly engaged in such an ambitious project if its legitimacy was to be ensured. The results represent a compromise between different world views and ideologies but have nevertheless endured as the foundation of the entire international human rights system.

The initial membership of the Commission was set at 18, a number periodically increased over its existence to reflect growth in UN membership. At the time of its dissolution the Commission's membership was 53.[65] Over the first two decades of its existence the Commission was effectively dominated by the United States, other Western countries, and their allies, as was indeed the United Nations as a whole. Eleanor Roosevelt, representing the United States, was the chair of the Commission for its first six years. No Sub-Saharan African state sat in the Commission until 1964.[66] From the 1960s, however, with the inflow of new states from the process of decolonization, their representation increased significantly in the Commission as in other UN bodies. By 1992 the Commission's membership had increased from 43 to 53 giving the developing world an unassailable majority.[67]

The Commission was empowered to establish subordinate advisory bodies through which it was envisaged experts would contribute. One such body which operated throughout the history of the Commission was the Sub-Commission on Prevention of Discrimination and Protection of Minorities, later renamed the Sub-Commission on the Promotion and Protection of Human Rights.[68] At the time of its dissolution the Sub-Commission was made up of 26 independent

63 Tolley, n 13 above, at 10.

64 For a contrary view, see Lempinen, n 62 above, at 44.

65 Membership was expanded to 21 in 1962, 32 in 1967, and 43 in 1980 and 53 members in 1992, P Alston, n 62 above, at 194.

66 Tolley, n 13 above, at 14.

67 Alston, n 62 above, at 194.

68 A Eide 'The Sub-Commission on Prevention of Discrimination and Protection of Minorities' in P Alston (ed) *The United Nations and Human Rights : A Critical Appraisal* (1992) 211–64.

unpaid human rights experts, with a balance of representation from the UN's five regional groups.[69] The difficult relationship that had developed between the Commission and its Sub-Commission revolved around the efforts of the latter to claim greater independence in its work than the majority of the Commission could accept.

The former Sub-Commission had achieved in earlier years freedom to initiate its own research and in many instances standard setting taken up by the Commission began with the work of the experts on the Sub-Commission. It pioneered thematic working groups including on minorities, indigenous populations, and contemporary forms of slavery. In recent years its work on business and human rights norms and its annual Social Forum reflected its creative potential in advancing human rights protection.[70] However, its powers had been progressively reduced by the Commission and its Commission appointed membership were viewed as decreasingly independent or expert.[71] The replacement body for the Sub-Commission, the Advisory Committee on Human Rights, is firmly subordinate to the Human Rights Council. It will be elected under rules designed to ensure that its members act in a personal capacity but will not exclude entirely government officials.[72]

Another initially subordinate body of the Commission on Human Rights was a Sub-Commission on the Rights of Women. It was virtually immediately reconstituted as a full Commission under ECOSOC and has played a major role in promoting standards and protecting women's rights since.[73] The Commission on the Status of Women remains the one human rights body under the aegis of ECOSOC. Its working relations with the new Human Rights Council remain to be developed.[74]

B. Mandate of the Commission

The mandate given to the Commission was that of standard setting beginning with 'the formulation of an international bill of rights'. It was also tasked with the

[69] As of 2005, there were seven members from Africa, five from Asia, five from Latin America (GRULAC), three from Eastern Europe, and six from Western Europe and other States (WEOG).

[70] M Robinson, Opening Remarks, Fifty-Third Session of the Sub-Commission on Human Rights, Geneva, 30 July 2001, in K Boyle (ed), *A Voice for Human Rights Mary Robinson* (2006) 238–44.

[71] Abraham (2006), n 48 above, at 16.

[72] See the Advisory Committee, below.

[73] R. Leandra 'The Commission on the Status of Women' in P Alston (ed), *The United Nations and Human Rights: A Critical Appraisal* (1992) 265–303.

[74] The President of the Council Luis Alfonso de Alba (2006–7) pledged to strengthen the relationship. See, 'Commission on Status of Women discusses need for greater harmony in talks with presidents of Economic and Social, Human Rights Councils', UN Department of Public Information, (press release 7 March 2007). See, V Goyal, 'The United Nations Commission on Status of Women: Status in the United Nations Reform Process', (2007) (LLM thesis on file University of Essex, United Kingdom).

protection of minorities and the prevention of discrimination and with a residual authority that allowed the Commission to address 'any other matter concerning human rights'.[75] The Commission's achievement across the bulk of this range of tasks, particularly in standard setting, is accepted even by its fiercest detractors as impressive. Most of the agreements that constitute modern international law on human rights involved the Commission and its Sub-Commission. The Universal Declaration and the two International Covenants that together constitute the International Bill of Human Rights are the most famous, but the work of the Commission and its Sub-Commission on questions of discrimination and equality should also be recorded. The first international treaty to come into force in 1966, the International Convention on the Elimination of Racial Discrimination (ICERD), was drafted within the Sub-Commission and Commission.

C. Complaints Machinery

As already noted, while the intergovernmental engagement with establishing binding norms in international law has worked effectively, the opposite has proved the case in seeking to involve the same states in exercising judgment over each other in respect of compliance with such norms. From the outset the new Commission resisted taking on the function of examining the numerous individual complaints and petitions which streamed into the United Nations from all over the world appealing for action over human rights violations. The Commission resolved that it had 'no power to take any action in regard to any complaints concerning human rights'.[76] Complaints which raised labour rights issues were referred to the International Labour Organisation Committee on Freedom of Association, but otherwise the thousands of petitions which flooded into the UN remained un-opened and unanswered.[77] To understand the evolution of attitudes towards addressing complaints it should be recalled that the initial resistance to giving the new Commission any investigative or protective function came from the major Powers, including the United States, USSR, and the United Kingdom.[78] As noted above, those states which had crafted Article 2(7) of the Charter intended to rule out UN involvement in domestic affairs saw the Commission's role as confined to proposing and promoting international standards and as a forum for debate on such standards. This stance was challenged as early as 1949 by the UN Secretary General concerned that the result was 'bound to lower the prestige and authority not only of the Commission but of the United Nations as a whole'.[79] But to no avail.

[75] E/38.Rev.1 (1946) 7.

[76] ECOSOC Res 75(V) (1947), 5 August 1947.

[77] Alston, n 62 above, at 139–45.

[78] Tolley, n 13 above, at 17.

[79] Report on the Present Situation with Regard to Communications Concerning Human Rights, E/CN.4/165 (1949), 6 June 1948.

The Commission's denial to itself of jurisdiction to address complaints was to persist for two decades ending only when the process of decolonization from the 1960s brought the newly independent African and Asian countries a majority in the General Assembly. These countries pushed for action on issues of relevance to them, especially South Africa and the Apartheid system, and in pressing for the comprehensive achievement of self-determination of peoples. The greater number of newly independent states came to be reflected in their presence in UN bodies, including the Commission on Human Rights. With membership of an expanded Commission, African and Asian countries operating also through the Non-Aligned Movement (NAM) pressed successfully for Apartheid and racism to be treated as human rights issues. One key way was to ensure that the Commission addressed the human rights violations flowing from the discriminatory and oppressive policies of the South African state and also the colonial regime in Southern Rhodesia.

It was thus developing countries that were the progenitors of Commission Resolution 1215 (1967) establishing mechanisms for the Commission and its Sub-Commission to publicly debate situations of large-scale human rights violations, 'including policies of racial discrimination and segregation and apartheid in all countries'.[80] It was the same states which sponsored Resolution 1503 (1970) that gave the Commission the competence to receive and adjudicate on communications alleging gross and systematic violation of human rights.[81] It was equally the pressure for action on Apartheid which began what became known as the Commission's system of special procedures. In 1967 the Commission voted to establish an ad hoc Working Group on South Africa with an explicit mandate to investigate and report back on charges of torture and ill-treatment of prisoners, detainees, or persons in police custody in South Africa.[82]

While the NAM countries—supported primarily by the USSR—had in mind racism and Apartheid, their success created the precedent for the development of the Commission's mandate to address any situation of human rights violation in the world. The new Human Rights Council retains that competence of the former Commission in its permanent agenda.[83] In turn, the Council inherited the confidential complaint mechanism of the Commission. It has replaced the '1503 procedure' with a new complaint mechanism which is largely similar in nature. It is considered below. From these beginnings, the system of special procedures was also developed for individual and groups of experts to investigate, monitor, and report on human rights violations both in respect of thematic issues and particular countries. Apart from its standard setting activities, the special procedures

[80] ECOSOC Res 1235 (XLII) adopted 6 June 1967; Alston, n 62 above at 143–45.

[81] ECOSOC Res 1503(XLVIII) of 27 May 1970 revised by ECOSOC Resolution 2003/3 of 9 June 2000.

[82] E/CN4/Res/2 (XXIII), 6 March 1967.

[83] Item 4, Human rights situations that require the Council's attention. Agenda and Framework for the Program of Work, A/HRC/Res/5/1.

system represents the most important contribution of the Commission to the protection of human rights.[84]

D. Politicization of the Commission

One of the complaints over the Commission on Human Rights was that it was 'politicized' or 'over politicized' in its treatment of human rights. It is not entirely easy to deconstruct that word.[85] But it became the principal charge that finally brought the Commission down. Behind the issue lay the question of its composition. The role of regional groups and political caucuses in the United Nations system has already been discussed. Much of the progress, or absence of it, on human rights within the United Nations has flowed from the diplomatic resolution of the conflicting agendas and interests of its members as expressed through these groups. It has also been noted that the process of securing agreement through compromises has been remarkably successful at the level of drafting new human rights standards and establishing mechanisms such as the system of special procedures. The major challenges which led to serious crises in the Commission emerged in the past as they do today when the question of protection arises. States large and small resent or reject 'finger pointing' or attention being drawn to their shortcomings. The awareness of serious human rights suffering in member states, with the Commission pressed to act by NGOs, brings the political differences between blocs openly to the surface. One part of the resentment concerns complaints of 'selectivity' that certain states which are less powerful are targeted for condemnation where no such measures are addressed to the powerful.[86]

The problem of politics in the Commission is hardly a new one. The Commission functioned throughout the four decades of the Cold War and inevitably the ideological competition between East and West was constantly reflected in its deliberations and exchanges. For its first two decades the Commission was dominated by Western states led by the United States. Throughout that period no member of the Eastern bloc ever held the Chair of the Commission and there was little African participation.[87] In its early years it suited both the Western and the Eastern powers to steer the Commission away from addressing violations or developing a protection function. But with the growth of the NAM

[84] Amnesty International 'United Nations Special Procedures: Building on a cornerstone of human rights protection', IOR 40/017/2005, October 2005. See also in this volume, N Rodley 'United Nations Human Rights Council, Its Special Procedures and Their Relationship with the Treaty Bodies—Complementarity or Competition?'

[85] Oberleitner, n 62 above, at 44–8.

[86] See, for example, the view of Pakistan; 'Politicization and selective targeting... the arbitrary naming of countries and submission of country-specific resolutions, mostly against developing countries, especially Islamic countries, is the most negative feature of the Commission's work'. Statement by Ambassador Munir Akram, Permanent Representative of Pakistan to the United Nations at the Human Rights negotiations on the Establishment of Human Rights Council, New York, 18 October 2005. For an appraisal of the selection of countries in the Commission see, Alston, n 62 above, at 162–64.

[87] Tolley, n 13 above, at 187–203.

during the late 1960s and in later years, developing states achieved a majority on the Commission as on other UN bodies and a new era began with an emphasis on addressing racial discrimination and self-determination. The irony remarked upon frequently was that the NAM countries proved equally reluctant as other states to see the Commission deal with situations of violations within their own member states under the mechanisms they had engineered for Apartheid, colonialism, and Israel.

The United States spearheaded the accusation regarding the politicization of the Commission in the final years of the Commission. Its concerns reflected a similar phase of complaints in the 1970s by the then US Ambassador to the United Nations, Daniel Patrick Moynihan, who castigated the Soviet Union and other totalitarian states for constantly attacking the democracies and Israel in the Commission while ignoring egregious violations at home.[88]

In May 2001 the United States lost its seat on the Commission in disputed circumstances.[89] Three European member states in addition to the United States had gone forward for membership of the Commission within the 'Western European and Others' group, resulting in an ECOSOC election which the USA lost.[90] This was the first time that the United States had not been represented on the Commission since 1946. In 2003 when the US returned to the Commission, Jean Kirkpatrick, who had led the US delegation to the Commission's 58th session, renewed the attack on the election of human rights violating countries to the Commission.[91] The US forced a vote, which it lost, on the choice of Libya, nominated by the African Group, to take the chair of the Commission.[92] In 2004, over a US protest, Sudan was re-elected to the Commission despite its actions in Darfur. The accusation was that states which were notorious human rights violators sought membership of the Commission to shield themselves from accountability. What evidence there is for such a proposition is hard to come by, but it was clearly true that the voting arrangements ensured that a 'slate' proposed by the group for its allocated seats would be approved without vote and that the convention in ECOSOC was not to challenge a member put forward by any regional group.[93]

[88] D. Moynihan, 'The Politics of Human Rights', Commentary (May 1977).

[89] Kirkpatrick: The UN Commission on Human Rights a Review of its Mission Operations and Structure Testimony to the Sub Committee on International Operations and Human Rights, Washington, 6 June 2001.

[90] France obtained 52 votes, Austria 41, Sweden 32, and the United States 29.

[91] Jeane Kirkpatrick 'UN human rights panel needs some entry standards', *International Herald Tribune*, 14 May 2003.

[92] 'Libya takes human rights role' <http://news.bbc.co.uk/2/hi/africa/2672029.stm>. The vagaries of international politics are reflected in the fact that Libya was elected to the Security Council for a two-year term in 2008 taking the role of President for the month of January 2008. US Secretary of State Condoleezza Rice met with the Libyan ambassador in the same month.

[93] See S E Sach's paper, 'Sins of Commission: Repressive Regimes and the UN Commission on Human Rights'. Sachs examined membership of the Commission 2000–2003 and concluded 'In the past three years, regimes with the worst or near-worst human rights records have been substantially over-represented on the Commission, a trend that is statistically significant and in certain ways historically unprecedented.' <http://www.stevesachs.com/papers/paper_hrc.html>.

The Commission had sought to address its own reform, in particular the system of special procedures, on many occasions over the previous decade.[94] A major review and its recommendations were adopted in full in 2000.[95] While these reform efforts did not prevent the demise of the Commission, they did provide the basis for the comprehensive review of the inherited procedures and systems later implemented through the new Human Rights Council.

3. The Human Rights Council

A. Origins

The proposal to replace the Commission on Human Rights with a Human Rights Council was contained in the former Secretary General Kofi Annan's report, 'In Larger Freedom', published in March 2005 in preparation for the World Summit in September of that year.[96] This was something of a surprise. The preceding High Level Panel report on which the proposals were built had focused in its recommendations on strengthening the role of the High Commissioner for Human Rights.[97] It had considered the question of reform or replacement of the Commission but opted for the former. As a longer term option, it saw the idea of a Human Rights Council functioning alongside the Security Council and the Economic and Social Council as a Charter body.[98]

The High Level Panel spelled out the grounds for concern over the performance of the Commission. It adopted what had become common criticisms of the body:

> In recent years, the Commission's capacity to perform [its tasks] has been undermined by eroding credibility and professionalism. Standard-setting to reinforce human rights cannot be performed by States that lack a demonstrated commitment to their promotion and protection. We are concerned that in recent years States have sought membership of the Commission not to strengthen human rights but to protect themselves against criticism or to criticize others. The Commission cannot be credible if it is seen to be maintaining double standards in addressing human rights concerns.[99]

The Panel saw the main issue as that of the membership of the Commission. Their view was that changing membership criteria was unlikely to remove the politicization of the Commission. It opted for the idea of universal membership.

[94] Compilation of recent documents in relation to the enhancement of the working methods of the Commission on Human Rights (1999–2005), Non-Paper, Office of the High Commissioner for Human Rights Secretariat of the Commission on Human Rights, 17 January 2006.

[95] Decision 2000/109 of the Commission on Human Rights adopting the report of the Intersessional open-ended working group on enhancing the effectiveness of the mechanisms of the Commission, E/CN4/2000/112.

[96] Report of the Secretary General, 'In Larger Freedom: Towards Development, Security and Human Rights for All', UN Doc A/59/2005.

[97] Report of the High Level Panel on Threats, Challenges and Change, A More Secure World: Our Shared Responsibility, UN Doc A/59/565 (2004).

[98] Ibid, para 291. [99] Ibid, para 283.

Switzerland, which had joined the United Nations only in 2002, was a key actor in the genesis of the Council.[100] Switzerland's Foreign Ministry commissioned a study in March 2003 to explore options for reform of the Commission.[101] While this study recommended deeper reform, it also mooted as a longer term option a Human Rights Council. One of the consultants, Professor Walter Kälin, was commissioned to further develop the idea of a Council. His report on a proposed Council[102] was then brought by the Swiss to the Secretary General and placed before the High Level Panel. The support for the idea of replacing the Commission by the UN Secretariat should be seen in the context of the particularly stormy relations between it and the United States Administration, which in turn was quick to adopt the proposal.[103]

'In Larger Freedom' called for a Council smaller in size than the Commission to be either a principal organ of the United Nations or to be created under the General Assembly.[104] In either case members of the Council should be elected by a two-thirds majority of the General Assembly and should undertake to abide by the highest human rights standards. In an Addendum to his Report, circulated to all states, the Secretary General set out in greater detail his arguments for replacing the Commission and the functions envisaged for the new Council.[105] On the status of the Council he argued for the Council being a standing body and a principal organ alongside the other Councils of the UN, the Security Council, and the Economic Social and Cultural Council. Thus the three fields of activities of the United Nations, peace and security, development, and human rights would have equal status in the organization's architecture. The Council should continue the mandate of the Commission in receiving and responding to complaints of large-scale violations of human rights. This would be in parallel to its new peer review system that would thoroughly consider the human rights situation in all states. The Council should have the mandate to address human rights emergencies whether in regular or special sessions. The Human Rights Council should work closely with the other components of the international human rights system, the treaty bodies, and the High Commissioner for Human Rights. It should preserve and develop the role of NGOs and National Human Rights Institutions. The Human Rights Council would continue to play a central role as the Commission had in the further development of the international law of human rights.

[100] 'Course of a diplomatic initiative for the creation of a UN Human Rights Council; historical background', Département Fédéral des Affaires Étrangères, Bern, March 2006.

[101] W Kälin and C Jimenez, *Reform of the UN Commission on Human Rights, Study Commissioned by the Swiss Ministry of Foreign Affair* (Institute of Public Law University of Bern, Bern/Geneva, 2003).

[102] W Kälin 'Towards a Human Rights Council: Options and Perspectives', August 2004

[103] The Iraq 'Oil for Food' scandal which brought fierce criticism of the UN from the US Congress and of the Secretary General was ongoing throughout 2005. Traub, n 52 above, at 250–9.

[104] 'In Larger Freedom', n 96 above, para 183.

[105] Human Rights Council Explanatory Note by the Secretary General A/59/2005/Add1, 23 May 2005.

In April 2005 Kofi Annan travelled to Geneva to address the Commission on the new proposals including the proposed peer review function of a Human Rights Council. He told the Commission that its ability to perform its tasks had been undermined by the politicization of its meetings and the selectivity of its work.

> We have reached a point at which the Commission's declining credibility has cast a shadow on the reputation of the United Nations system as a whole, and where piecemeal reforms will not be enough.[106]

The plan had been to have the proposed core features of the new body—its status, size, and the election threshold of two-thirds of the General Assembly members, debated and agreed between states and ready for adoption before the September 2005 World Summit. Thereafter the detailed modalities of how it would function could be worked out by the General Assembly following the Summit.[107] But despite intense negotiations between all regional groups and the Secretariat, it proved impossible to reach agreement before the Summit or during it as to composition of the proposed institution, its status, or the election system.

The Summit Outcome document contained agreement in principle to create the Human Rights Council and that it should address situations of gross violations of human rights. But it left issues of 'mandate, modalities, functions, size, composition, membership, working methods and procedures of the Council' to a round of post summit negotiations through the General Assembly.[108]

Thereafter, states negotiated these elements of the Human Rights Council in over five months of consultations chaired by President of the Assembly, Jan Eliasson and co-Presidents, Ambassador Dumisani Kumalo of South Africa and Ambassador Ricardo Alberto Arias of Panama. Despite the differences between the regional and political groups, a final compromise text or draft resolution was agreed upon by the end of February 2006. However, John Bolton, the United States Ambassador who had largely stayed away from the negotiations, objected to the draft resolution.[109] The key sticking point for the United States concerned membership and the mode of election to the new body. The United States had backed Kofi Annan's preference for a much smaller body than the former Commission. However, the compromise agreed in the General Assembly was for a 47-member body, a reduction of only six from the membership of the Commission. The Secretary General and the Western Group, including the United States, pushed for election to the Council to require a two-thirds majority vote (128 votes in favour) whereas the formula finally agreed upon was that candidates would be elected

[106] Secretary General Office of the Spokesperson, Geneva, 7 April 2005; Secretary-General's Address to the Commission on Human Rights, New York.

[107] Addendum, n 105 above.

[108] 2005 World Summit Outcome, UN Doc A/60/1 (2005), paras 157–60.

[109] For a journalist's account of the negotiations over the Summit Outcome document and the extraordinary obstructiveness of the US Ambassador John Bolton, see Traub, n 52 above, at 373–98.

'directly and individually by secret ballot by the majority of the members of the General Assembly' (96 votes in favour).[110] The United States had unsuccessfully proposed exclusion of any country subject to measures under Chapter VII of the UN Charter, 'related to human rights abuses or acts of terrorism'. This condition was not acceptable but it was agreed that an elected member of the Council could be removed by a two-thirds vote of the General Assembly (of members present and voting), if found responsible for gross and systematic violations of human rights. In the end however, the United States was not prepared to join a consensus on the draft resolution.[111] It called a vote which was taken on 15 March 2006. Resolution 60/251 creating the Human Rights Council was passed with a vote of 170 in favour to four against (Israel, US, Palau, and Marshall Islands). There were three abstentions (Belarus, Iran, and Venezuela).[112]

B. Resolution 60/251 and the Mandate of the Human Rights Council

Resolution 60/251 of the General Assembly is the constitutional basis of the Human Rights Council and sets out its mandate.[113] The mandate is prefaced by a number of principles that will guide the work of the Council. These are; 'universality, impartiality, objectivity and non-selectivity, constructive international dialogue and cooperation'.[114]

1. *Protection and Prevention*

The Council is given an explicit protection role. It will be responsible 'for promoting universal respect for the protection of all human rights and fundamental freedoms for all, without distinction of any kind and in a fair and equal manner'.[115] Its protection role importantly extends to prevention. The Council is required to 'contribute through dialogue and cooperation to the prevention of human rights violations and respond promptly to human rights emergencies'.[116] The Council's protection mandate also requires it to 'address situations of violations of human rights, including gross and systematic violations, and make recommendations thereon'.[117] On that foundation a new complaint mechanism based on the 1503 procedure of the former Commission has been built.

[110] Human Rights Council Election Note by Secretariat, A/INF/60/6, 30 March 2006.

[111] Burci, n 21 above, at 33.

[112] See, 'Explanation of Vote on the Human Rights Council Draft Resolution' by Ambassador John Bolton, US Permanent Representative to the United Nations, Statement in the General Assembly, 15 March 2006, available at <http://www.state.gov/p/io/rls/rm/63143.htm>. In this statement, Ambassador Bolton said that the test of the new body would be if it took action on serious abuse cases like Sudan, Cuba, Iran, Zimbabwe, Belarus, and Burma.

[113] GA/Res/60/251, Human Rights Council, 3 April 2006.

[114] GA/Res/ 60/251, para 4.

[115] Ibid, para 2. [116] Ibid, para 5(f). [117] Ibid, para 3.

2. *Promotion*

The Council's promotion mandate largely codifies the practice of the former Commission. It shall, amongst other things:

1. Promote human rights education and learning as well as advisory services, technical assistance, and capacity-building, to be provided in consultation with and with the consent of member states concerned;
2. Serve as a forum for dialogue on thematic issues on all human rights;
3. Make recommendations to the General Assembly for the further development of international law in the field of human rights;
4. Promote the full implementation of human rights obligations undertaken by States and follow up the goals and commitments related to the promotion and protection of human rights emanating from United Nations conferences and summits.[118]

3. *Coordination and Mainstreaming of Human Rights*

The World Summit Outcome document directed the Council to 'promote the effective coordination and the mainstreaming of human rights within the United Nations System'.[119] This role is now incorporated in Resolution 60/251. The Council has yet to address this aspect of its mandate and it does give rise to some issues. The goal of integration (or mainstreaming) of human rights throughout the activities of the United Nations is also given to the UN High Commissioner for Human Rights.[120] In 1997 Kofi Annan, as Secretary General at the outset of his reform drive, asked the then High Commissioner Mary Robinson to lead on the task of mainstreaming.[121] In principle there is nothing wrong with directing different bodies to promote coordination but the Council will need to pursue this mandate in dialogue with the High Commissioner.

4. *Working with 'Stakeholders'*

The Council is directed to work in close cooperation with 'Governments, regional organisations, national human rights institutions and civil society'. National Human Rights Institutions (NHRIs) and NGOs had developed strong and effective roles before the Commission on Human Rights and that *acquis* is now formally recognized by Resolution 60/251. Thus the Preamble acknowledges that 'non governmental organizations play an important role at national regional and international levels'. The role of NGOs and NHRIs in the work of the new Council is discussed further below.

[118] Ibid, para 5.
[119] 2005 World Summit Outcome, UN Doc A/60/1 (2005), para 159.
[120] GA Res 48/141 (1993), para 4(i).
[121] Boyle, n 70 above, 299–318.

5. *Universal Periodic Review*

Most interest has been sparked by the Council's function of reviewing the human rights performance of all states.[122] The universal periodic review (UPR) process is governed by Resolution 60/251 but more detailed modalities of UPR have been adopted by the Human Rights Council and are discussed below.[123]

6. *First Elections to the Council*

The first elections to the 47 member Council were held on 9 May 2006. NGOs were active in pressing the candidate states to make 'voluntary pledges' on upholding human rights. All states ultimately did so and according to observers the pledge may have also dissuaded states with notorious records from standing.[124] The Council's marginally smaller membership than the former Commission (47 rather than 53) resulted in a more pronounced redistribution of seats between the five regional groupings under the equitable geographical distribution formula. The reduction of Latin American and Caribbean seats (15 compared to 21) and the Western Group seats (10 to eight) meant that these countries 'have lost the power to win a vote... unless their proposals attract the support of at least three African and Asian States'.[125]

C. Institution Building: Human Rights Council Resolution 5/1

Following the elections and after informal consultations, states agreed that Ambassador Luis Alfonso de Alba, Mexico's Permanent Representative to International Organisations in Geneva, would hold the position of President of the Council for the first year. The bureau would comprise four vice-presidents selected from the other four regional groups, one of whom would serve as the rapporteur. Under the much praised leadership of Ambassador de Alba, the newly elected Council spent a large portion of its first year 2006–7 in agreeing on the architecture of the body.[126] The results, referred to as the Institution Building text, were published and endorsed by the Council on 17 June 2007 and adopted by Resolution on 18 June 2007.[127]

[122] Ibid, para 5(e).

[123] Institution-building of the United Nations Human Rights Council, Universal Periodic Review Mechanism, A/HRC/Res/5/1, 18 June 2007.

[124] Abraham (2006), n 48 above, at 18. For the states elected see <http://www.un.org/ga/60/elect/hrc>.

[125] Y Terlingen, 'The Human Rights Council: A New Era in UN Human Rights Work' (2006) 21 Ethics and International Affairs 167, 171, cited in M Abraham, 'Building the New Human Rights Council Outcome and analysis of the institution-building year', Occasional Paper 31, the Geneva Office, Friedrich Ebert Stiftung (2007) at 12.

[126] The institution-building process was carried out through three open ended inter-sessional working groups. NGOs and national human rights institutions (NHRIs) participated in the working group sessions along side member and observer states. Abraham, n 124 above, at 9.

[127] A/HRC/Res/5/1, Human Rights Council Resolution 5/1, United Nations Human Rights Council Institution Building, 18 June 2007, paras 1–38.

The text prescribes in considerable detail the following: the Universal Periodic Review Mechanism; Special Procedures; the Complaint Procedure; the Agenda of the Council; Methods of Work, and the Rules of Procedure.

1. Universal Periodic Review Mechanism

The Council has published a calendar time tabling the review of all member states over a four-year cycle. The mechanism's main elements are summarized here.[128]

(a) Principles and objectives

Some twelve principles are set out in Resolution 5/1 to guide UPR. Only some can be touched upon here. Participation of the country under review is axiomatic but the need to involve NGOs as well as National Human Rights Institutions (NIHRIs) is noteworthy. UPR should ensure a gender perspective and also take into account 'the level of development and specificities of countries'. The review should be conducted in 'an objective, transparent, non-selective, constructive, non confrontational and non-politicized manner'. The objectives of the review include improvement of human rights on the ground as well as fulfilment of the state's human rights obligations and at the state's request enhancement of capacity and technical assistance.

(b) Periodicity and order of the review

The cycle for review of all states will be four years, which will require 48 states to be reviewed each year over three sessions of the Council. All members of the Council are to be reviewed during their period in office and the equitable geographic distribution principle will operate in the selection of countries for review.

(c) Sources for UPR

Resolution 5/1 provides that there will be three documents generated as the basis of the review of the state. First, a national report is prepared by the state with a maximum length of 20 pages. The second document will be information from treaty bodies and the Special Procedures prepared by the OHCHR with a maximum length of 10 pages. A third 10-page document also prepared by the OHCHR will be based on information provided by 'other stakeholders', including NGOs and National Human Rights Institutions. In Decision 6/102 the Council provided guidelines for the preparation of this documentation.[129] Notably the states are advised to provide information on what consultation took place within the country in preparing a national report. They are also advised to give the legislative

[128] See also chs 2 and 3 in this volume; Gaer, 'A Voice Not an Echo: Universal Periodic Review and the UN Treaty Body System' (2007) 7 Human Rights Law Review 109; Abraham, n 124 above, at 34–41.

[129] Decision 6/102 Follow-up to the Human Rights Council Resolution 5/1 adopted 27 September 2007.

background of the country especially for the promotion and protection of human rights as well as information on human rights infrastructure, including national human rights institutions. Furthermore, the states should include information on implementation of international human rights obligations as well as, among other data, action on voluntary commitments made on election to the Council and cooperation with human rights mechanisms. States are also encouraged to identify achievements, best practices, challenges, and constraints, as well as how they propose to overcome challenges and 'improve the human rights situation on the ground'. Finally, states might indicate what their capacity building needs are and any request for technical assistance.

(d) Review hearing

The review hearing is conducted in a plenary working group of the Council chaired by the President with member and observer states being free to participate in the interactive dialogue. NGOs and other stakeholders may attend but may not participate at this stage. The rules provide for three rapporteurs chosen by drawing lots from different regional groups (the troika) who have the task of facilitating the review and preparing the working group report on the state in question. The review hearing is allocated three hours and a further hour is allocated for the adoption of the working group's report. The outcome report considered by the plenary Council at a later meeting comprises a summary of the review process along with recommendations and/or conclusions and voluntary commitments. The opportunity is also provided for NGOs to comment at this stage. Prior to the adoption of the 'outcome' document of the review, the state is to be fully involved and may make further comments on the draft report. Recommendations accepted by the state in question will be identified and those which it does not accept will also be recorded.

(e) Follow-up

The true test of the effectiveness of UPR will emerge only with evidence of fulfilment of commitments made by states. UPR will be a standing item on the Council's agenda and it is the intention that there should be scrutiny on the extent to which recommendations are implemented by the state reviewed. In formal terms, that must await the second cycle of UPR, namely after four years, when it is planned that the focus will be on the implementation of commitments. Proposals in the negotiations that a follow up rapporteur might be appointed or that the state reviewed might report to the Council on implementation of the review were not accepted.[130] Persistent non-cooperation by a state with the mechanism, including failure to fulfil recommendations accepted, will be addressed by the Council.[131] The international community would be asked to be involved

[130] Abraham, n 124 above, at 41.
[131] A/HRC/Res/5/1, para 36.

where capacity-building and technical assistance is required in consultation and with the consent of the state.[132]

The first session of the UPR mechanism involving some 16 states was held from 7–18 April.[133] A second session again involving 16 states was held from 5–19 May 2008. While the mechanism is at an early stage it is clear that states under review and Council members in the three hours of interactive dialogue have made serious efforts to give the process meaning and depth. The atmosphere has been constructive and the issues raised for scrutiny have addressed both strengths and weaknesses of the countries in question. What is most interesting and of longer term significance, has been the extent to which countries under review have been both self-critical and have accepted recommendations made by other states for positive action, including the ratification of international instruments. The frankness with which some countries accepted that they have human rights problems and agreed to address them is genuinely new and encouraging.[134] The United Kingdom, considered in the first session, accepted most of the UPR recommendations in whole or in part.[135] Pakistan, considered in the second session of UPR, announced that it was in the process of ratifying the United Nations Civil and Political Covenant and the Convention against Torture. It had ratified the Covenant on Economic and Social and Cultural Rights on its election to the Council. It is also establishing a Human Rights Commission and had incorporated a human rights education curriculum in schools. The interactive dialogue with Pakistan did address many issues including the violation of rights of women, the rights of religious minorities, and capital punishment, subjects which were also documented powerfully in the NGO submissions to the review. These issues, among others, are reflected in the recommendations made by the working group and were said to be given serious consideration by the Government.[136]

2. *Special Procedures*

The most important institutional creation of the former Commission on Human Rights was that of the system of Special Procedures and it is an institution that

132 A/HRC/Res/5/1, para 38.

133 The first group of states selected was: Bahrain, Ecuador, Tunisia, Morocco, Indonesia, Finland, the United Kingdom, India, Brazil, the Philippines, Algeria, Poland, the Netherlands, South Africa, the Czech Republic, and Argentina.

134 The Report of the Human Rights Council on its Eighth Session, 2–18 June 2008, A/HRC/8/L10/Add1, 26 June 2008 contains summaries of the UPR sessions to date. Full documentation relating to the sessions of UPR as well as summaries of the dialogue between the state under review and the Council are available on the OHCR extranet. The extranet also stores archives of the web casts of all UPR sessions.

135 Report of the Working Group on the Universal Periodic Review United Kingdom of Great Britain and Northern Ireland. Addendum, Views on conclusions and/or recommendations, voluntary commitments and replies presented by the State under review, A/HRC/8/25/Add2, 18 June 2008.

136 Report of the Working Group on the Universal Periodic Review Pakistan, A/HRC/8/42, 4 June 2008.

has been preserved in the new Human Rights Council. The Special Procedures are discussed further in Chapter 2 and only a brief account is offered here.[137]

The Special Procedures (Special Rapporteurs, Representatives, Independent Experts, and Working Groups) are independent and unpaid experts appointed by the Commission and now the Council, who have a variety of protection functions including monitoring, investigating, advising, reporting, and making recommendations on the implementation of human rights by governments. They are categorized as thematic, dealing globally with specific human rights or human rights concerns or are appointed in respect of the human rights situation in particular countries. In addition to protection functions the special rapporteurs, as they are most commonly known, have played a significant role in developing international human rights law standards through their analysis of particular norms and their conceptualization and reflections on the problems of securing protection of those norms. However, the work of the experts has not always been appreciated and some states represented on the Council harbour reservations and hostility to the special procedures system, especially those appointed to monitor and investigate violations in particular countries. The negotiations on the special procedures in the Council were a matter largely of preserving rather than advancing the system.[138] Some states did press for the abolition of country rapporteurs based on the argument that the system of UPR rendered them unnecessary.[139] Among the first decisions of the Council was not to re-appoint the country rapporteurs for Cuba and Belarus. However, the remaining 39 rapporteurs had their mandates renewed for one year.[140] UN Resolution 60/251 had directed the Council to 'review and where necessary improve and rationalize' the system of special procedures, a process which is ongoing. The Council has now adopted a Code of Conduct for Special Procedure mandate holders.[141] The Council has also set out rules to ensure transparent selection and appointment of qualified mandate holders.[142] Given that more time is available, the experience of the interactive dialogue with the special procedures during the presentation of their reports in the Council sessions to date has been a considerable improvement in terms of time and content, compared with the former Commission.[143]

[137] See ch 2 in this volume, N Rodley, 'United Nations Human Rights Council, Its Special Procedures and Their Relationship with the Treaty Bodies—Complementarity or Competition'. See also, G Oberleitner, *Global Human Rights Institutions* (2007), 54–60; J Gutter, 'Special Procedures and the Human Rights Council: Achievements and Challenges Ahead', (2007) 7 Human Rights Law Review 93. An extensive source on the special procedures is the dedicated page on the OHCHR site at <http://www.ohchr.org>.

[138] Abrahams, n 124 above, at 33.

[139] Algeria (on behalf of the African Group), Bangladesh, Belarus, China, Cuba, the Democratic People's Republic of Korea, India, Iran, Malaysia; Abrahams, n 124 above, at 27.

[140] Human Rights Council, Decision 102, 29 June 2006.

[141] A/HRC/Res/5/2, 18 June 2007. [142] Ibid, paras 39–64.

[143] R Brett 'Neither Mountain Nor Mole Hill: Review of the Human Rights Council One Year On', Quaker United Nations Office, Geneva, August 2007 at 8; M Lempinen, n 62 above, at 248–59.

3. *The Human Rights Council Advisory Committee*

This new body replacing the former Sub-Commission on the Promotion and Protection of Human Rights will consist of 18 experts and is explicitly termed a think tank for the Council.[144] It will work at the Council's direction and under guidelines set out in the institution-building resolution. The clear subordination of the Advisory Committee to the Council spelled out in these guidelines is the culmination of what had been happening to the autonomy of its predecessor body.

The Advisory Committee is elected by the Council in secret ballot based on a set allocation by geographical region.[145] All member states of the UN may nominate candidates for the Advisory Committee but from their own region only. While civil society organizations may not nominate, the guidelines recommend that states consult with NHRIs and NGOs and that the names of those supporting proposed candidates should be included with the nomination. Due consideration should be given in nominations and elections to gender balance and 'an appropriate representation of different civilizations and legal systems'.[146]

Members of the Advisory Committee are required to have recognized competence in the field of human rights, to be of high moral standing, and to have independence and impartiality. Regrettably, the guidelines do not exclude candidates holding government appointment but rather only where such individuals hold positions that could give rise to a conflict of interests with their responsibilities in the Advisory Committee.[147] Members will serve for three years and may be re-elected once.

The Advisory Committee may not adopt resolutions or decisions and its work, studies, and research-based advice, will be requested by the Council. However, it may suggest further research proposals for approval by the Council. At its abolition, the Sub-Commission met for a single session of three weeks. The Advisory Committee is reduced to two weeks of meetings, which should be different sessions, although it may request approval for additional ad hoc sessions from the Council. In addition to states, NGOs, NIHRIs, intergovernmental organizations and others are encouraged to participate in the Committee's meetings on the same basis as their involvement with the Council. The Advisory Committee will have a function under the new complaints procedure of the Council (see below).

4. *Social Forum and the Minorities Forum*

The Council has decided that the Social Forum, an initiative of the former Sub-Commission, will continue to be convened.[148] The Forum is designed to allow

[144] The first meeting of the Advisory Committee is scheduled for August 2008 in Geneva.

[145] A/HRC/Res/5/1, paras 70–84. The regional allocation on the Advisory Committee is: African States 5; Asian States 5; Eastern European States 2; Latin American and Caribbean States 3; Western European and other States 3. The High Level Panel had envisaged independent experts would be nominated for appointment jointly by the Secretary General and High Commissioner for Human Rights, n 53 above, para 287.

[146] A/HRC/Res/5/1, para 72. [147] A/HRC/Res/5/1, para 68.

[148] A/HRC/Res/6/13, 28 September 2007. This Forum is scheduled to meet for three days in September 2008.

dialogue about global poverty themes between the UN human rights system as well as relevant UN agencies and grass roots civil society. A further initiative of the former Sub-Commission was the Working Group on Minorities established as a forum within the Sub-Commission for dialogue between different minorities and with governments.[149] It was distinctive in allowing full participation from minorities and NGOs. The Human Rights Council has now approved, in replacement of the Working Group, a Forum on Minority Issues with a similar mandate and similar participation.[150] The Forum will meet annually for two days for thematic discussions. Its mandate is directed at promoting dialogue and cooperation on minority issues as well as the further implementation of the UN Declaration on Minorities. The independent expert of the Council on minority issues will guide the work of the Forum and report on its deliberations to the Council.

5. *Complaint Procedure*

Resolution 5/1 sets out a complaint procedure, 'to address consistent patterns of gross and reliably tested violations of all human rights and all fundamental freedoms occurring in any part of the world and under any circumstances.'[151] In effect, the complaint procedure reproduces the 1503 complaint procedure of the former Commission on Human Rights.[152] However, it is expressed to be 'improved where necessary so as to ensure that the complaint procedure be impartial, objective, efficient, and victims-oriented and conducted in a timely manner'. The entire procedure will remain a confidential one 'with a view to enhancing cooperation with the State concerned'. The mechanism is directed at situations of violation and is not for a complaint of an individual violation for which there are other avenues at national and international levels.

As under the 1503 procedure, there are two stages in the process of addressing a complaint. The Human Rights Advisory Committee will constitute a five-member Working Group on Communications, with one member from each regional group. Its function is to determine the admissibility and merits of a communication. The other body, the Working Group on Situations, is made up from the Council itself. It receives from the Advisory Committee a file of all admissible communications with its recommendations. The Working Group on Situations may then provide a report to the Council with recommendations on a course of action. The range of actions open to the Council are, as with the former Commission, to keep the matter under review, appoint an expert to monitor and to report back to the Council, or to decide to discontinue the confidential procedure and bring the case before the Council in public session. The Council may recommend that the OHCHR provide capacity-building assistance or advisory services to the state concerned. A positive improvement on the 1503 procedure is

[149] ECOSOC Res 1995/31 of 25 July 1995.
[150] A/HRC/Res/6/15, 28 September 2007 and see Alfredsson, ch 6 in this volume.
[151] A/HRC/Res/5/1, paras 85–109.
[152] Abraham, n 124 above, at 61–72.

that the complainant is to be kept informed at all stages of the process, including being informed as to the outcome.

6. *Special Sessions*

The idea of mandating the new Human Rights Council to convene special sessions outside its agreed schedule of meetings was intended to increase its relevance and that of the United Nations in addressing human rights emergencies. For most of its existence, the former Commission on Human Rights had no such competence. However, in 1990, exceptional sessions were authorized by ECOSOC subject to approval by half of Commission members.[153]

The Human Rights Council was authorized to hold special sessions at the request of a member of the Council with the support of one-third of the membership.[154] Within a period of less than two years the Council has convened in special session no less than seven times. These sessions can only be addressed here briefly. The first six sessions concerned what would be recognized as human rights emergencies where civil and political rights had been grossly violated or were at risk.[155] The seventh, held in May 2008, was a novel initiative at the request of Cuba to consider a different emergency affecting an economic and social right—the impact on the right to food of the sudden rise in food prices. The request for the session had the support of members from all regional groups and the resolution concluding the session which emphasized the right to food and the respondent duties of states to secure it in the current crisis passed without dissension.[156] The special session on Myanmar also concluded without a vote in the Council. It passed a strong resolution condemning the military regime and its massive repression of protest.[157] However, that could not be said about the other special sessions. The dire situation in the Occupied Territories was before the Council on three occasions following Israeli military incursions.

Each session resulted in condemnatory resolutions passed with a significant number of votes against and also abstentions. In each case the division in the Council over the question of including condemnation of both Israeli and Palestinian violence reflected the constant regional divisions to be found in all UN fora over the Occupied Palestinian Territories. A similar division was reflected in the session on Lebanon, which followed the sudden outbreak in July 2006 of armed conflict between Israel and Hezbollah.[158] The special session on

[153] ECOSOC Res 1990/48 of 25 May 1990. The Commission held five special sessions to discuss the situation in former Yugoslavia (August and December 1992); Rwanda (1994); East Timor (1999); and violations of the human rights of the Palestinian people by Israel (2000).

[154] GA/Res/60/251, para 10.

[155] Three of these concerned the Occupied Palestinian Territories, a fourth, the 2006 Lebanon war, and the others, the situations in Darfur and in Myanmar.

[156] A/HRC/S/7/1, 22 May 2008.

[157] A/Res/HRC/S-5/1: Situation of human rights in Myanmar , 2 October 2007.

[158] A/HRC/S-2/1, The grave situation of human rights in Lebanon caused by Israeli military operations, 11 August 2006.

Sudan over Darfur was called by Finland and the European Union, after considerable criticism over the excessive focus on Israeli violations compared with other human rights emergencies. After much negotiation, which removed condemnatory language in respect of the Sudan's responsibility for the Darfur human rights crisis, a resolution was passed without a vote which nevertheless did agree to send a high level mission to Darfur.[159] As it happened, the mission was unable to visit Darfur as the Sudan did not issue visas.[160] One positive feature of practice from these sessions results from the General Assembly's direction that the Council be 'action-oriented'. This has meant that compared to the former Commission, the Council has focused more on utilizing mechanisms for investigation including the special procedures, as well as engaging with governments (as in the case of Sudan) and following up the reports of missions.[161]

7. NGOs and National Human Rights Institutions (NIHRIs)

A positive feature of the institutional building process has been the explicit recognition extended to civil society and NIHRIs. General Assembly Resolution 65/251 directed that the participation of NGOs would be based on the existing rules that had applied to the Commission as well as Commission practice.[162] Practice had allowed considerable freedom to NGOs beyond what would be obtained before the General Assembly or other UN bodies in the circulation of documents and opportunities to speak, as well as to interact with government delegates.[163] NGOs welcomed the creation of the Human Rights Council and a coalition of NGOs for an effective Council has been vital in ensuring that the best of the inheritance from the former Commission was preserved, particularly the special procedures. They participated in the negotiation of the institutional package through the working groups of the Council. NGOs also participate in the interactive dialogue with the special procedures and, as noted above, have an explicit input into the UPR, including the opportunity to speak during the consideration of the final outcome of the review by the plenary session of the Council. The parallel sessions held by NGOs (and by NIHRIs) during lunch breaks attract not only civil society but also governmental representatives.

NGO activism has also been evident in the General Assembly over the election of states to the Human Rights Council. Thus the Coalition of NGOs for the Human Rights Council at the initiative of Sri Lankan NGOs lobbied effectively

159 S-4/101, Situation of human rights in Darfur, 9 March 2007.

160 A/HRC/4/80 Report of the High-Level Mission on the situation of human rights in Darfur pursuant to Human Rights Council decision S-4/101, 9 March 2007.

161 Brett, n 143 above, at 5.

162 ECOSOC Res 1996/31 establishes a scheme of different categories of consultative status for NGOS and encourages the participation of NGOs from developing countries. See, A/HRC/Res/5/1, Rule 7. The Conference of Non-Governmental Organisations in Consultative Status with the United Nations, (CONGO) is the key body which facilitates the participation of NGOs before the Council, <http://www.ngocongo.org/>.

163 Prove, n 57 above, at 11.

against the re-election of Sri Lanka to an Asian vacancy based on its human rights record.[164] African NGOs across the continent also lobbied African governments against Egypt assuming the position of Presidency of the Council by rotation for 2008–9, successfully promoting Nigeria instead.[165] The central importance to global human rights protection of a continuing strong NGO presence at the Human Rights Council is recognized by all. However, concern has been voiced over future NGO participation given the financial and other demands on them that a three-session Council now imposes.[166]

NIHRI participation had grown significantly over the final years of the former Commission and these independent national level human rights bodies have equally proved active before the Human Rights Council.[167] These bodies, which are accredited as in compliance with the Paris Principles[168] by the International Co-ordinating Committee of National Institutions, may contribute documentation and participate orally in Council sessions.[169]

8. The United Nations High Commissioner and the Human Rights Council

The position of the UN High Commissioner for Human Rights along with the Office of the High Commissioner was established by resolution of the General Assembly in 1993.[170] Resolution 48/141 provides that the High Commissioner holds the rank of Under Secretary General and is described as 'the United Nations official with principal responsibility for United Nations human rights activities'. The High Commissioner is appointed by the Secretary General following approval by the General Assembly, is answerable to the Secretary General, and carries out activities 'under the direction and control of the Secretary General'. The High Commissioner holds office for four years, renewable for one further term of four years. In selecting a candidate the Secretary General must have due regard to geographical location. At the same time the High Commissioner works with the main UN human rights organs, including the Human Rights

[164] 'UN: Sri Lanka's Defeat a Victory for Human Rights Council UN Vote Upholds Council Membership Standards on Rights' <http://www.hrw.org/effectiveHRC/SriLanka/>, 21 May 2008.

[165] Ted Picoone 'Score One for the NGOs', *Washington Post*, 5 July 2008. Egyptian NGOs had challenged Egypt's candidature for the Human Rights Council in 1997—'19 Egyptian Human Rights NGOs Appeal to the United Nations Egypt is Not Fit for Membership of the UN Human Rights Council', Cairo Institute for Human Rights, 14 May 2007.

[166] Brett, n 143 above, at 14. According to the OHCHR, between 110 and 179 NGOs took part in the first seven sessions of the Human Rights Council—OHCHR(2007) Report Activities and Results, 10.

[167] The basis of their participation is Commission Resolution 2005/4, 20 April 2005.

[168] Principles relating to the status and functioning of national institutions for protection and promotion of human rights were endorsed by the General Assembly by A/Res/48/134, 20 December 1993.

[169] Interventions by NIHRIs can be found in the OHCHR extranet. See also the official website National Human Rights Institutions Forum, <http://www.nhri.net>.

[170] GA/Res/48/141 of 20 December 1993.

Council and the General Assembly. The High Commissioner is a department of the UN secretariat, not an independent agency or body of the organization. The High Commissioner must undertake the tasks these organs request, but at the same time has the right to make recommendations on policy and action. The High Commissioner reports annually to the Human Rights Council and to the General Assembly. Resolution 60/251 establishing the Human Rights Council refers to the Council assuming 'the role and responsibilities of the Commission on Human Rights relating to the work of the Office of the United Nations High Commissioner for Human Rights as decided by the General Assembly in its Resolution 48/141 20 December 1993.'[171]

The precise role and the responsibilities of the former Commission and now the Council have never been entirely clear and the ambiguities in the relationship between the new Council and the High Commissioner have been a source of some tension between the two bodies.[172] The Council has assigned the role of secretariat to the Office of the High Commissioner in its institution-building resolution.[173] The OHCHR also fulfils such support functions for the treaty bodies and the special procedures. However, successive High Commissioners have also built up an independent protection role mandated by the General Assembly resolution establishing the post. The strengthening of OHCHR was a major element of the reforms that Kofi Annan had pressed for and achieved at the 2005 UN Summit. A doubling of the budget of the Office was approved.[174] The OHCHR had published an Action Plan in 2005 which envisaged the growth of its work by expanding its country missions in different world regions.[175]

The former High Commissioner Louise Arbour[176] had been a strong supporter of UPR as one potential means to reduce politicization and selectivity in the work of the Human Rights Council and advance human rights protection on the ground. The mechanism of UPR calls heavily on the resources of the OHCHR as it is responsible for the preparation of the substantial documentation involved which will necessitate increased staff.[177]

The High Commissioner has also had to endure pressure from the General Assembly and the Human Rights Council on the geographic composition of OHCHR staff to the effect that it is too Western and offends the principle

[171] See para 4.

[172] See for example the High Commissioner Louise Arbour's reported remarks in Washington in 2007, 'The Office of the Human Rights Commissioner is not the Human Rights Council . . . for those who have lost faith in the council, it is very important that they don't write off the office of the high commissioner', Marc Perelman 'U.N. Rights Chief Takes Her Case to Congress', *The Forward*, 11 July 2007.

[173] A/HRC/Res/5/1, Rule 14.

[174] 2005 World Summit Outcome UN Doc A/60/1 (2005) para 124.

[175] A/59/2005/Add3, 26 May 2005.

[176] Louise Arbour completed her four-year term on 30 June 2008. The new High Commissioner is Navanethem (Navi) Pillay of South Africa, who will take up her post on 1 September 2008.

[177] OHCHR (2007) Report Activities and Results, 9.

of equitable geographic distribution.[178] There is concern that such pressure is intended by some member states to reduce the autonomy of OHCHR and of the High Commissioner. At one point in the negotiations over the Council, China had proposed that the Council might 'supervise the work of the Office of the High Commissioner for Human Rights by regularly reviewing its annual work programme and budget as well as their implementation'. The proposal was not pursued but gave rise to considerable concern.[179] It is clear nevertheless that the majority of states recognize that the new Council needs to work cooperatively with OHCHR respecting the different competences of each body. The OHCHR is an indispensable and autonomous part of the United Nations human rights system and its work is vital for the Human Rights Council's future.

4. Prospects

A. 'Neither Mountain nor Molehill'

A perceptive and experienced observer of the transition from Commission on Human Rights to Human Rights Council summed up the first year of the Council as 'neither a mountain nor a mole hill'.[180] That continues to be an apposite verdict after the second year of its existence. The Human Rights Council has neither fulfilled the highest expectations nor has it dashed them completely. The United States however, has become disenchanted. It appears for now to have lost confidence in the Human Rights Council. It did not put itself forward for election to the Council in its first or second year and in June 2008 announced its withdrawal as an observer from the Council citing, amongst other issues, the disproportionate focus on condemnation of Israel compared to other countries.[181] The decision to withdraw from the Council has been criticized. Human Rights Watch condemned the decision as failing victims and noted that human rights abuses in US counter-terrorism policies had undermined its credibility in defending human

[178] A/Res/61/159, 16 February 2007; Human Rights Council A/HRC/7, 27 March 2008. The Council resolution was introduced by Cuba and was adopted by a recorded vote 34 to 10. The European Union and other states, while agreeing with the goal of the resolution, voted against it on the grounds that significant advances had been made by the High Commissioner on geographical balancing of staff and that human resource questions were a matter for the Fifth Committee of the General Assembly and for the Secretary General. According to internal statistics, as of 31 December 2007, 13.1% of all OHCHR professional staff were from Africa; 12.6% from Asia; 11.9% from Latin America-Caribbean Group; 4.8% from Eastern Europe, and 57.5% Western Europe and Other group. This should be compared with the overall UN Secretariat ratios: Africa: 13.2%; Asia: 19%; LAC: 11.2%; EE: 9.3%; WEO: 47%. A Frazer 'Law Vision and Tightrope Walking: OHCHR in the Context of UN Reform and the International Politics of Human Rights' (2007) (LLM thesis on file University of Essex, United Kingdom).

[179] Prove, n 57 above, at 25.

[180] Brett, n 143 above.

[181] n 24 above.

rights before the Council.[182] The current US Administration's negative posture towards the new Human Rights Council from its inception has been as damaging to the historical legacy of the United States as the architect of the former Commission on Human Rights as it has been for its fledgling successor. Whether a new administration following the presidential election in the United States in November 2008 will lead to a change in policy is unknown, but the long-term absence of the United States from engagement with the United Nations Human Rights Council can only have negative implications for its prospects and for the international human rights system as a whole.

The Council's achievements in making a successful transition from the former Commission, by establishing its own institutional architecture, procedures, and agenda for work is rightly praised. This could not have been achieved without the commitment of its members to a considerable degree of cooperation and willingness to compromise especially across geographic and political blocs. That is not to say that there are not major differences within the Council over human rights, as has been evident in its sessions to date. But members understand that the credibility of the Council requires that differences are negotiated through dialogue, particularly across regions. The membership of the Council is by a considerable majority representative of the developing world. The Western members cannot dominate its decisions and need to negotiate to achieve their goals. But the commitment to a culture of dialogue and cooperation must not lead to a position where the Council avoids addressing the realities of states flagrantly violating human rights. The efforts to abolish country rapporteurs have been resisted so far, but if the pressure to do so from some states (including China) succeed, not only the credibility, but also the relevance, of the Council could come into question.

The long-term success of the Council rests with the one true innovation achieved through its creation: the system of Universal Periodic Review. UPR is at an early stage but the success to date of the non-adversarial but frank and detailed dialogue between states holds real promise for the advancement of universal human rights protection. The continued engagement of civil society and of other 'stakeholders' such as NIHRIs with the Council, is vital for the effectiveness of UPR. Their engagement across the entire mandate of the Council is equally vital if its potential as a new beginning in the promotion and protection of universal human rights is to be realized.

1. The Council and other Components of the UN Human Rights System

In his note to the General Assembly, setting out his thoughts on the proposed Human Rights Council in 2005, the former Secretary General, Kofi Annan, identified a range of issues which would need to be addressed once the Council

[182] 'Leaving UN Rights Council Fails Victims of Abuse', *Human Rights Watch Press Release*, Geneva, 6 June 2008.

was established. These concerned the Council's relationship with other parts of the United Nations human rights system and represent a considerable agenda for the Council over its next years:

Another set of issues requiring further elaboration concerns the role and mandate of the Human Rights Council vis-à-vis the other components of the United Nations human rights system, in particular the Office of the High Commissioner, other United Nations agencies and programmes dealing with human rights, the treaty monitoring bodies, the General Assembly, the Security Council, the Economic and Social Council and the proposed new Peace-building Commission. The creation of the Human Rights Council would reinforce and strengthen the human rights work of those other components. For example, the Human Rights Council would provide an opportunity to rationalize the agenda of the Third Committee of the General Assembly with the work of the Human Rights Council, as well as to strengthen the General Assembly's ability to analyse and draw attention to continuing gaps in the implementation and mainstreaming of human rights throughout the United Nations system.[183]

As anticipated by Kofi Annan, an unresolved issue concerns the respective functions of the Council and the Third Committee of the General Assembly which considers human rights and humanitarian issues. Resolution 60/251 requires that the Council submit an annual report to the General Assembly. The concern is over duplication of functions between the Human Rights Council and the Third Committee which could undermine the Council.[184] Ambassador Luis Alfonso de Alba, the Human Rights Council's first President, has voiced the worry that, 'the possibility of the Third Committee reopening decisions of the Council weakens the status of the Council and pays little credit to its work. A good and logical division between the Council and the Third Committee remains to be solved.'[185]

The relationship between the Council and the High Commissioner for Human Rights has already been discussed. One of the tasks given to the Council is to promote the effective coordination and mainstreaming of human rights within the United Nations system, a function, as already noted, that is also given to the High Commissioner for Human Rights. The experience of OHCHR in the field, including as part of peace missions,[186] has relevance for the Council's preventive mandate. Its duty to respond to human rights emergencies offers a foundation

[183] Explanatory Note by Secretary General, n 105 above, para 17.

[184] For criticism of the incoherence of the Third Committee's human rights work see, G Oberleitner, n 62 above, at 86–8.

[185] 'From the Commission on Human Rights to the Human Rights Council: Reflections on the Transition' public lecture, University of Essex, Human Rights Centre, 7 March 2008. <http://www2.essex.ac.uk/human_rights_centre/news/Essex-Remarks%20LADA.pdf>. See also, 'Third Committee suspends consideration of the first-ever report of Human Rights Council' General Assembly, GA/SHC/3865, UN Department of Public Information, 11 November 2006.

[186] By the end of 2007, OHCHR had 11 country offices, nine regional offices, and 13 human rights advisers in UN Country Teams, and also supported human rights components in 17 peace missions, OHCHR (2007) Report Activities and Results, 6.

for a relationship with the Security Council. A constructive relationship with the treaty bodies can develop through the UPR mechanism which already draws on their reports. But all such relationships with other components of the United Nations human rights system will require leadership and commitment in the Council as well as time to develop.

2

The United Nations Human Rights Council, Its Special Procedures, and Its Relationship with the Treaty Bodies: Complementarity or Competition?[1]

Sir Nigel Rodley

1. Introduction

For historical reasons, the United Nations (UN) is presently endowed with two sets of human rights monitoring procedures: those established under human rights treaties[2] and those under the UN Human Rights Council, variously called

[1] This is an updated and expanded version of 'United Nations Human Rights Treaty Bodies and Special Procedures of the Commission on Human Rights—Complementarity or Competition', 25 Human Rights Quarterly 882 (2003); reprinted in N Ando (ed), *Towards Implementing Universal Human Rights—Festschrift for the Twenty-Fifth Anniversary of the Human Rights Committee* (2004) 3.

[2] The eight core treaties and treaty bodies are: International Convention on the Elimination of All Forms of Racial Discrimination, 660 UNTS 195 (entered into force 4 January 1969), (1966) (ICERD)/Committee on the Elimination of Racial Discrimination (CERD); International Covenant on Economic, Social and Cultural Rights, GA Res 2200 (XXI), (1966) (entered into force 3 January 1976) (ICESCR)/Committee on Economic, Social and Cultural Rights (CESCR); International Covenant on Civil and Political Rights, GA Res 2200 (XXI) (1966) (entered into force 23 March 1976) (ICCPR)/Human Rights Committee (HRC); Convention on the Elimination of All Forms of Discrimination Against Women, GA Res 34/180, (1980) (entered into force 3 September 1981), (CEDAW)/Committee on the Elimination of Discrimination Against Women (CEDAW Committee); Convention Against Torture and Other Cruel, Inhuman or Degrading Treatment or Punishment, GA Res 39/46, (1985) (entered into force 26 June 1987), (CAT)/Committee Against Torture (CAT Committee); and Convention on the Rights of the Child, GA Res 44/25 (1989) (entered into force 2 September 1990) (CRC)/Committee on the Rights of the Child (CRC Committee); International Convention on Protection of the Rights of All Migrant Workers and Members of their Families, GA Res 45/158 (1990) (entered into force on 1 July 2003) (ICRMW)/Committee on Migrant Workers (CMW), Convention on the Rights of Persons with Disabilities, GA Res 61/106 (2006)/Committee on the Rights of Persons with Disabilities (entered into force 3 May 2008). A further core treaty has since been adopted, but is not yet in force; International Convention for the Protection of All Persons from Enforced Disappearance, GA Res 61/177 (2006)/Committee on Enforced Disappearances. The following works deal with the treaty system as a whole: P Alston and J Crawford (eds), *The Future of UN*

'non-treaty procedures', 'extra-conventional mechanisms', or 'Charter-based mechanisms'. The latter may be divided into procedures at the level of the Council itself (public and private) and the 'special procedures', that is, those the Council has established to be discharged by appointed experts acting in their individual capacities. These, in turn, may be divided into country-specific and thematic procedures. In practice, the country-specific special procedures are generated directly by the Council's own country discussions and only last as long as the Council considers (for whatever reason) that it should continue to scrutinize the human rights situation in the state in question. The thematic special procedures have a more stable status, being renewed for three-year periods and rarely discontinued.[3]

The Charter-based procedures as a whole only began to develop after the first human rights treaties were adopted. The International Convention on the Elimination of All Forms of Racial Discrimination (ICERD) was adopted in 1965; the International Covenant on Civil and Political Rights (ICCPR) and on Economic, Social and Cultural Rights (ICCSCR) were adopted in 1966. The first country-specific engagement of the Council's predecessor, the Commission on Human Rights, came with the adoption in 1967 of Economic and Social Council ('ECOSOC') Resolution 1235 (XLII). This permitted the Commission to con-

Human Rights Treaty Monitoring, (2000); A F Bayefsky (ed), *The UN Human Rights System in the 21st Century* (2000); A F Bayefsky, *The UN Human Rights Treaty System* (2001).

[3] The following thematic mandates are in existence at the time of writing: Working Group on Enforced or Involuntary Disappearances; Working Group on Arbitrary Detention; Working Group on People of African Descent; Special Rapporteur on Extrajudicial, Summary or Arbitrary Executions; Special Rapporteur on the independence of judges and lawyers; Special Rapporteur on the question of torture; Representative of the Secretary General on Internally Displaced Persons; Special Rapporteur on Religious Intolerance; Special Rapporteur on the Question of the Use of Mercenaries; Special Rapporteur on the Promotion and Protection of the Right to Freedom of Opinion and Expression; Special Rapporteur on Contemporary Forms of Racism, Racial Discrimination, Xenophobia and Related Intolerance; Special Rapporteur on the Sale of Children, Child Prostitution and Child Pornography; Special Rapporteur on Violence against Women, its Causes and Consequences; Special Representative of the Secretary General on the Situation of Human Rights Defenders; Special Rapporteur on the Adverse Effects of the Illicit Movement and Dumping of Toxic and Dangerous Products and Wastes; Special Rapporteur on the Human Rights of Migrants; Independent Expert on the Effects of Economic Reform Policies and Foreign Debt on the Full Enjoyment of Human Rights; Special Rapporteur on the Right to Education; Special Rapporteur on the Right to Adequate Housing; Special Rapporteur on the Right to Food; Special Rapporteur on the Situation of Human Rights and Fundamental Freedoms of Indigenous People; Independent Expert on the Question of Human Rights and Extreme Poverty; Independent Expert on the Right to Development; Special Rapporteur on the Right to Health; Independent Expert on Minority Issues; Independent Expert on Human Rights and International Solidarity; Special Rapporteur on Human Rights and Terrorism; Special Rapporteur on Trafficking in Persons; and Special Representative of the Secretary General on Human Rights and Transnational Corporations and Other Business Enterprises. The following works deal with the special procedures system: J Carey, *UN Protection of Civil and Political Rights* (1985); T J M Zuijdwijk, *Petitioning the United Nations* (1982); M E Tardu, *Human Rights: the International Petition System* (1979); A Dormenval, *Procédures onnusiennes de mise en oeuvre des croits de l'homme* (PUF, Paris, 1991); M Lempinen, *Challenges Facing the System of Special Procedures of the United National Commission on Human Rights* (2001), ch 8 of which also addresses the relationship between the special procedures and the treaty bodies; I Nifosi, *The UN Special Procedures in the Field of Human Rights* (2005); J Gutter, *Thematic Procedures of the United Nations Commission on Human Rights and International Law* (2006).

sider consistent patterns of human rights violations and investigate gross human rights violations. In 1970, the well-known 1503 procedure (named after the ECOSOC Resolution 1503 (XLVIII) establishing it) was adopted to permit the Commission to deal, in closed session, with complaints from non-governmental sources of consistent patterns of gross violations of human rights. It was not until 1980 that the Commission established its first thematic mechanism, the Working Group on Enforced or Involuntary Disappearances, that is, some 35 years after the founding of the UN.

This delay reflected a belief by many of the member states of the organization in its early days that scrutiny of any individual state's human rights practices constituted improper intervention in matters essentially within the domestic jurisdiction of states, as excluded by Article 2(7) of the Charter of the United Nations. Even though, as early as 1950, the bold and pioneering commentator Sir Hersch Lauterpacht argued that mere discussion of a state's human rights performance was not precluded under the Charter's non-intervention rule,[4] that view was not to prevail for some two decades.

On the other hand, no such problem existed if a state voluntarily agreed to the monitoring activity by means of adherence to a treaty that provided for it. In the words of one of the most renowned framers of the Universal Declaration of Human Rights,

> *il aurait été difficile de contester que les Etats pouvaient par la voie d'instruments juridiques particuliers prendre des engagements qui faisaient ressortir les obligations qu'ils assumaient ainsi en matière des droits de l'homme du domaine de leur compétence interne.*[5]

Thus, supervisory procedures were envisaged as a necessary part of the two treaties that, with the Universal Declaration, were to complete the International Bill of Human Rights: ICESCR[6] and the ICCPR.[7] As it happened, the protracted process of agreeing on the Covenants made it possible for the specialized ICERD[8] to be adopted a year earlier, with its own supervisory body. The drafting of three of the four other specialized conventions now in force—the Convention on the Elimination of All Forms of Discrimination against Women (CEDAW),[9] the Convention against Torture and Other Cruel, Inhuman or Degrading Treatment

[4] H Lauterpacht, *International Law and Human Rights* (1950), at 168–73.

[5] René Cassin, *Hague Recueil* (1951), 27, 310. 'It would have been difficult to disagree that States could, by way of particular juridical instruments, take on commitments that entail assuming obligations, including in the field of human rights within their domestic jurisdiction.'

[6] See generally M Craven, *The International Covenant on Economic, Social and Cultural Rights* (1995).

[7] See generally D McGoldrick, *The Human Rights Committee: Its Role in the Development of the International Covenant on Civil and Political Rights* (1990); I Boerefijn, *The Reporting Procedure under the Covenant on Civil and Political Rights* (1999); S Joseph, J Schultz, and M Castan, *The International Covenant on Civil and Political Rights—Cases, Materials and Commentary* (2nd ed, 2004); M Nowak, UN *Covenant on Civil and Political Rights—CCPR Commentary* (2nd ed, 2005).

[8] See generally N Lerner, *The UN Convention on the Elimination of All Forms of Racial Discrimination* (2nd ed, 1980).

[9] CEDAW, n 2 above; see generally L Rehof, *Guide to the Travaux Préparatoires of the United Nations Convention on the Elimination of All Forms of Discrimination against Women (1993).*

or Punishment (CAT),[10] and the Convention on the Rights of the Child (CRC)[11]—began before the beginnings of the thematic special procedures.

This history permits speculation as to whether the treaty bodies would have been created had extra-conventional mechanisms with a comprehensive mandate been achievable at the birth of the UN.

Similarly, the existence of the treaty bodies, once on the horizon, led to early concerns that special procedures should not duplicate their work and, indeed, that the very existence of the special procedures should be reviewed once the treaty bodies were in operation.[12]

In fact, we seem now to be at the stage where, despite occasional reviews of each of the two systems—treaty bodies[13] and non-treaty procedures[14]—there is no serious proposal to roll back one system in favour of the other. Rather, the chapter will first look at the country-specific work of the Human Rights Council, comparing and contrasting it with the relevant working methods of the treaty bodies. Here the potential for overlap between, on the one hand, the new Council procedure of Universal Periodic Review (UPR) and, on the other, the treaty body review of periodic reports will be identified and its significance assessed. Subsequently, the work of the treaty bodies and that of the thematic special procedures will be compared and contrasted, in respect of which there is surprisingly little duplication and overlap.

2. Country Work of the Council and Review of Periodic Reports by Treaty Bodies

The country work of the Commission on Human Rights traditionally raised no problems of duplication or overlap with that of the treaty bodies. First, the decision to consider a country situation under either the 1235 or 1503 procedures was one taken by a group of government representatives, whereas the treaty bodies are

[10] CAT, n 2 above; see generally J H Burgers and H Danelius, *The United Nations Convention against Torture: a Handbook on the Convention against Torture and Other Cruel, Inhuman or Degrading Treatment or Punishment* (1988); A Boulesbaa, *The UN Convention on Torture and the Prospects for Enforcement* (1999); C Ingelse, *The UN Committe against Torture* (2001).

[11] CRC, n 2 above; see generally A G Mower, Jr, *The Convention on the Rights of the Child* (1997); S Detrick, *A Commentary on the United Nations Convention on the Rights of the Child* (1999).

[12] See ECOSOC Res 1235 (XLII), para 4; ECOSOC Res 1503 (XLVIII), para 10.

[13] See, eg, P Alston, Independent Expert, *Effective Functioning of Bodies Established Pursuant to United Nations Human Rights Instruments (Final Report)*, UN Doc E/CN.4/1997/74 (1997); Concept Paper on the High Commissioner's Proposal for a Unified Standing Treaty Body, UN Doc HRI/MC/2006/2.

[14] See *Enhancing the effectiveness of the mechanisms of the Commission on Human Rights*, UN Doc E/CN.4/DEC/2000/109 (2000); *Report of the Intersessional open-ended working group on enhancing the effectiveness of the mechanisms of the Commission on Human Rights*, UN Doc E/CN.4/2000/112; Human Rights Council Res 5/1 (2007), *Institution-Building of the United Nations Human Rights Council.*

composed of individual experts.[15] Secondly, the treaty bodies are not normally looking at an overall situation; rather they are focusing on specific issues. This is evidently the case for the specialized treaty bodies but it is also largely true for the treaty bodies with a more general mandate: the Human Rights Committee (HRC) under the ICCPR and the Committee on Economic, Social and Cultural Rights. Typically, they look at states from an article-by-article perspective, not a global one. Thirdly, and of special importance, the treaty bodies do not usually take up states on an ad hoc basis; they pursue a standard agenda, applying their procedures as state reports come up for consideration, apart from the rarely used option retained by some treaty bodies of asking for special reports. What it boils down to is that the traditional country work of the Commission/Council has involved unmistakably political decision-making, while that of the treaty bodies is impartially selected and institutionally determined.

Indeed, it was the very politically selective nature of the Commission's work that was asserted to be a central reason for seeking to replace it with another body—the Council. Others will assess how successfully in general this objective appears to have been achieved.[16] Here, we are concerned only with one dimension of the Council's processes, the UPR. However, it was precisely the UPR process that was seen as a key innovation in addressing the political selectivity charge. Since UPR was something that would apply to all UN member states, it would be impossible to argue that the Council was applying double standards. Universality is the opposite of selectivity.

The relevance of this to the treaty bodies lies in the fact that the one procedure common to all the treaty bodies and obligatory on all states party to the treaties is the periodic review process, involving states party submitting reports that are then considered and assessed by the treaty body in question on the basis of a 'constructive dialogue'. This sounds suspiciously close to UPR which, according to General Assembly Resolution 60/251,[17] is to be 'a cooperative mechanism, based on an interactive dialogue'. The Assembly was evidently alert to the issue, since it

[15] Of course, when the Commission/Council appoints a body, such as (rarely) a working group or (typically) a special rapporteur to undertake country-specific scrutiny, the mandate-holders serve as individual experts. Note, however, that there was a substantial role for the now dissolved Sub-Commission on Prevention of Discrimination and Protection of Minorities (later Sub-Commission on the Promotion and Protection of Human Rights) in the early phases of the 1503 procedure. By 2000, the Sub-Commission's function had been reduced to providing a Working Group on Communications that reviewed and forwarded direct to the Commission communications (from NGOs) appearing 'to reveal a consistent pattern of gross and reliably attested violations of human rights' (ECOSOC Res 200/3). The Human Rights Council Advisory Committee that replaced the Sub-Commission now appoints a similar working group for the Complaints Procedure that effectively continues the 1503 procedure (HR Council Res 5/1, Annex (2007), paras 65–108). The Sub-Commission's role in adopting country-specific resolutions in public session was terminated by the Commission in 2000 (Dec 109/2000, Annex, para 52).

[16] See in this volume, K Boyle, 'The United Nations Human Rights Council: Origins, Antecedents and Prospects', ch 1; see also, M Abraham, *Building the New Human Rights Council*, Dialogue on Globalization, Occasional Paper No 33, Friedrich Ebert Stiftung (2007).

[17] GA Res 60/251 (2006), para 5(e).

provided that 'such a mechanism shall complement and not duplicate the work of treaty bodies'.[18]

What it did not do was lay down how this was to be achieved. This was left to the Council which, after a year of deliberations, adopted Resolution 5/1 (2007), its institution-building package. The first 38 paragraphs of the package are devoted to the UPR mechanism. The mechanism is explored further in both Chapters 1 and 3 of this volume.

The salient elements are that every four years states are to submit a 20-page information document which 'can take the form of a report' on the fulfilment of its human rights obligations and commitments, and the Office of the High Commissioner for Human Rights (OHCHR) will prepare two reports of up to 10 pages each, one on the findings of UN treaty bodies and special procedures and one that summarizes information from 'stakeholders' (read 'NGOs and national human rights institutions'). On the basis of these reports, a working group of the whole Council will conduct the main interactive dialogue with the state concerned, lasting some three hours. A further hour of Plenary discussion, in which NGOs will be able to participate will conclude the discussion. A 'troika' of rapporteurs from Council members, chosen by lot, may help prepare the dialogue and perhaps the outcome document for discussion in the Plenary.

The outcome is to consist, amongst other matters, of 'conclusions and/or recommendations' and 'may include... [an] assessment... of the human rights situation in the country under review'. This again sounds suspiciously like the conclusions and recommendations typically found in the Concluding Observations of treaty bodies adopted after their constructive dialogue with states party.

Any reader familiar with human rights work will know that since, in most cases, the only international sanction for human rights violations is the verdict of the court of public opinion, duplication of work can be helpful in getting a hearing before that court. Accordingly, more is better. It may therefore be asked what problem there is with the UPR in fact duplicating treaty body periodic reviews, at least with respect to states party to each treaty. Might not their submission of information under the UPR process make it somewhat harder for states to claim a 'reporting burden' that leaves them overdue in their reporting to the treaty bodies? Might it even encourage states to adhere to treaties they are not yet party to as a means of eliciting the appreciation of their peers in the UPR?

The potential problem lies in how the results of the two processes compare. For if there is a real basis for comparison, then comparisons will be made. It is surely not too cynical to suggest, for example, that if the outcome of UPR is less critical of a state than the concluding observations of treaty bodies in respect of the same state, then the state will invoke the gentler diagnosis of UPR to discredit the

[18] Ibid. See generally in this volume, N Bernaz, 'Reforming the UN Human Rights Protection Procedures: a Legal Perspective on the Establishment of the Universal Periodic Review Mechanism', ch 3; for a thorough background analysis of the issue, see Gaer, 'A Voice Not an Echo: Universal Periodic Review and the UN Treaty Body System', 7 Human Rights Law Review (2007) 109.

harsher diagnosis of the treaty bodies. Nor would it be inconsistent with experience to expect that a process led by governments with an outcome elaborated and adopted by government representatives, on the basis effectively of a three-hour dialogue, is likely to yield a gentler diagnosis than one arrived at by individual experts on the basis of a (typically) six-to-nine-hour dialogue on a more limited range of issues.

Various suggestions were made aiming at avoiding this situation. One, considered but not retained during the discussions leading to the institution-building package, would have focused UPR on the extent to which states had actually implemented recommendations of the treaty bodies and special procedures. According to one commentator this would, even after adoption of the institution-building package, have been consistent with that package.[19] Another suggestion, a variation on the previous idea, would have been for UPR to avoid reviewing an issue covered by a treaty obligation with regard to which the state is up to date with its reporting obligations, limiting such a consideration to the activities of the state to give effect to the recommendations.[20] Yet a further variation, offered by the present author during informal gatherings of relevant actors would have been for the outcome to avoid arriving at 'conclusions' in respect of the treaty obligations just mentioned, restricting the outcome to recommendations. This was based on the probability that competing assessments of human rights performance as could be expected to be reflected in 'conclusions' could be more harmful to the promotion of human rights than would non-identical recommendations on how to address a specific human rights problem.[21]

In fact, the model adopted was one that had neither conclusions nor corporate recommendations. The key element is the list of recommendations submitted by different delegations during the dialogue in the Council's Working Group, together with any reaction by the state in question. This seems at first to have avoided all the originally feared concerns regarding competition between the outcomes of the two processes. However, a third possible problem may have arisen: some delegations look to recommendations of other parts of the system, notably those of the treaty bodies and special procedures. If the state under review can then feel free to announce that it does not accept a particular such recommendation, this could then affect the authority of the original recommendation, be it a treaty body or a body of the Council itself. In any event, the system is sufficiently new that it may be premature to assume that it has achieved its mature shape.

[19] Scheinin, 'Elements of the Universal Periodic Review', presentation made during The New Human Rights Council: The First Two Years, Workshop—European University Institute, Florence, 7–8 November 2007.

[20] Hampson, 'An Overview of the Reform of the UN Human Rights Machinery', 7 Human Rights Law Review (2007) 7, at 17.

[21] eg at Wilton Park Conference, 'Building on 60 Years of the Universal Declaration of Human Rights: The Way Forward', 17–19 January 2008.

3. Treaty Bodies and Thematic Special Procedures

The main common element of the work of the treaty bodies and the thematic special procedures is that both are in the hands of individual experts. As such both may reasonably be expected to deliver more impartial assessments of compliance with human rights obligations than may states.[22]

A. Purpose of Activities

While there might be extensive overlap or potential overlap in the mandate of treaty bodies on the one hand, and special procedures on the other, there is little, if any, in their purpose.

The treaties are silent as to the purpose of the functions attributed to the treaty bodies, as are the resolutions establishing or continuing the mandates of the special procedures. Nevertheless, there are differences in context that clearly elucidate their respective purposes. Essentially, it is suggested that the treaty bodies should be conceived of as functioning on a bilateral plane, while the special procedures operate on the multilateral plane. While mainly a matter of formality, the distinction has substantive implications.

In formal terms, the treaty bodies are typically elected by one multilateral cluster and report to another. That is to say, they are elected by a meeting of states parties and report to the General Assembly.[23] Since the reports of the treaty bodies are not before the meetings of states parties (substantive items on their agendas are usually confined to electing the treaty bodies' members), it is understandable that those meetings not be concerned with the treaty bodies' conclusions and views of compliance or otherwise with the respective treaties.[24] Meanwhile, the General Assembly similarly ignores the country-specific substance of the reports. Arguably, it may be thought inappropriate, unless the treaty were to provide otherwise,[25] for a body, like the Assembly, composed of members not confined to states parties, to take positions on the behaviour of those states that have assumed the respective treaty obligations.

[22] The election/appointment processes differ. Treaty body members are elected by states party to the treaty, while special procedures mandate-holders are appointed by the Council on recommendation of the Council President. The latter is presented with possible candidates by a consultative group of five, composed of individuals nominated to serve in their individual capacities by each UN regional group.

[23] The CESCR is anomalous in this respect, as it is established by the Economic and Social Council (ECOSOC), the original body designated to receive and consider states' periodic reports (ICESCR, n 2 above, arts 16–17). Accordingly, it is elected by and reports to ECOSOC.

[24] It should be noted, however, that some members of the HRC have hinted that a more country-specific substantive role for the meetings could be appropriate: CCPR/C/SR 1999 (2002).

[25] As the formally constituted treaty body for the ICESCR is ECOSOC, it evidently could have members not states parties reviewing reports of states parties.

Accordingly, it may be inferred that the essential relationship as regards the treaties is between the treaty bodies and each individual state party. This view is underlined by the current core function of all of them, namely, the consideration, in dialogue with each state party, of the reports submitted to the treaty bodies by the states parties.

By contrast, the special procedures are typically elected by and report to the same multilateral body, the Human Rights Council. Their reports frequently provide the subject matter of discussion, not least in respect of their country-specific reporting, which may even be invoked in debates on whether or not to adopt country-specific resolutions.

In addition, as far as the thematic procedures are concerned, they are expected to make recommendations aimed at states generally (these are often reflected in resolutions on the subject matters of the mandates) and, through the Council, to other parts of the UN and the international community, including non-governmental organizations.[26]

Of course, in response to the political impossibility, in their early days, of the treaty bodies' adopting country-specific observations, they developed the techniques of the 'general comment'. These are expositions of the treaty body's understanding of the scope and nature of states' obligations under the treaty in question. They have proved to be important, authoritative guides to states, especially when preparing their periodic reports. As such they may cover similar territory to that covered by the special procedures in the recommendations that may be found in their annual reports.

Space does not allow for a detailed comparison of the two types of contribution. Any interested reader is invited to compare the HRC's general comment on ICCPR Article 7 with the compilation of recommendations made by the Special Rapporteur on torture,[27] to perceive the different nature of both exercises. In brief, the general comment adopts an expository style, identifying key obligations perceived to be explicit or implicit in the prohibition of torture or cruel, inhuman or degrading treatment or punishment.

The compilation of recommendations uses more lapidary language and goes into greater detail with respect to desirable measures. Indeed, the very fact that the Special Rapporteur's functions include not just identifying the specifics of legal obligation, but also proposing the measures that might be considered good practice with a view to prevention, inevitably affects the content and nature of the two approaches.

So, while much of the work of the special procedures is carried out by means of bilateral communication between each special procedure and individual UN member or observer state, it is done with a view to informing the action of a

[26] See, eg Report of the Special Rapporteur on torture, UN Doc E/CN.4/2002/76 (2001) Annex I.

[27] Ibid; Compilation of General Comments and General Recommendations Adopted by Human Rights Treaty Bodies: UN Doc HRI/GEN/1/Rev 5 (2001) at 139.

multilateral body. That action may be country-specific, but need not be. The procedures' function of permitting the Council to understand certain phenomena on a comparative and global basis is at least as important, for then it is able to address further the phenomena on the same basis.

In this context—the essentially bilateral focus of the treaty bodies and the essentially multilateral focus of the special procedures—an examination of working methods of both type of mechanism needs to be situated.

B. Working Methods

An examination of the working methods of each type of mechanism shows that there is little in the way of overlap and duplication of function.

The treaty bodies currently in existence have up to four types of activity. First, as has been seen, all have a core function in common: they examine reports to be submitted periodically by states parties. Second, three may consider interstate complaints: CERD, on an obligatory basis (ICERD Articles 11–3),[28] the HRC (ICCPR Articles 41–43),[29] and CAT Committee (CAT Article 21),[30] on an optional basis. Third, on an optional basis, four committees may consider complaints of violations of the rights of individuals (CERD under ICERD Article 14,[31] HRC under ICCPR Optional Protocol,[32] CAT Committee under CAT Article 22,[33] CEDAW Committee under CEDAW Optional Protocol).[34] Fourth, two committees, the CAT Committee (CAT Article 20)[35] and the CEDAW Committee (CEDAW Optional Protocol)[36] may investigate of their own motion apparent systematic torture practices or violations of CAT and CEDAW respectively. These investigations may include on-the-spot visits to particular state parties, with the parties' permission.[37]

The special procedures that engage in systematic actions on alleged violations within their mandates typically undertake the following actions: first, transmittal of allegations of violations and legislative, or institutional aspects conducive to violations, to governments for their comments; second, sending urgent appeals (usually in individual cases)[38] to prevent possible imminent violations; and, third,

[28] ICERD, n 2 above, Arts 11–13.

[29] ICCPR, n 2 above, Arts 41–3.

[30] CAT, n 2 above, Art 21.

[31] ICERD, n 2 above, Art 14.

[32] Optional Protocol to the International Covenant on Civil and Political Rights, GA Res 2200A (XXI) (1966) (entered into force 23 March 1976).

[33] CAT, n 2 above, Art 22.

[34] Optional Protocol to the Convention on the Elimination of All Forms of Discrimination against Women, GA Res A/54/4 (1999) (entered into force 22 December 2000).

[35] CAT, n 2 above, Art 20.

[36] CEDAW Optional Protocol, n 34 above.

[37] While the CAT Art 20 procedure is automatically applicable in principle, it may be excluded by a reservation made under Art 28. CAT, n 2 above, Arts 20, 28. Similarly, the CEDAW procedure may be excluded by means of a reservation made under Optional Protocol art 10. CEDAW Optional Protocol, n 34 above, Art 10.

[38] The technique may also be used for more general urgent matters: see n 54 below and accompanying text.

undertaking on-the-spot visits to countries with an apparent extensive problem, with the permission of the state in question.

The interrelatedness or otherwise of the activities of both sets of bodies may best be understood by approaching them from two perspectives: general country work and case-specific work.

General country work may itself be divided between routine work, investigation work—usually involving on-the-spot fact-finding missions—and, occasionally, urgent appeals. Beginning with routine general country work, it is evident that the styles of work between the two types of bodies are markedly dissimilar. The typical core work of the treaty bodies involves an examination of reports, article by article, submitted periodically by states parties. The reports, whose quality assuredly varies, are usually dealt with according to a standard formula. The committee in question or a designated sub-group will approve written questions to the government of the state party which then sends a delegation to a session of the committee to present the report and respond to the questions, as well as to oral questions members may choose to put by way of follow-up. Thus, the report is the basis of the exercise and the main formal source of information.

Except for the CESCR and the CRC Committee, NGOs will have no formal role and their information no formal status. In practice, the Secretariat makes arrangements to facilitate the transmission of NGO information to individual committee members and to permit NGOs to brief interested committee members.[39] It is evident that the NGO information looms large in the ability of the Committee and its members to pose the kinds of questions necessary to elicit from the state party's delegation a fuller sense of the actual practice in that state than typically is apparent from the state party's report. The questions, particularly written ones, normally will be formulated in general terms, although they may well be based on individual cases. Of course, individual cases taken up by the committees that have dealt with such cases in their optional procedures may well figure in the questions. Despite having no formal status, NGO information effectively provides a sort of continuing education or refresher course to enhance the expertise of committee members for the purposes of the exercise at hand. As will be seen below, treaty bodies, or at least their members, increasingly have access to other independent sources of information, such as the findings of other treaty bodies and of the special procedures themselves.

The centrepiece of the exercise is the dialogue with the government delegation.[40] In response to the written and oral questions, the delegation is

[39] This of itself represents an evolution: in the early days of the HRC, for example, NGOs had to post or distribute personally to individual members willing to receive it, any material they wished to be considered; the argument was that since the material had no official status, the Secretariat should not be involved in processing or disseminating it. See Boerefijn, n 7 above, at 216–20.

[40] There has been a tentative trend towards conducting a review where the state party fails over a long period to submit a due report or where it constantly delays sending a delegation. The main purpose here is to prod the state into submitting the report or appearing, not to have a hearing in

able to clarify legal and factual questions and give important contextual orientation. Follow-up oral questions can elicit direct responses, prevarication, or no response, all of which permit the committee in question to assess the reality sought by the questions.

Even in the days before the committees began formulating concluding observations on the basis of the exchange, there were, as there remain, at least three important outcomes of the exercise. One was the learning process for the state party preparing the report, as it examined its own legal system from the perspective of the requirements of a seriously undertaken international instrument. The second outcome was having to submit to and absorb critical reactions by members from all parts of the world, to whose election they had been a party. The third, however intangible and unsusceptible of measurement, yet perhaps the most important, was the dialogue itself. A delegation, typically consisting of senior officials responsible for law enforcement and the administration of justice, and diplomats, flanks the committee chairperson and faces the committee in a formally arranged chamber; it has come for the purposes of undergoing an act of formal and public accountability regarding the extent to which the state party it represents has given effect to a set of obligations that it has solemnly assumed by ratifying or acceding to the treaty in question. No individual special rapporteur, special representative, or advisory services expert under the special procedures system has anything comparable. Certainly, the few special procedures working groups may, like their one-person counterparts, have meetings with representatives of states, in respect of which they are seeking to elucidate facts or arrange possible missions. But these are ad hoc, informal, and private. They have nothing of the ceremonial nature of the reviews by treaty bodies of state reports.

For the last 16 or so years, there has been a much more concrete outcome of the review process carried out by the treaty bodies, namely, the concluding observations.[41] The crucial parts are their findings under the notion of 'subjects of concern' and the recommendations made to the state party to address the concerns. Where the concerns relate to factually contested matters, they will usually refer to 'allegations' of violations rather than to 'violations' *tout court*. Nevertheless, the very inclusion of the allegations will at least signify that the state party has failed effectively to refute their credibility. Moreover, in a practice developed by the HRC, the seriousness of the concerns will be reflected in the follow-up information or action requested of the state party in the concluding observations. The actual follow-up may also affect the timing of the subsequent periodic report.[42]

absentia: see Rules of Procedure of the Human Rights Committee (Basic Reference Document), UN Doc CCPR/C/3/Rev 6 (2001).

[41] Until 1992, the HRC was not prepared to interpret its power to make 'general comments', under ICCPR Art 40(4), as empowering it to make country-specific comments, as opposed to comments of a general nature. See Boerefijn, n 7 above, at 303–6.

[42] See HRC Rules of Procedure, n 40 above, Rule 70A.

The approach of the action-oriented special procedures is very different. Most of the material they transmit to governments is in the form of individual case allegations, to which the governments may or may not respond. The main source, which will be authorized as a source by the resolutions establishing their mandates,[43] will be NGOs. Where the allegations they receive include general material, for instance, assessing the scope of the practice or describing legal impediments to the prevention of the phenomenon, then states will also be invited to comment on these. In the early years of their mandates, the country entries in their reports to the Commission on Human Rights tended to restrict themselves to a summary of allegations transmitted and any replies received. To the extent that this represented a dialogue, it was primarily a written one. Many subsequently formulated observations on the correspondence, in the way of provisional judgment and rather general recommendations. These generally consist of a few sentences. They are inevitably limited by the fluctuating information they may receive in any given year and the limited nature of the information on the political and legal context in which the allegations of individual violations are said to occur. Accordingly, while their reporting is annual, they have little of the sustained consideration of the issues that the treaty bodies' reviews of periodic reports evince. On the other hand, the wealth of case-specific material can give a sense of the scope and gravity of a problem that is missing from the process of periodic reporting to the treaty bodies.

Only two of the existing treaty bodies are expressly empowered to engage in investigative country work, including the use of on-the-spot visits. So any area of potential overlap with the special procedures only applies to the CAT Committee (Article 20)[44] and the CEDAW Committee (Optional Protocol).[45] The CAT Committee's power applies to all states party except the few which have availed themselves of the option in CAT Article 28 to exclude the power.[46] Yet, here too the experience is limited. It is understood that there have been seven inquiries into suspected systematic practices of torture, the reports of which are in the public domain: Turkey,[47] Egypt,[48] Peru,[49] Sri Lanka[50] and Mexico,[51] Serbia/Montenegro,[52] and Brazil.[53] The reports on all except Egypt are based on on-the-spot fact-finding visits. Egypt availed itself of the right to refuse to receive a committee delegation.

[43] See, eg summary or arbitrary executions, ECOSOC Res 1982/35 (1982), which, on the recommendation of the Commission, established the mandate of the Special Rapporteur on summary or arbitrary executions and determined that the Special Rapporteur would seek and receive information from governments and international governmental and non-governmental organizations.

[44] CAT, n 2 above, Art 20.

[45] CEDAW Optional Protocol, n 34 above.

[46] CAT, n 2 above, Art 28.

[47] UN Doc A/48/44/Add1 (1993).

[48] UN Doc A/51/44 (1996), paras 180–222.

[49] Report of the Committee against Torture, UN Doc A/56/44 (2001), paras 144–93.

[50] UN Doc A/57/44 (2002), paras 117–95.

[51] UN Doc CAT/C/75 (2003).

[52] UN Doc A/59/44 (2004).

[53] UN Doc CAT/C/39/2.

Most of the published reports tend to show the value of sustained study. They deal with a broad range of allegations and consider in detail the legal and institutional framework in which the problem is manifested. They suggest that the in-country experience permits the Committee to make less tentative conclusions (the Egypt report makes greater use of 'allegations' to qualify its assessment), more detailed analysis of the legal issues, and more specific recommendations reflecting the greater understanding of the local scene. Indeed, the CEDAW Committee's only public report of a country visit focusing on the murder and disappearance of women in Ciudad Juarez, Mexico, is a fine example of comprehensive human rights reporting.[54] In sum, they demonstrate the undoubted value of an on-the-spot visit to come to grips with the legal and practical realities of the human rights situation.

The country visit has become routine for most special procedures. Of course, states remain free to refuse access, but a substantial number set a more positive example. Indeed, there is now a practice of states giving blanket prior agreement to visits by any special procedure, some 60 having done so as of October 2007.[55] The interest of the special procedures in country visits is assuredly because of the benefits described above. Direct access to civil society and most relevant levels of officialdom permits an 'immersion course' in the historical, constitutional, legal, and operational framework of the problems being studied. Insistence on the conditions of access contained in the standard terms of reference for fact-finding visits make possible, in this writer's experience, substantial uncovering of those aspects of the reality that governments prefer to conceal and which, indeed, may be unknown to important higher level decision-makers, whether by preference or inadvertence.

So far the potential for overlap applies only to the CAT Committee acting under CAT Article 20 and the Special Rapporteur on Torture and to the CEDAW Committee and the Special Rapporteur on Violence against Women. Any such overlap or duplication on the torture issue has been avoided by the Special Rapporteur's policy of not seeking to visit a country in respect of which the CAT Committee has initiated an Article 20 inquiry. On the other hand, there is evidently room for complementary action. Thus, in 1997, five years after the CAT Committee visited Turkey, the Special Rapporteur also sought a visit, which took place in 1998.[56] Since neither mechanism has the resources that would make follow-up visits practicable, the Special Rapporteur's visit was able to serve as a de facto follow-up to the Committee's visit. Similarly, the CAT Committee's visits to Mexico and Brazil were able to build on earlier ones of the Special Rapporteur.[57]

[54] UN Doc CEDAW/C/2005/OP8/Mexico (2005). Unlike the CAT Committee, the CEDAW Committee is not restricted to publishing only a summary report (see CAT Art 20(5)). In fact, Mexico consented to publication of the CAT Committee's full report.

[55] See the website of the Office of the High Commissioner for Human Rights: <http://www.ohchr.org>, go to 'special procedures'.

[56] UN Doc E/CN4/1999/61/Add1 (1991). The Special Rapporteur sought the invitation in 1995 UN Doc E/CN4/1996/35 (1996), para 178. The Committee's visit had taken place in 1992.

[57] UN Doc CAT/C/75 (2003), para 7 (Mexico); UN Doc CAT/C/39/2 (2007), paras 45–6 (Brazil).

In addition, in the light of Egypt's refusal of access to the Committee, the Special Rapporteur on torture did not hesitate to seek an invitation to visit that country,[58] albeit no such invitation was forthcoming. On the other hand, a visit to Mexico by the Special Rapporteur on Violence against Women only seven months after that of CEDAW, half of the report of which deals with the Ciudad Juarez situation,[59] should perhaps be seen as testifying to Mexico's particular openness to international attention to this notorious problem.

One final aspect of special procedure activity relevant to general country work, for which there is no counterpart in the methods of the treaty bodies, is the urgent appeal. As will be noted below, urgent appeals are normally used by special procedures in individual cases, by way of seeking to avert harm to individuals feared to be at risk. However, the technique may occasionally be resorted to for a more general purpose. For instance, four procedures jointly appealed to Peru to refrain from adopting a constitutional amendment aimed at permitting an amnesty for crimes committed by security forces in counter-emergency operations.[60] The only analogous treaty body measure available is the request for a special report from the state party.[61]

To the extent that some treaty bodies and several special procedures are engaged in *case-specific work*, this at first sight could be a source of overlap and duplication. A closer look reveals that the perception is so far largely illusory. The area of potential overlap is, in any event, limited. It covers only individual cases that could be the subject of communications to the HRC in respect of state parties to the Optional Protocol to the ICCPR;[62] to the CAT Committee in respect of states parties that have made the requisite declaration under CAT Article 22;[63] to the CERD in respect of states parties that have made the requisite declaration under ICERD Article 14;[64] and to the CEDAW Committee in respect of states parties to the CEDAW Optional Protocol.[65] Moreover, the nature of the activity of the two types of mechanism is generally different. The treaty bodies, when considering individual cases, do so for the purpose of formulating 'views' as to whether or not there has been a violation. This is the practice of only one of the special procedures. While, as noted earlier, they seek information from states in respect of allegations of individual violations, they do so in the framework of reporting the dialogue and perhaps making observations on the problem in general in the state. Except for the Working Group on Arbitrary Detention (WGAD), they do not systematically engage in formulating judgmental conclusions on each case.

[58] The Committee reported in 1996 (see n 48 above) and the Special Rapporteur sought the invitation in 1997 UN Doc E/CN4/1998/38 (1998), para 4.

[59] UN Doc E/CN4/2006/61/Add4.

[60] The four procedures were the Working Group on Enforced or Involuntary Disappearances and the Special Rapporteurs on extrajudicial, summary or arbitrary executions, on torture, and on the independence of judges and lawyers. See, UN Doc E/CN4/1996/35 (1996), paras 133–6.

[61] For example, the Committee against Torture sought a special report from Israel in 1996, which was submitted in 1997; UN Doc CAT/C/33/Add2/Rev.1 (1997).

[62] ICCPR Optional Protocol, n 32 above.

[63] CAT, n 2 above, Art 22.

[64] ICERD, n 2 above, Art 14.

[65] CEDAW Optional Protocol, n 34 above.

The HRC, tellingly, does not generally consider the activities of the special procedures as 'procedures of international investigation or settlement', as precluded by ICCPR Optical Protocol Article 5(2)(a).[66]

The WGAD, on the other hand, has from the beginning had a specific mandate of 'investigating' cases of arbitrary detention.[67] In the light of this wording, it makes reasoned findings (currently called 'opinions')[68] on whether the case involves a violation of the right not to be subjected to arbitrary detention. This could evidently involve overlap with a case coming before the HRC, especially under ICCPR Article 9. Indeed, in respect of one case submitted to both bodies, the WGAD transmitted the case to the HRC, once it became aware of the situation.[69] It is also understood that attempts are made in the Secretariat to steer cases in the right direction. For example, in a case where domestic remedies have been exhausted, the Secretariat may process it under the Optional Protocol, while in one where they have not, it may be processed for the attention of the WGAD. Here, however, much will depend on the familiarity of staff members with the different procedures, a task rendered more difficult by the fact that the relevant staff work in separate branches.

As far as the treaty bodies and special procedures are concerned, the duplication is not of function, but of potential inconvenience to a state receiving multiple requests. This can be a problem *within* the cluster of special procedures, as well as between them and the treaty bodies. Ideally, systems in the Secretariat would ensure that in such cases, states are invited to make their responses to each of the mechanisms involved.

As noted earlier, the special procedures have developed the method of issuing urgent appeals to states in circumstances where a violation within their mandates is feared to be about to take place or to be taking place. They constitute routine preventive work for several of the procedures that use them, especially the Working Group on Enforced or Involuntary Disappearances (WGEID), the Special Rapporteurs on Extrajudicial, Arbitrary or Summary Executions, and on Torture, and the Special Representative on Human Rights Defenders.[70]

[66] eg the HRC was not precluded from dealing with a case also under study by the Special Rapporteur on summary or arbitrary executions. See *Baboeram and ors v Suriname* (146/1983 and 148–54/1983), Annex X, UN Doc A/40/40 (1985), para 9.1.

[67] Commission Res 1991/42, 5 March 1991.

[68] Commission on Human Rights Resolution 1997/50, para 7, required the Group to give 'views', rather than 'decisions'. In response, it has chosen the word 'opinions'.

[69] *Arredondo Guevara v Peru*, UN Doc E/CN4/2001/14/Add1 (2000), paras 61–2; the HRC considered that the case remained admissible in the light of the group's reference of the case to the HRC without any expression of its views. See Report of the Human Rights Committee, UN Doc A/55/40, Vol II Annex IX E (2000).

[70] Office of the High Commissioner for Human Rights, Seventeen Frequently Asked Questions about United Nations Special Rapporteurs, Fact Sheet No 27 (2001), 9; Rodley, 'Urgent Action', in G Alfredsson and ors (eds), *International Human Rights Monitoring Mechanisms—Essays in Honour of Jakob Th. Möller* (2nd rev edn, 2009 forthcoming); Van Boven, 'Urgent Appeals on Behalf of Torture Victims', in *Mélanges en homage au Doyen Gérard Cohen-Jonathan* (2004) 1651.

The only comparable measure currently used by the treaty bodies is the interim measure, whereby the body seeks suspension of a formal measure believed to be imminent in a state party, pending its consideration of the substance of the complaint. Thus, for example, the HRC, through its Special Rapporteur on New Communications, is empowered under Rule 86 of its Rules of Procedure to request interim measures by a state party to avoid irreparable damage, for instance, an execution taking place before the HRC is able to assess the compatibility of the penalty with the state party's obligations under the ICCPR.[71] The HRC and CAT Committee act similarly in the case of threatened expulsions from states parties to states where the alleged potential victim would be at risk of torture.[72]

It is not impossible to conceive that the treaty bodies, resources permitting, might adopt an urgent appeals system similar to that of the special procedures. However, it is unlikely that they would do so outside the formal framework of action on individual cases pursuant to the optional individual complaints procedures. Since the latter involves compliance with the rule of exhaustion of domestic remedies and the maintenance of confidentiality until the case is either declared inadmissible or is the subject of final views, any urgent action would presumably be likely to be constrained by the domestic remedies rule and the same confidentiality. For the special procedures, there are no similar constraints. They can take up a case, regardless of the stage it may be at in the domestic legal system. They may not, following a mandated requirement to use 'discretion' in their work,[73] usually report publicly on the actions until they issue their annual reports, but there is no rule of confidentiality and some have also used press releases to draw public attention to the appeal.[74] Indeed, if the work of the treaty bodies is, as has been seen, characterizable by its formality, the work of the special procedures is more notable for its flexibility.[75]

4. Extent of Direct Cooperation

One factor representing a pull towards common endeavour is the very existence of the relevant treaties. These establish the mandates of the treaty bodies, but

[71] A de Zayas, 'The Examination of Individual Complaints by the United Nations Human Rights Committee under the Optional Protocol to the International Covenant on Civil and Political Rights', in *International Human Rights Monitoring Mechanisms*, n 70 above, 67, 79–81.

[72] See HRC Rules of Procedure, n 40 above, Rule 108(9); see, *S H v Norway* (121/1998), UN Doc A/55/44, Annex VIIIB4 (2000), para 1.2.

[73] eg Commission Res 1985/33, para 6 (establishing the mandate of the Special Rapporteur on Torture). See now Human Rights Council Res 5/1 (2007), Annex.

[74] As part of its 'institution-building package', the Human Rights Council adopted a Draft Code of Conduct for Special Procedures Mandate-Holders of the Human Rights Council (Human Rights Council Res 5/1 (2007), Annex.

[75] However, the new International Convention on Enforced Disappearance, n 1 above, gives its Committee an urgent action function which certainly could duplicate that of the Council's Working Group on Enforced Involuntary Disappearances (Art 30). This will require policy decisions to be taken by both bodies, preferably by agreement.

they are also essential sources of legitimacy for the activities of the special procedures. Thus, the CAT will frequently be invoked by the Special Rapporteurs on Torture and on Violence Against Women, as will the ICERD by the Special Rapporteur on Racial Discrimination and the CRC by the Special Rapporteur on the Sale of Children.[76] Of course, it is essential that the special procedures not seem to arrogate the role of guardians of the treaties, a role that belongs to the treaty bodies. Rather, they base themselves on general international law or normative standards. These may be reflected in various sources, such as declarations, resolutions, and other manifestations of acceptable state practice. For example, the Special Rapporteur on Torture will frequently invoke the 1975 General Assembly Declaration against Torture,[77] especially vis-à-vis states not party to the CAT, as well as other 'soft law' instruments.[78] Yet, where a particular rule or type of recommended behaviour promoted by the Special Rapporteur is covered by the CAT, it would be perverse for him to refrain from invoking the relevant CAT provision in communication with states that are, in fact, parties to the Convention. Certainly, a special procedure should be careful in adopting a controversial interpretation of a human rights treaty monitored by a treaty body, especially if that interpretation is at odds with that of the treaty body. Yet, the silence of the treaty body need not necessarily preclude the special procedure from staking out a position. For instance, the Special Rapporteur, where constrained to address the appropriateness of including corporal punishment within his mandate, could not but explore the relevance of the CAT in support of his contention that the practice did fall within the mandate.[79] The CAT Committee appears subsequently to have taken the same view.[80]

The special procedures also typically promote ratification of the treaties of most concern to their mandates, with some also advocating acceptance of their optional complaints procedures.[81] This is a role proper to them that would be

[76] Report of the Special Rapporteur on torture: Visit to Brazil, UN Doc E/CN4/2001/66/Add2 (2001), paras 149–51; Report of the Special Rapporteur on violence against women: UN Doc E/CN4/2000/68/Add3 (2000), para 76; Report of the Special Rapporteur on contemporary forms of racism, racial discrimination, xenophobia and related intolerance, UN Doc E/CN4/1994/66 (1994), para 10, describing ICERD as 'the basic international legal instrument' relevant to his mandate; Report of the Special Rapporteur on the sale of children, child prostitution and child pornography, UN Doc E/CN4/2002/88 (2002), para 13, describing the CRC and its Optional Protocol on the sale of children, child prostitution, and child pornography as 'the foundation for determining and developing the scope of the mandate'.

[77] These references will be in letters transmitting allegations to governments, but do not appear in the heavily summarized versions found in the annual reports; it also figured in his analysis of the relevance of his mandate to the problem of corporal punishment. See Report of the Special Rapporteur [on torture] UN Doc E/CN4/1997/7 (1997), para 3.

[78] eg UN Doc E/CN4/1994/31 (1994), para 135, referring to the Body of Principles for the Protection of All Persons under Any Form of Detention or Imprisonment, adopted by GA Res 43/173 (1988).

[79] UN Doc E/CN4/1997/7 (1997), paras 6–8.

[80] See Conclusions and recommendations of the Committee against Torture: Saudi Arabia, UN Doc CAT/C/CR/28/5 (2002), para 3(e).

[81] eg Report of the Special Rapporteur on torture: Visit to Pakistan, UN Doc E/CN4/1997/7/Add2 (1996), para 102; Report of the Special Rapporteur on contemporary forms of racism,

minimally appropriate for the treaty bodies themselves. In doing so, they are inevitably promoting the importance of the work of the treaty bodies. After one visit (to Sierra Leone), the Special Rapporteur on Violence Against Women even recommended that the authorities submit a report to the CEDAW.[82]

While they may not formally invoke the country-specific findings of the special procedures, the treaty bodies routinely have access to and cite in the oral dialogue the findings of special procedures. This is especially the case where the findings are those of a country-specific special procedure or of a thematic one which has recently reported on a country visit. For example, the report of the Special Rapporteur on Torture on his visit to Brazil in 2000 was referred to in the CAT Committee's dialogue with that country in 2001.[83] While in view of the confidentiality of Committee discussions of the list of issues to be presented to a state party in advance of the review and of their concluding observations, the point cannot be documented, it is this writer's experience with the HRC that the findings and recommendations of these special procedures reports will also influence the issues identified in the list of issues and recommendations in the concluding observations. It is also understood that the same is true for other treaty bodies, notably the CAT Committee.

The work of the treaty bodies may also inform that of the special procedures. Thus, the findings of the CAT Committee's mission to Turkey and its concluding observations on Mexico loomed large in the discussions with the authorities during the visit of the Special Rapporteur on torture to those countries.[84] The same Special Rapporteur routinely included in his observations at the end of country visits entries in his annual report reference to the findings of the HRC and the CAT Committee in their concluding observations.[85] While this may not be standard practice for the special procedures, the work of the treaty bodies may inform their recommendations

racial discrimination, xenophobia and related intolerance: Mission to South Africa, UN Doc E/CN4/1999/15/Add1, para 90(6); Report of the Special Rapporteur on violence against women: Mission to Haiti, UN Doc E/CN4/2000/68/Add3 (2000), para 76; Report of the Special Rapporteur on the sale of children, child prostitution and child pornography: Mission of the Special Rapporteur to the United States of America on the issue of commercial sexual exploitation of children, UN Doc E/CN4/1997/95/Add2 (1997), ch VII; inexplicably the former Special Rapporteur on the sale of children omitted to recommend that the Russian Federation ratify the Optional Protocol to the Convention on the Rights of the Child on the sale of children, child prostitution, and child pornography, adopted by GA Res 263, 25 May 2000, after her visit to that country in October 2000 (Report of the Special Rapporteur: Mission to the Russian Federation, UN Doc E/CN4/2001/78/Add2 (2001)).

[82] See UN Doc E/CN4/2002/83/Add2 (2002), para 115.

[83] In its concluding observations, the Committee requested 'information concerning measures taken by the public authorities to implement throughout the country, the recommendations…of the Special Rapporteur on torture to which the state party delegation referred during the dialogue with the Committee'. See UN Doc CAT/C/SR 471 (2001), para 39 (Gaer); see Report of the Committee against Torture: UN Doc A/56/44 (2001), para 120(i).

[84] See Report of the Special Rapporteur: Visit to Turkey, UN Doc E/CN4/1999/61/Add1 (1999), para 104; the report of the visit to Mexico is, regrettably, silent on the point, which is a matter of the author's personal recollection; see Report of the Special Rapporteur: Visit to Mexico, UN Doc E/CN4/1998/38/Add2 (1998).

[85] eg Report of the Special Rapporteur: UN Doc E/CN4/2001/66 (2001), paras 50 (Argentina), 63 (Armenia), 68 (Australia), 167 (Belarus), 231 (Cameroon), 235–6 (Chile), 330–1 (China), 349 (Congo), 475–6 (Egypt), 688 (Kyrgyzstan), 843 (Peru), 857 (Portugal), 1223 (United States). The

in other ways. For instance, in the report of her visit to Colombia, the Special Rapporteur on Violence against Women urged the Government to comply with the CEDAW recommendations after its review of Colombia's fourth periodic report.[86] On the other hand, the CERD in 1999 took the unusual step of publicly lamenting that the Special Rapporteur on Racism 'appears to completely overlook the relevance' of the ICERD.[87] While it is unfortunately true that he had apparently overlooked the CERD's concluding observations in the reports on several country visits,[88] in that very year he did refer to them in his annual report in respect of the scheduled tribes and castes of India.[89] It may be speculated whether this reflected an awareness of the concern within CERD. Certainly, by 2001, the report of his visit to Australia made reference to CERD's concluding observations.[90]

As far as direct contact between the special procedures and the treaty bodies is concerned, the Special Rapporteur on Torture and the CAT Committee have consistently held joint meetings.[91] The main topic of these is to ensure precisely that the two mechanisms maximize the complementarities of their work and minimize duplication. On one occasion, responding to a Committee member's question, the Special Rapporteur gave reasons why he thought there would be difficulties for the Special Rapporteur to submit situations that the Committee might study under CAT Article 20.[92] At a later meeting, cooperation in respect of Article 20 was further explored.[93] Another topic of the meetings has become agreeing on a joint text, together with the Voluntary Fund for Victims of Torture and the High Commissioner for Human Rights, to commemorate the International Day in Support of Victims of Torture (26 June).[94] The second Special Rapporteur on the Sale of Children recently had a meeting with the CRC Committee with a view to seeking closer cooperation with the Committee and attended a thematic meeting convened by the Committee.[95] His predecessor had attended similar thematic meetings.[96]

present Special Rapporteur seems no longer to be including country observations in his reports of transmittal of allegations and state responses: UN Doc A/HRC/7/3 and Add1 (2008).

[86] See UN Doc E/CN4/2002/Add 2, para 120.

[87] Boyle and Baldaccini, 'A Critical Evaluation of International Human Rights Approaches to Racism', in S Fredman (ed), *Discrimination and Human Rights—The Case of Racism* (2001) 135, 183–4; see Report of the Committee on the Elimination of Racial Discrimination, UN Doc A/52/18 (1997), para 666.

[88] See Van Boven, 'United Nations Strategies to Combat Racism and Racial Discrimination; A Sobering but not Hopeless Balance Sheet', in M Castermans-Holleman and ors (eds), *The Role of the Nation-State in the 21st Century* (1998) 251, fn 261.

[89] See UN Doc E/CN4/1999/15 (1999), paras 88–100.

[90] See UN Doc E/CN4/2002/24/Add1 (2002), para 1.

[91] eg UN Docs E/CN4/1995/34 (1995), para 6; A/61/259 (2006), para 29.

[92] See UN Doc CAT/C/SR 187 (1994), paras 19–21.

[93] Press Release, UN Comm. against Torture, Committee against Torture Holds Dialogue with Special Rapporteur on Torture (28th session 25 May 2002).

[94] eg Report of the Committee against Torture, Annex V, UN Doc A/55/44 (2000), paras 17–18.

[95] See UN Doc E/CN4/2002/88 (2002), para 34.

[96] She attended the CRC Committee's day of discussion on state violence against children; see UN Doc E/CN4/2001/78 (2001), para 6; so did the Special Rapporteur on torture: see UN Doc E/

In general, a recent study considered the cooperation between Special Rapporteurs and both Committees to be an exception.[97] It found that the same does not apply to the relationship between the CEDAW Committee and the Special Rapporteur on Violence against Women or that between CERD and the Special Rapporteur on Racism.[98] The same source indicates dissatisfaction by these treaty bodies with the absence of contact,[99] although it is this writer's understanding that the Special Rapporteur on Violence against Women had sought such contact with the CEDAW Committee.[100] By 2004 a meeting had taken place.[101] Except for an initial, apparently positive, exploratory meeting in 1995,[102] the first meeting between CERD and the Special Rapporteur on Racism that the author has been able to identify took place in 2006.[103] On the other hand, the Special Rapporteur apparently had a meeting in 2001 with the Secretary of the CERD which considered ways and means of enhancing cooperation between them.[104] In the light of the positive relationship between the torture-related and child-related mechanisms, it is difficult to comprehend why that of the others should not be similar. It cannot be excluded that a (misplaced) perception of potential competition is a factor.

There is no doubt that the HRC has not sought systematic contacts with the special procedures, respectful as it may be of their contribution, through their reports, to its work. Since most of them are relevant to its work, a practice of holding meetings with them would be an added burden on an already overcharged agenda. Presumably juridical considerations do not loom large. It is true that there is nothing in the ICCPR envisaging such contacts, but a similar absence in the ICERD, CAT, and the CRC has not prevented the contacts referred to. Certainly, the CESCR, as a sub-organ of ECOSOC, has no formal inhibitions, nor does it apparently have practical ones. In 2001 it had an exchange of views with the Special Rapporteur on Adequate Housing 'with a view to exploring the scope of appropriate cooperation between the Committee and the Special Rapporteur'.[105] In the same year, evidencing that this was no isolated incident, the Committee announced that it would

'[L]ook into ways of further strengthening its cooperation with the relevant special rapporteurs of the Commission on Human Rights (including the special rapporteurs on adequate housing, on the right to education, on the right to food, on violence against women, its causes and consequences, on the sale of children, child prostitution and child

CN4/ 2001/66 (2001), para 15.

[97] See A F Bayefsky, *The UN Human Rights Treaty System* (2001), 56.

[98] Ibid. [99] Ibid.

[100] Information kindly provided by the human rights officer who services the mandate of the Special Rapporteur, on file with the author.

[101] See UN Doc E/CN4/2005/72, para 4.

[102] See UN Doc A/50/476 (1995), paras 26–32; see also Boyle and Baldaccini, n 87 above.

[103] See UN Doc A/HRC/4/19 (2007), para 20.

[104] Information kindly provided by the human rights officer who services the mandate of the Special Rapporteur, on file with the author.

[105] UN Doc E/2002/22, UN Doc E/C12/2001/17 (2002), para 1066.

pornography and on the human rights of migrants) and with its independent experts (on the right to development, on the question of human rights and extreme poverty and on structural adjustment and foreign debt).'[106]

What is clear is that at the group level both sets of procedures have been keen to develop an annual consultation. Starting with the attendance in 1996 of the chairperson of the third annual meeting of special procedures at the seventh session of the meeting of persons chairing human rights treaty bodies,[107] the chair of that session of the treaty body meeting attended the fourth special procedures meeting in 1997, as did the chair of the CESCR.[108] The following year the chair of the Committee against Torture attended.[109] By 1999, the scheduling of both meetings was such as to permit the first joint session of the chairs of treaty bodies and the special procedures, which is now an annual event.[110]

It is beyond the scope of this article to examine the details of this evolving cross-system dialogue. Perhaps the most significant aspect of it is that it manifestly corresponds to a shared perceived need. One facet of the need is that of improving mutual knowledge and understanding of each group of mechanisms. Inevitably, the meetings can only help partially: each of the eight treaty bodies can convey what it wishes to the assembled special procedures, but not all the special procedures can do the same in a brief meeting, nor can the treaty body chairs reasonably be expected to be an effective conduit to the whole membership of the Committee they represent. Moreover, the regular turnover of special procedures mandate holders and treaty body chairs limits the possibility of entrenching the information and ideas exchanged.

A recurrent theme in the reports of their first three joint meetings was the intense focus on the importance of promoting full awareness by mechanisms of each group of the activities and output of the mechanisms of the other group. The key role of the Secretariat in making that happen was evidenced by increasingly insistent demands for feedback on the recommendations, notably, those requesting the Secretariat to put in place systems that would facilitate the desired information exchange.[111]

The joint meetings have, with some nuance that doubtless reflects a certain diffidence by some treaty bodies, given their blessing in principle to the notion of bilateral meetings between treaty bodies and relevant special procedures. In the words of the recommendation from the first meeting: 'The joint meeting encouraged the treaty bodies to call, as they felt necessary, for the cooperation of the

[106] Ibid, para 1050. The author is grateful to University of Essex colleague Professor Paul Hunt, who at the time was Rapporteur of the CESCR, for providing him with this information.

[107] See UN Doc A/51/482 (1996), para 8, 53.

[108] See UN Doc E/CN4/1998/45, paras 9, 34–43.

[109] See UN Doc E/CN4/1999/3, paras 10, 33–42.

[110] eg UN Docs E/CN4/2000/5 (1999), paras 30–1; E/CN4/2001/6 (2000), paras 71–6; E/CN4/2002/14 (2001), paras 69–75. The latest report is to be found in UN Doc A/63/280 (2008), at paras 7–10.

[111] Ibid.

special procedures, including the possibility of a direct exchange of information during their respective sessions.'[112]

By the third joint meeting, the tone, albeit in the passive voice, seemed somewhat less doubtful: 'Increased emphasis should be placed on organizing meetings between special procedures mandate holders and the treaty bodies.'[113]

In terms of the overall theme of this essay, the will towards cooperation rather than competition was best stated in the first sentence of the first recommendation of the first joint meeting: 'The joint meeting emphasized that the work of each group of mechanisms is equally and mutually important.'[114]

Subsequent meetings have permitted exchanges on the shared concerns about the impact of anti-terrorism measures on human rights and the more internal issues, notably the transition from the Commission on Human Rights to the Human Rights Council and proposals for reform of the treaty body system.[115]

5. Conclusion

It may be that, had the UN from the beginning been ready to establish a human rights monitoring system analogous to that found in the current Charter-based system, it would not have then gone on to create the system of treaty bodies. Certainly, there would have been little likelihood that any treaty body system would have been endowed with the core function of reviewing states' periodic reports, alongside UPR. The current challenge will be to find ways of indeed making the two processes complementary and productive, rather than competitive and injurious to the promotion of the better enjoyment of human rights. This not insignificant dimension apart, the existence of the two systems cannot be properly understood as creating substantial duplication and overlap.

The treaty bodies have nothing resembling the Human Rights Council's public discussion procedures or confidential procedures for looking at situations of consistent patterns of gross violations of human rights. It is the systems of thematic special procedures mandates and those of the treaty bodies, both driven by experts, that bear comparison. The implicit purpose of each system is substantially different. The structural features of the elective and reporting constituencies of the type of mechanism places them on essentially separate planes: bilateral for the treaty bodies, multilateral for the special procedures. This is connected with a different style of communication; characterized by dialogue, in the case of the treaty bodies, and fact-elucidation, in the case of the special procedures. The main

[112] See UN Doc E/CN4/2000/5 (1999), para 31(b). The present author chaired that year's meeting of special rapporteurs and co-chaired the joint meeting.

[113] See UN Doc E/CN4/2002/14 (2001).

[114] See UN Doc E/CN4/2000/5 (1999), para 31(a).

[115] eg UN Doc E/CN4/2005/5 (2004), paras 64–68 (anti-terrorism and human rights); UN Doc A/HRC/43 (2006), paras 56–9.

focus of the treaty bodies, particularly through their core function of reviewing states' reports is to promote enhanced respect for the human rights enshrined in the treaty obligations, with general comments being merely an attendant product aiming to give states guidance on the nature and scope of other obligations for their reports. A main focus, if not the only one, of the thematic special procedures is to provide the whole UN membership with comparative and global understanding of the human rights problem in question, as well as with guidance on how to deal with it.

As far as case work is concerned, the special procedures, with one exception (the Working Group on Arbitrary Detention) do not pursue individual cases to a formal conclusion on whether or not there has been a violation, whereas the treaty bodies do just that. In the case of the exception, the problem has been solved in the one case it has arisen, by the Working Group on Arbitrary Detention's deferring the case to the HRC. If that had not happened, it cannot be excluded that such an incident could lead to the HRC's considering the case to be inadmissible by reason of having been submitted to an alternative procedure of international investigation or settlement. That no such thing happens in respect of cases submitted to the other special procedures, testifies to the difference in function between the two types of procedure. Also, improved information management systems within the Secretariat can contribute substantially to the avoidance of duplicative case work.

By contrast, the special procedures' use of urgent appeals has no real counterpart in the current treaty bodies' methods. In the rare cases where an apparent similar practice exists, it is used by the treaty bodies to preserve the possibility of determining whether or not a violation could occur. The purpose of the special procedures' urgent appeals is to prevent, inhibit, or stop any feared violations.

In general, the activities of the treaty bodies reflect the formality of the solemn legal instruments that gave birth to them; those of the special procedures have the flexibility appropriate to their genesis in a UN political body. This does not mean that the special procedures should consider themselves free to act inconsistently, without an established (common or procedure-specific) methodology. Rather, a key aspect for the special procedures is to seek to have some effect and give some guidance in a short time frame, whereas for the treaty bodies the very nature of periodic reports and the necessarily protracted process of reaching views on individual cases require a longer term perspective.

This analysis suggests that any area of potential overlap and duplication of work between the two types of mechanism is largely illusory. Where occasionally, it is real, it is avoidable by the application of the treaties' rules on admissibility, by improved information management systems in the Secretariat, and by a spirit of cooperation, whereby the special procedures defer to the activities of the treaty bodies.

Underlying any legitimate concern of potential cross-system duplication and overlap is the assumption that the state whose activity in question is a party to the relevant treaty and that, where optional, it has accepted the treaty bodies' scrutinizing or complaints functions. It is, therefore, axiomatic that there can be no such duplication or overlap in respect of states that have not adhered to the treaty or accepted the optional procedures. That acceptance would also have to be, as is not presently the case, irrevocable.[116] Pursuing the same logic, it would also be necessary for the treaty bodies that do not at present engage in on-the-spot fact-finding visits to do so. This would raise the question as to whether they have the implied power to do so or would need a treaty amendment or optional protocol to give them that power (the CEDAW Optional Protocol may be put forward as suggesting, *a contrario*, that there is no such implied power.) The treaty bodies would also have to be able to engage in urgent appeals beyond those merely aimed at preserving their adjudicative functions.

It will be evident that this sort of evolution would in fact involve a transformation in the nature of the treaty body system to approximate that of the special procedures system. Any transformation of this sort cannot reasonably be expected in the near future. Universal ratification of the treaties is still a depressingly distant goal, despite sustained attempts at promoting it.[117] Presumably universal acceptance of the optional procedures is yet further off.

It would appear that, for the foreseeable future, the two systems will remain what they have been so far, highly complementary means of promoting accountability for compliance with human rights norms. The complementarity is increased by the ability of each system to build on the work of the other. Of course, from the perspective of the state, interest from more than one body, however different the basis of that interest, represents probably unwanted, increased pressure to address the problem. The human rights perspective must, however, particularly in view of the non-coercive nature of the actions, be that of the potential victim. From that perspective, multiple activity can only be supportive of the broader human rights project.

[116] For example, Guyana, Jamaica, and Trinidad and Tobago have denounced the Optional Protocol to the ICCPR.

[117] See Roadmap towards the implementation of the United Nations Millennium Declaration: UN Doc A/56/326 (2001), para 204.

3

Reforming the UN Human Rights Protection Procedures: A Legal Perspective on the Establishment of the Universal Periodic Review Mechanism

Nadia Bernaz[1]

1. Introduction

Recent reform of the UN human rights machinery has become one of the most paper-consuming topics in the international human rights academic world.[2] The situation appears all the more striking since arguably, the creation of the Human Rights Council in March 2006[3] and the correlative abolition of the UN Commission on Human Rights has not resulted in groundbreaking institutional decisions. The mere creation of the Council, in itself, does not *fundamentally* change the way human rights are guaranteed at the international level.

The reorganization of the different procedures[4] has followed separate paths. A first set of reforms can be viewed in the context of the overall UN reform, formally discussed since 2003 when the Secretary General set up a High Level Panel on Threats, Challenges and Change 'to assess current threats to international peace

[1] The author wishes to thank Judge Jakob Möller and Ms Mara Steccazzini for their help in accessing older UN documents, as well as Dr Vinodh Jaichand and Dr Katarina Månsson for their useful comments on earlier drafts.

[2] Special issues Human Rights Brief (vol 13, issue 3, Spring 2006) and Human Rights Law Review (vol 7, issue 1, 2007). See also Ghanea, 'From UN Commission on Human Rights to UN Human Rights Council: One Step Forward or two Steps Sideways?', 55 International and Comparative Law Quarterly (2006) 695; Alston, 'Richard Lillich Memorial Lecture: Promoting the Accountability of Members of the New Human Rights Council', 15 Journal of Transnational Law and Policy (2005–6) 49; Tait, 'The United Nations Human Rights Council', 8 Human Rights and UK Practice (2007) 34. See also P Alston, J Crawford (eds), *The Future of UN Human Rights Treaty Monitoring* (2000).

[3] GA Res 60/251, 15 March 2006.

[4] As a preliminary comment, it must be pointed out that the UN human rights implementation mechanisms—intergovernmental and treaty based—are not unified. As such, one cannot talk about a system, a term that implies a certain unity or at least an interconnectedness that is lacking in the present case. This is the reason why the term 'procedures' will be used throughout the chapter.

and security; to evaluate how . . . existing policies and institutions have done in addressing those threats; and to make recommendations for strengthening the UN so that it can provide collective security for all in the twenty first century'.[5]

The Panel's report and subsequent negotiations within the UN resulted in the creation of a new intergovernmental body, the UN Human Rights Council, the successor to the Commission on Human Rights.[6] A first round of discussions concerned the future of the procedures carried out by the former Commission, in particular the special procedures and the complaint procedure, as well as the modalities of the new universal periodic review process the Council is to undertake, following the terms of its founding resolution.[7] These discussions lasted a year and ended on 18 June 2007 with the adoption by the Human Rights Council of the Institution Building Resolution.[8]

A second set of envisaged reforms concerns the human rights treaty bodies, as many commentators are of the opinion that the reporting system and the complaint procedures before these bodies ought to be at least rationalized, if not overhauled.[9] However, the likelihood of action on such reform appears rather low at the moment.[10]

The UN human rights protection procedures remain first and foremost part of the UN nebula. As such, they can hardly be viewed outside a very politicized context: the choice of a voting system, geographical representation, the seemingly arbitrary decision to establish one special procedure while discontinuing another, the reform of the treaty bodies; in other words most issues related to the UN human rights protection procedures carry with them the overwhelming weight of politics.

[5] Note by the Secretary-General introducing the Report of the High-level Panel on 'Threats, Challenges and Change, A More Secure World: Our Shared Responsibility', A/59/265, 2 December 2004, para 3.

[6] The panel did not come up with the idea of creating this new body. It had been first mooted by Professor Kälin and Cecilia Jimenez from the Bern Institute of Public Law. See Brülhart, 'From a Swiss Initiative to a United Nations Proposal (from 2003 until 2005)' in L Müller (ed), *The First 365 Days of the United Nations Human Rights Council* (2007) at 16.

[7] GA Res 60/251, 15 March 2006, para 5 (e).

[8] HRC Res. 5/1, 18 June 2007 and see, Boyle, ch 1 and Rodley, ch 2, in this volume.

[9] Scheinin, 'The Proposed Optional Protocol to the Covenant on Economic, Social and Cultural Rights: a Blueprint For UN Human Rights Treaty Body Reform—Without Amending the Existing Treaties', 6 Human Rights Law Review (2006) 131; Nowak, 'The Need for a World Court of Human Rights', 7 Human Rights Law Review (2007) 251; Bowman, 'Towards a Unified Treaty Body for Monitoring Compliance with UN Human Rights Conventions? Legal Mechanisms for Treaty Reform', 7 Human Rights Law Review (2007) 225; O'Flaherty and O'Brien, 'Reform of UN Human Rights Treaty Monitoring Bodies: a Critique of the Concept Paper on the High Commissioner's Proposal for a Unified Standing Treaty Body', 7 Human Rights Law Review (2007) 141.

[10] The High Commissioner for Human Rights Louise Arbour championed the idea of a unified standing treaty body, see Plan of action submitted by the UN High Commissioner for Human Rights, Annex to, 'In Larger Freedom: Towards Development, Security and Human Rights for All', Report of the Secretary-General, UN Doc A/59/2005/Add3, 26 May 2005, para 147, and OHCHR, Concept Paper on the High Commissioner's Proposal for a Unified Standing Treaty Body, UN Doc HRI/MC/2006/2, 22 March 2006. However this radical proposal failed to garner sufficient support, see, Chairperson's Summary of a Brainstorming Meeting on Reform of the Human Rights Treaty Body System 'Malbun II' (Triesenberg, Liechtenstein), A/HRC/2/G/5 Annex, 14–16 July 2006.

Yet the UN, as an international organization, remains a public international law institution. Beyond its politicization, the UN is undoubtedly a laboratory for international law-making. For instance, the General Assembly appears to be a preferred forum for the adoption of treaties, classical public international legal instruments. Based on decision-making processes, the resolutions adopted or the state representatives' interventions, conclusions as regards the crystallization of a rule of customary law, or the development of a practice contrary to the existing law may be drawn. Therefore, despite the dominant political flavour of the UN, it can still be viewed and properly studied from a public international law standpoint. The purpose of this chapter is precisely to discuss the current reforms of the UN human rights procedures, in particular those related to the universal periodic review mechanism, (UPR), from a public international law perspective. It does not aim at providing an exhaustive overview of the reform process.[11] Rather, it intends to discuss some aspects of the current and proposed reforms that may seem most relevant for an international jurist. The central argument in this respect is that in an ideal system modelled by law, human rights protection would enjoy both clear standards and efficient monitoring mechanisms. Although these two elements remain highly theoretical and should not be viewed as realistic goals, the purpose of this short contribution is to assess the substantial and procedural aspects of the new Council's universal periodic review mechanism against these ideal features and to shed specific legal light on the new mechanism. Evidently, given the politicized context in which the mechanism is likely to function, one should not be too severe while appraising it from a purely legal perspective.

As mentioned earlier, whereas safeguarding human rights at the international level entails clear substantive and procedural law, one has recently witnessed the adoption by the Human Rights Council of a rather uncertain basis for the new universal periodic review, notably, but not exclusively, because both binding and non-binding law are presented as formal standards for the review. In addition, the establishment of this new monitoring mechanism could lead to the questioning of the very existence of another mechanism, namely the human rights treaties' reporting system, which indicates that, perhaps, the time has come to re-examine the different UN human rights procedures with a view to rationalizing them.

The first part of this chapter focuses on the substantive issue of the universal periodic review's standards, the determination of which proved extremely thorny. In the end, both binding and non-binding human rights law will be used to assess states' human rights records, a practice that was already afoot within the former Commission on Human Rights through its relying on soft law texts as standards for complaint procedures. While soft law standards have an important role to play in the field of human rights protection, notably because they may evolve as true legal obligations, using them as review standards will certainly be difficult in practice. In other words, blurring the frontier between binding and non-binding law

[11] See Boyle, ch 1 in this volume for such an overview.

with the view to encouraging states to better respect human rights is not necessarily the best approach. The second part of this contribution concentrates on procedural matters and points out that the new UPR mechanism will necessarily encroach on existing mechanisms and, as a consequence, may provide for an opportunity to rethink thoroughly the UN human rights monitoring procedures.

2. Substantive Legal Aspects of Universal Periodic Review: States' Obligations and Commitments as Applicable Standards

General Assembly Resolution 60/251 states that the Human Rights Council is to 'undertake a universal periodic review, based on objective and reliable information, of the fulfilment by each State of its human rights obligations and commitments.'[12] During its first regular session in June 2006, the Council decided 'to establish an inter-sessional open-ended intergovernmental working group to develop the modalities of the universal periodic review mechanism',[13] which work was to be completed 'within one year after the holding of its first session' (by June 2007).[14] The facilitator of the working group, H E Mohamed Loulichki from Morocco, identified six elements for discussion based on the various contributions he received. One was the determination of a basis of review.[15]

As noted earlier, this basis ought to be each state's 'human rights obligations and commitments'.[16] The Institution Building Resolution, finally adopted by the Council on 18 June 2007, specifies the sources for UPR on which a consensus had emerged among states: the Charter of the UN, the Universal Declaration of Human Rights, human rights instruments to which a state is party, and voluntary pledges and commitments made by states, including those undertaken when presenting their candidatures for election to the Human Rights Council.[17] Also, interestingly, 'in addition to the above and given the complementarity and mutually interrelated nature of international human rights law and international humanitarian law, the review shall take into account international humanitarian law'.[18] This last point, formulated in a rather convoluted way, is the result of a compromise. The facilitator had proposed to include international humanitarian law, 'as and where applicable',[19] but agreement was hard to reach. Whereas some states argued that

[12] GA Res 60/251, 15 March 2006, para 5(e).

[13] A/HRC/DEC/1/103, 30 June 2006, para 1. Records of the Working Group are available on the OHCHR extranet, <http://www.ohchr.org>.

[14] GA Res 60/251, 15 March 2006, para 5(e).

[15] A/HRC/4/CRP3, 13 March 2007, para 4. The other five elements are: the principles and objectives of the review, the periodicity and order of review, the process and modalities of review, the outcome of the review and the follow-up to the review.

[16] GA Res 60/251, 15 March 2006, para 5(e).

[17] HRC Res 5/1, 18 June 2007, para 2.

[18] Ibid.

[19] Non-Paper on the Universal Periodic Review Mechanism prepared by the facilitator, 27 April 2007. See also Non-Paper on the Universal Periodic Review Mechanism, 6 June 2007, OHCHR extranet.

international humanitarian law was undoubtedly relevant for human rights protection, others pointed out its specificity and the practical difficulties the Council would face in assessing compliance with international humanitarian law given the troubled contexts in which it applies.[20] In a later non-paper, the facilitator also proposed to include as additional bases of review national constitutions, legislation and domestic laws. No agreement could be reached on these elements.[21]

Hence, consensus has emerged that the UPR will be based on the UN Charter, the human rights treaties to which the state is a party, and 'applicable' international humanitarian law—a formulation that seems to include both treaties and customary rules—binding instruments of international law or binding customary rules, as well as on the Universal Declaration of Human Rights and voluntary pledges and commitments undertaken by the state, that is to say soft law instruments. Founding a review mechanism both on binding and non-binding legal commitments is not a problem in principle. Indeed, by broadening the scope of the standards that states ought to conform to, human rights protection could be enhanced, which is the ultimate goal. However, blurring the distinction between binding and non-binding law is likely to complicate the assessment work in practice. In the course of negotiations, states were insistent that the distinction between the two must be upheld. The contents of each category—obligations and commitments—were also forcefully discussed.

A. States' Human Rights Obligations: A Much-Questioned Basis of Review

During the UPR working group sessions, states emphasized the obvious point that their obligations only arise from treaties to which they are parties, simply because it cannot be different.[22] Finland, speaking on behalf of the European Union, had proposed that compliance be discussed regarding all treaties, whether or not the State under scrutiny had ratified it. It suggested 'for those states that have not ratified treaties, the mechanism will provide a forum for discussing human rights compliance on the basis of the information from different sources, compiled by the Office of the High Commissioner for Human Rights'.[23] But this position was rejected, notably by Algeria, speaking on behalf of the African states[24] and Singapore, in rather bold terms.[25]

The latter position rests on a solid legal basis, namely Article 34 of the Vienna Convention on the Law of Treaties of 1969, which states that 'a treaty does not create either obligations or rights for a third State without its consent'.[26] This

[20] A/HRC/4/CRP3, 13 March 2007, para 15. [21] Ibid, para 19.

[22] Ibid, para 13.

[23] Updated Compilation of Proposals and Relevant Information on the Universal Periodic Review, 5 April 2007, at 30–1, OHCHR extranet, <http://www.ochr.org>.

[24] Ibid at 10. [25] Ibid at 86.

[26] Vienna Convention on the Law of Treaties, 1151 UNTS 331(1969).

provision reflects one of the most deeply entrenched rules of customary international law. It is not surprising, then, that previous attempts within the UN human rights machinery to hold states accountable on the basis of treaties they did not adhere to had failed. In the 1990s, a special procedure of the former Commission on Human Rights, namely the Working Group on Arbitrary Detention, began to base its recommendations on the International Covenant on Civil and Political Rights even when the state under review was not a party to it. They considered themselves to be 'justified in referring... to... the International Covenant on Civil and Political Rights, even if the Working Group has before it a case concerning a non-party State, in view of the tenacity of the declaratory effect of the quasi-totality of its provisions'.[27] The Commission on Human Rights formally asked the Working Group to renounce this practice in 1996,[28] which was complied with and acknowledged in its report a year later.[29] Other mechanisms of periodic review, such as that of the International Labor Organization, when dealing with treaties, are also limited to reviewing how states parties to those treaties comply with them.[30]

Treaties, even human rights treaties, only apply to states that are parties to them. Binding international human rights law arises exclusively from two formal sources of law, treaty and custom.[31] Apart from treaty law and customary law there cannot be any legally binding obligation. There may be law, as exemplified by General Assembly resolutions, but it is then non-binding and cannot be referred to as an obligation, but merely as a soft law commitment.[32] It should be noted, in this respect, that the facilitator of the working group on UPR had proposed to use customary human rights law as a basis of review but that there was no consensus on this.[33] The exclusion of customary rules of human rights law appears unfortunate but is not surprising in the sense that the determination of customary rules is a very complex process, subject to debate, and in any case is to be undertaken by proper judicial organs. Consensus was nevertheless reached concerning 'applicable humanitarian law', which seems to include customary humanitarian law.

In this context, the inclusion of the Universal Declaration of Human Rights (UDHR) in the list of standards states ought to comply with is worth commenting on. Embodied in a General Assembly resolution,[34] the UDHR is not binding in

[27] Report of the Working Group on Arbitrary Detention, E/CN4/1993/24, 12 January 1993, Deliberation 02, para 23. See also, Decisions 42/1992 (Cuba) para 6(b) and 44/1992 (Cuba), para 6(c) in the same report.

[28] Commission on Human Rights, Resolution 1996/28, 19 April 1996, para 5.

[29] E/CN4/1997/4, 17 December 1996, para 49.

[30] Comparative summary of information on existing mechanisms for periodic review, 11 December 2006, OHCHR extranet, <http://www.ochr.org>.

[31] General principles of law, common to virtually all national legal systems, are also a formal source of international law, but were apparently not discussed within the working group on universal periodic review.

[32] See V Degan, *Developments in International Law: Sources of International Law* (1997) 194.

[33] A/HRC/4/CRP3, 13 March 2007, para 19.

[34] GA Res 217 A (III), 10 December 1948.

itself. Its normative status nonetheless is unquestionable. In addition it has become an undeniable material source of international human rights law, either through the adoption of treaties or the development of customary rules.[35] Its absence from the list of standards would have damaged the periodic review process even if, from a strict legal point of view, states are not bound to comply with it.

In the course of undertaking the review in the field of international human rights law, as opposed to international humanitarian law, the Council is then left with only one formal source of legal obligation: treaties to which the state is a party. Although simple at first glance, this situation appears in fact rather problematic for two main reasons. First, by relying only on the human rights instruments to which the state is a party, the Council runs the risk of putting itself in an uncomfortable position. Indeed, a state which is party to no human rights treaties will only see its records appraised according to the Charter or the Universal Declaration of Human Rights. The fewer standards, the less likely it is that violations of those standards will be pointed out. This would in the end mean that states that did not ratify human rights treaties would be judged less severely than those who did, a rather awkward situation to say the least. The whole point of human rights treaties is to ensure human rights protection, at least this is the desired goal. As a result, states who agree to commit themselves through such binding instruments ought to be supported. Conversely, states who refuse to be bound by human rights treaties should be encouraged to join such treaties and put under greater scrutiny. By focusing on states parties to human rights treaties, as opposed to third states, the Human Rights Council could easily miss the point.

Second, if the Council uses only ratified treaties as standards for UPR, the risk of duplicating the treaty bodies' role, a concern specifically addressed by Resolution 60/251, increases.[36] In order to prevent this risk from materializing, some states had proposed to focus the Council's work on the issue of states' reservations to treaties and 'any action undertaken to withdraw them',[37] as well as on 'any action undertaken to follow-up and implement the concluding observations of relevant treaty bodies'.[38] Such focus would avoid encroaching too obviously on the treaty bodies' work, and would in fact ensure follow-up of their recommendations, an apposite complementary work. None of these options are mentioned in the Institution Building Resolution, which nevertheless reaffirms that one of the principles of the mechanism is that it should 'complement and not duplicate other human rights mechanisms, thus representing an added value'.[39] Arguably, this suggests that in fact the review will not focus so much on the treaty obligations as such but rather, possibly, on reservations and follow-up of the treaty bodies' work.

However, this would mean that the universal periodic review is not based on substantive legal obligations arising from treaties to which states have adhered.

[35] See H Steiner, P Alston, R Goodman, *International Human Rights in Context* (2008) 160.
[36] GA Res 60/251, 15 March 2006, para 5(e).
[37] A/HRC/4/CRP3, 13 March 2007, para 13.
[38] Ibid. [39] HRC Res 5/1, 18 June 2007, para 3(f).

Reservations are unfortunate but are a well-rooted international legal practice. Discussing states' reservations to human rights treaties and encouraging them to withdraw those reservations is a useful exercise. Yet, it should be clearly distinguished from assessing states' actual human rights records, unless, of course, the reservations are closely related to the very human rights abuses committed. Similarly, concluding observations made by treaty bodies are not binding and do not impose formal obligations on states. Discussing how states fulfil them, hence ensuring their follow-up, would clearly be valuable, but it must be said that this exercise would remain entirely outside the sphere of binding international law.

In addition, because customary human rights law seems to be excluded as well, if the prohibition to duplicate existing mechanisms implies that the review will focus on reservations and follow-up of concluding observations, in practice this would amount to eliminate legally binding obligations as the basis of review, a regrettable situation as human rights treaties represent one of the most important achievements of human rights law. Aside from discussions relating to reservations, the Council would then only assess how States fulfil their non-legally binding commitments. But on this point also consensus was difficult to reach, as will be discussed in the next section.

B. States' Commitments: A Debatable Basis of Review

Consensus eventually emerged among states that voluntary pledges when they present themselves for election to the Human Rights Council, and other voluntary commitments given by states should form part of UPR.[40] Some countries were very reluctant and pointed out that 'these may not apply equally to all states and thus, would not be consistent with the principles of universality of coverage and equal treatment of states'.[41] In addition, it could be that by using such pledges and commitments to conduct the review, the Human Rights Council could trigger negative side-effects. By voluntarily undertaking mere commitments, as opposed to binding commitments, states wish to remain within a non-formal setting. Therefore utilizing mere commitments as standards to formally assess state practice seems inappropriate as they are not meant to be used this way. If, by voting in favour of a General Assembly resolution, a state can then be reproached by the Council for not having respected it, chances are that states will be even more cautious than they currently are in voting in favour of such resolutions, and may end up not voting for them at all. The same reasoning may be applied in respect of states' commitments to the final declarations of conferences, which are usually adopted by consensus. States may become reluctant to participate in international conferences if their presence and non-express opposition to a final declaration adopted by consensus could be used to criticize them

[40] HRC Res 5/1, 18 June 2007, para 2

[41] A/HRC/4/CRP3, 13 March 2007, para 14.

in the future. During the course of the negotiations on UPR, reservations were expressed on the reference to commitments arising from 'UN conferences and summits' because on the one hand, they would be very difficult to identify and on the other, even when identified, the outcomes of such conferences 'did not achieve universal support in some cases' and, being 'inspirational' in nature, they could not constitute a proper basis for review.[42]

In any case, the practical feasibility of use of mere commitments arising from the outcomes of summits in the review process is questionable. Their wording is often very general and they set up goals rather than precise obligations. As a result, to utilize them as assessment standards for human rights records appear quite difficult, at least for situations not involving gross violations. Indeed, the former Commission on Human Rights, in the course of a 1503 complaint procedure used both binding and non-binding texts as standards for states' action. In particular, use was made of the Universal Declaration of Human Rights while appraising gross violations of human rights.[43] In such a context, when the violations are dramatic, even texts lacking precision may be used, since one can easily conclude that a violation occurred, provided the fact-finding was correctly undertaken. In addition, as mentioned earlier, the Universal Declaration of Human Rights, given its symbolic value, cannot be put on the same plane as any other commitment. But UPR is not meant to focus on gross violations. Such violations require quick reaction. Periodic review is intended to evaluate the improvements and/or the drawbacks of states in the area of human rights, based on widely accepted and fairly precise standards. From this perspective, one may question the appropriateness of including soft law commitments as a basis for review without however finally specifying in Resolution 5/1 what these commitments might be.

This is without prejudice to the fact that soft law instruments, such as General Assembly resolutions, may serve as a basis for the development of future hard law norms, treaty embodied or of a customary nature. In that sense, including mere commitments in the list of standards appears to be a good idea, as the universal periodic review will provide an interesting forum for discussion on developing norms. However, it is worth mentioning that formally reviewing the fulfilment by a state of its obligations and commitments and discussing soft law standards with the view to encouraging the state under review to agree to harder norms in the future are two rather different tasks. Yet, they do not necessarily exclude each other.

The contents of the pledges which member states made in standing for election to the Council raise certain questions. States pledge to promote and protect human rights. Yet, one may say that when a state promises, through a pledge, to respect rights that are embodied in treaties to which it is a party, it is in fact watering down the force of the binding obligation. For instance, in France's

[42] A/HRC/4/CRP3, 13 March 2007, para 17.

[43] E Lawson, M Bertucci, L Wiseberg, *Encyclopedia of Human Rights* (1996) 1507. The Human Rights Council will do the same: HRC Res 5/1, 18 June 2007, para 87.

pledge, one can read that it 'will continue to work towards ensuring full respect for all fundamental rights of women, the elimination of all forms of discrimination and violence directed at them and the representation of women in decision-making bodies'.[44] However, as a state party to the Convention on the Elimination of all Forms of Discrimination against Women, France is *bound* to do so. In other words, whereas it can be viewed as a proof of good faith to pledge itself to favour gender equality, it would be even better if France was simply respecting its existing international obligations. If it did, there would be no need for such a pledge. One may view the pledges positively, as proofs of the states' commitment to protect certain rights. Yet, it may also be the case that presenting commitments that are in fact legally binding as commitments states merely pledge to respect could constitute a substantial step backwards if, while assessing the state's records through the universal periodic review, the Council highlights the non-respect of the pledges and not the violation of an international legal obligation. In that sense, the pledges of certain states to become parties to human rights treaties they have not ratified yet makes more sense and constitutes a real added value.[45]

In sum, the idea that the UPR mechanism should be based on 'the fulfillment by each state of its human rights obligations and commitments',[46] raises many questions. Relying on the idea that 'All human rights are universal, indivisible, interrelated, interdependent and mutually reinforcing',[47] the General Assembly adopted a broad conception of the standards of review. It left the Human Rights Council with the task of deciding precisely which standards will provide the basis for review but allowed that both binding and non-binding law could be used. Yet this blurring is not necessarily useful for the purpose of enhancing human rights' promotion and protection in the sense that, in any case, states do not agree with the idea that obligations and mere commitments are the same thing. On the contrary, it could be argued that precise and clear legal standards would be needed for the review process. By leaving aside customary international human rights law, and perhaps even treaties—but this last option will hopefully not materialize—in order to avoid encroaching upon the treaty bodies' work, the Council is left with few options. Perhaps a better idea would have been to set up a follow-up procedure of the treaty bodies' concluding observations and of recommendations issued by the special procedures, as this was undoubtedly needed, instead of creating a new mechanism on such a fragile basis. Now that the Human Rights Council has been created, another solution to avoid duplication of the treaty bodies' work

[44] France's Candidacy to the Elections to the Human Rights Council, 9 May 2006 at 6, <http://www.un.org/ga/60/elect/hrc/france.pdf>.

[45] See for instance, Voluntary Pledges and Commitments, Indonesia, 8 March 2007 at 3, <http://www.un.org/ga/60/elect/hrc/indonesia.pdf>. Indonesia gave a detailed list of all the instruments it intends to become party to.

[46] GA Res 60/251, 15 March 2006, para 5(e).

[47] Ibid, Preamble. This formulation follows that of the Vienna Declaration and Programme of Action, A/CONF157/23, 12 July 1993, para 5.

would be to rethink the whole treaty body system, in particular the reporting procedures; in other words, to rationalize the UN's human rights mechanisms.

3. Procedural Aspects of UPR and Prospects for the Rationalization of the UN Human Rights Monitoring Mechanisms

For the moment, there are three main monitoring routes for human rights law within the UN: political (before the Human Rights Council and through the special procedures), administrative (through the presentation of state reports before the treaty bodies), and quasi-judicial (through complaint mechanisms before certain treaty bodies such as the Human Rights Committee). All have either recently experienced reform or attempted reform with the view to improving them. These mechanisms constitute great achievements despite the fact that they produce only non-binding recommendations. In the field of human rights, international jurists have learned to content themselves with soft law. In international law, where there is no centralized organ vested with enforcement powers and where, consequently, implementation is traditionally seen as a problematic issue, any mechanism that may favour implementation is a welcome addition. However, this does not mean that there is no room for improvement. As already discussed the UN's intergovernmental human rights body, the Commission on Human Rights, has now been replaced by the Human Rights Council, a new organ with an improved membership criteria[48] and, of more relevance to this chapter, a new human rights monitoring system, the universal periodic review mechanism. To what extent the establishment of this mechanism may advance the rationalization of the procedures needs to be discussed.

The universal periodic review mechanism aims at strengthening the existing monitoring system, by creating a new route for such monitoring. This is a good idea in principle, because it allows for a systematic and periodic scrutiny of every UN member state, notwithstanding potential problems associated with the basis of review, discussed above. It must also be pointed out that UPR is by no means a novelty. A similar procedure had been set up in 1956 and finally abandoned in 1980. Is it relevant to reinstall a comparable procedure less than 30 years later? This issue surely needs to be addressed for the future in the context of the rationalization of the UN human rights machinery. Might the universal periodic report toll the knell of the treaty bodies' reporting procedures? It seems as though it will

[48] The High Level Panel, in its report, emphasized that the Commission on Human Rights' credibility had decreased mainly because 'in recent years States have sought membership of the Commission not to strengthen human rights but to protect themselves against criticism or to criticize others', Report of the High-level Panel on 'Threats, Challenges and Change, A More Secure World: Our Shared Responsibility', A/59/265, 2 December 2004, para 283. On membership criteria see Boyle, ch 1 in this volume.

necessarily duplicate them. However, as will be suggested, that could turn out to be a positive development in the long run.

A. The Universal Periodic Review as an Old 'New Idea': Overcoming Past Errors

As a preliminary comment, it should be emphasized that review mechanisms do exist in several other systems, although, in practice, the actual procedures may differ a great deal. In fact, experience with existing comparable procedures served as a basis for the discussion in the Human Rights Council of the detailed provisions of the UPR mechanism which were finally adopted.[49]

The historical precedent for UPR operated by the former Commission on Human Rights was also important. It had been created in 1956 by ECOSOC,[50] and requested States 'to transmit to the Secretary General, every three years, a report describing developments and the progress achieved during the preceding three years in the field of human rights'.[51] The Secretary General was then 'to prepare a brief summary of the reports... for the Commission on Human Rights'[52] and the periodic reports were discussed during sessions of the Commission on Human Rights. Considered 'obsolete' and 'of marginal usefulness', the system was finally abolished in 1980.[53] Alston observed that, as far as this reporting procedure was concerned, 'its achievements could readily be measured in terms of trees destroyed, but it is doubtful whether it made any significant contribution to the promotion of respect for human rights'.[54] According to Farer, the failure of the system may be easily explained: 'Since the very making of a report, much less its content, was effectively left to the discretion of states, the reporting process was not calculated to roil any of the world's chancelleries'[55] and, as a result, had very little effect, a factor which undoubtedly played a role in its demise.

The Institution Building Resolution, adopted by the Human Rights Council on 18 June 2007, requires that the documents on which the review will be primarily based are 'information prepared by the state concerned, which can take the form of a national report'.[56] Additional information is to be compiled by the OHCHR based on the treaty bodies' and special procedures' reports in respect of

[49] Background Information & Presentations on Existing Mechanisms for Periodic Review, Human Rights Council, OHCHR Extranet page, <http://www.ohchr.org>, and, n 30 above.

[50] For an account of this procedure see, Alston, 'Reconceiving the UN Human Rights Regime: Challenges Confronting the New UN Human Rights Council', 7 Melbourne Journal of International Law (2006) 185, at 207–14.

[51] ECOSOC Res 624 B (XXII), 1 August 1956, para 1.

[52] Ibid, para 4. See also McDougal & Bebr, 'Human Rights in the United Nations', 58 American Journal of International Law (1964) 603, at 634.

[53] GA Res 35/209, 17 December 1980.

[54] Alston, n 50 above, at 213.

[55] Farer, 'The United Nations and Human Rights: More than a Whimper Less than a Roar', 9 Human Rights Quarterly (1987) 550, at 573.

[56] HRC Res 5/1, 18 June 2007, para 15(a).

the country under review as well as on 'credible and reliable information provided by other relevant stakeholders'.[57] Although the OHCHR will play an important role in the new system, the fact remains that the state reviewed will prepare the primary basic document for discussion, a self-written report.

In the end, the only actual difference between the new system of UPR, based on states' reports, and the one that was considered 'obsolete' and 'of marginal usefulness' less than 30 years ago, lies in the procedure set up for the actual review. In 1956, the states were to prepare a triennial report, to transmit it to the Secretary General who, in turn, was 'to prepare a brief summary of the reports... for the Commission on Human Rights'.[58] The system did not formally include any form of organized discussions between the reporting state and the Commission. Conversely, the working group on the universal periodic review came up with a detailed list of practical modalities.[59] Whether or not these will suffice to overcome the procedural problems encountered in the past remains to be seen.[60] For now, one can notice that the two systems appear quite similar at first glance. Hopefully, a better fate awaits the new universal periodic review.

Paradoxically however, it must be said that although human rights' protection warrants a reliable and legitimate international monitoring mechanism, its success may lead to certain difficulties. In fact, if the new UPR mechanism turns out to be satisfactory, it could have profound consequences for the entire UN human rights machinery, as the risks of duplicating the treaty bodies reporting procedures appear quite high.

B. The Universal Periodic Review: A Replacement for the Treaty Bodies Reporting Procedures?

The UPR mechanism, based on reports, should at the same time 'complement and not duplicate other human rights mechanisms, thus representing an added value'.[61] This goal of non-duplication has been a constant concern for the architects of the reform[62] and at first glance seems to be a valuable one. Human rights protection deserves clear methods of implementation and since duplication involves confusion and potentially a lower level of protection, it should be avoided.

Yet, given the way the reporting procedures before the treaty bodies currently work, the difference between these procedures and the UPR system appears rather tenuous. The process of considering states parties' periodic reports by the

[57] Ibid, para 15(c).

[58] ECOSOC Res 624 B (XXII), 1 August 1956, para 5.

[59] HRC Res 5/1, 18 June 2007, paras 18–25.

[60] The issue of the basis for review was also a major problem, see Alston, n 50 above, at 213.

[61] HRC Res 5/1, 18 June 2007, para. 3(f).

[62] Gaer, 'A Voice not an Echo: Universal Periodic Review and the UN Treaty Body System', 7 Human Rights Law Review (2007) 109, at 111–12 and 114–25.

different treaty bodies consists in examining the said reports together with government representatives.[63] 'Based on this dialogue, the Committee publishes its concerns and recommendations.'[64] The universal periodic review system consists in designating a group of three rapporteurs, which will prepare a report on each state report and other relevant information concerning that state,[65] then in gathering the 47 member states of the Council into a Working Group and in engaging in an 'interactive dialogue between the country under review and the Council'.[66] At the end of the process, the Council will adopt 'a report consisting of a summary of the proceedings of the review process; conclusions and/or recommendations, and the voluntary commitments of the State concerned'.[67] In view of the evident commonalities between the two mechanisms, it looks as though duplication, or at least significant overlap, will necessarily occur.

In fact, many states had warned against such a possibility during the course of the negotiations. Australia had emphasized that it did 'not support any proposal for a separate reporting process' as 'this would duplicate the reporting processes required under the treaty bodies and... [be] unnecessary'.[68] The Netherlands had pointed out that given 'the already heavy workload for states following from their treaty body monitoring obligations', they were 'not in favour of adding a new reporting obligation for states'.[69] Japan had proposed that a questionnaire be sent to every state under review. Their response to the questionnaire would then serve as a basic document to conduct the review.[70] This would have avoided additional reporting obligations. But the mechanism adopted in the end did not steer clear of this stumbling block: it will be based primarily on a self-written report.

This mechanism therefore lies within the scope of an already much criticized reporting process of the treaty bodies. This process is seen as onerous by states and because of the number of reports required under the different treaties there is already a tendency towards overlap, which is a waste of time and energy for every actor in the mechanism—the treaty bodies, the states, and consequently the beneficiaries.[71] A revolutionary system at the outset, the human rights treaty

63 'In addition to the government report, the treaty bodies may receive information on a country's human rights situation from other sources, including non-governmental organizations, UN agencies, other intergovernmental organizations, academic institutions and the press', OHCHR webpage on the human rights treaty bodies.

64 Ibid.

65 The groups of three rapporteurs (*Troikas*) to conduct the reviews for the first and second universal periodic review sessions were selected on 28 February 2008: List of Troikas for the First UPR Session, 7–18 April 2008 ; List of Troikas for the Second UPR Session, 5–16 May 2008.

66 HRC Res 5/1, 18 June 2007, para 21. See also HRC 8/PRST/1, Modalities and practices for the universal periodic review process, 8 April 2008.

67 Ibid, para 26.

68 Office of the High Commissioner for Human Rights, Secretariat of the Human Rights Council, Updated compilation of proposals and relevant information on the universal periodic review, 5 April 2007, at 68.

69 Ibid at 43.

70 Ibid at 78.

71 See generally, references, n 9 above.

regime is currently in difficulty due to 'its success in attracting the participation and involvement of states'.[72] Because the treaties have been widely ratified, states do produce many reports, which in consequence are often late. A huge backlog has developed before the treaty bodies themselves resulting in delays in processing reports. In seeking to process more reports per session, treaty bodies are inevitably allowing less time for the dialogue with the states, an unfortunate feature because if the dialogue is reduced, perhaps the whole mechanism is somewhat missing the point.[73]

In this context, when reporting has demonstrated both its potential strength but also its limits in practice, the practical requirements of the new universal periodic review mechanism, as they were adopted on 18 June 2007 appear problematic. Each state under review prepares and presents yet another report, (albeit of a maximum length of 20 pages)[74] while still bound by its obligation to produce reports for each treaty to which it is a party. Thus it must be assumed that the new mechanism will encroach on the treaty bodies' work as it concerns review of state reports. If the new mechanism proves to be a success the need for state reports to the treaty bodies could come to be questioned in the longer run. In fact, by focusing on seeking to avoid duplication and not acknowledging the fact that duplication—or at least considerable overlap—is inevitable, the architects of the Council reform may have lost sight of a significant concern, the need for rationalization.

It must be said, however, that simply replacing the treaty bodies' reporting procedures by the universal periodic review would give rise to substantial problems. First, whereas independent experts sit on the treaty bodies, the universal periodic review will be conducted by states themselves, in fact by all the Member states of the Council sitting in a Working Group. The often mentioned risk of politicization[75] within the Council in general, and in the course of the periodic review mechanism in particular, commonly raised against the former Commission on Human Rights, is real and should not be overlooked. As Felice Gaer put it:

> discussion of overlap with the treaty bodies in large measure reflects the fact that these bodies are seen as among the most credible and professional of the UN human rights mechanisms. The treaty bodies have operated separately from the political intergovernmental human rights bodies.[76]

In other words, for the periodic review to fully replace the treaty bodies' reporting procedures, the Human Rights Council would have to demonstrate its capacity to abide by the principle of equal treatment of each state. Whether or not

[72] Crawford, 'The UN Human Rights Treaty System: a System in Crisis?', in P Alston, J Crawford (eds), *The Future of UN Human Rights Treaty Monitoring* (2000) at 3.

[73] Ibid, 4–5.

[74] HRC Res 5/1, 18 June 2007, para 15(a).

[75] Gaer, n 62 above, at 133.

[76] Ibid at 138.

this constitutes a realistic possibility is a matter outside the scope of this chapter, and in any event will require close scrutiny over the next years of the Council's practice in conducting UPR. Second, since the reporting procedures are based on the treaties themselves, formally eliminating them would probably necessitate amendment of the treaties. To amend all the treaties, the most satisfying reform plan from a legal point of view, would require the consent of all the states parties,[77] a large-scale task since these treaties are in the case of some almost universally ratified.[78] Although difficult in theory, it must be noted that in order to amend all the treaties,[79]

> a crucial factor... resides in the levels of likely governmental support for, or opposition to, the proposals for reform. Should they command general and whole-hearted approval, concern over the legal niceties would be greatly diminished, since consent, or at least acquiescence, represents the antidote to most ostensible violations of process or form in this context.[80]

In reality, if states were to agree generally with a proposal that the universal periodic review could replace the treaty bodies reporting procedure in a satisfactory manner, then at least de facto such a replacement could occur. No additional obligation would be incurred. Simply, instead of reporting both to the Council and the treaty bodies, the states would report only to the Council through the universal periodic review mechanism.

Such a possibility could represent a major step on the way to the rationalization of the human rights monitoring mechanisms. Yet, the improvement of human rights protection and effective implementation does not necessarily call for such procedural rationalization. The issue of duplication is a complex one. On the one hand, having two similar reporting and review systems may yet attract criticism as being wasteful. It also creates the risk of having the Human Rights Council disregarding or questioning the treaty bodies' recommendations for political motives, which may lead to differences in interpretation and therefore to a

[77] For a discussion of the difficulties facing this option in a larger context, one of creating a unified treaty body, and not simply eliminating the reporting procedures, see Bowman, 'Towards a Unified Treaty Body for Monitoring Compliance with UN Human Rights Conventions? Legal Mechanisms for Treaty Reform', 7 Human Rights Law Review (2007) 225.

[78] International Convention on the Elimination of all Forms of Racial Discrimination, 660 UNTS 195 (1965) 173 parties; International Covenant on Civil and Political Rights, 999 UNTS 171 (1966) 160 parties; International Covenant on Economic, Social and Cultural Rights, 993 UNTS 3 (1966) 155 parties; Convention on the Elimination of All Forms of Discrimination against Women, 1249 UNTS 13 (1979) 185 parties; Convention against Torture and Other Cruel, Inhuman or Degrading Treatment or Punishment, 1465 UNTS 85 (1984) 144 parties; Convention on the Rights of the Child, 1577 UNTS 3 (1989) 193 parties; International Convention on the Protection of the Rights of All Migrant Workers and Members of Their Families, GA Res 45/158, 18 December 1990, 36 parties; Convention on the Rights of Persons with Disabilities, GA Res 61/106, 13 December 2006, 36 parties.

[79] Bowman envisages the creation of a unified treaty body, and not the end of reporting procedures. But his argument is all the more valid in this more restricted context.

[80] Bowman, n 77 above, at 229.

prejudicial lack of clarity. On the other hand, the treaty bodies, even if they have undoubtedly helped shape the contents of human rights' protection through their recommendations, remain expert bodies. As such, their recommendations cannot give rise to customary law, whereas the future recommendations of the Human Rights Council based on the universal periodic review will be a valuable tool for targeting the development of customary rules. In that sense, the duplication of procedures is not necessarily a problem but may represent an interesting division of labour: the treaty bodies may influence state practice but do not represent states' positions. The universal periodic review, as a mechanism conducted by an intergovernmental body, may favour the crystallization of customary rules. In other words, substantial overlap may entail a more positive consequence, namely cross-fertilization.[81]

4. Conclusion

This chapter was centred on the new mechanism of universal periodic review but also touched on the question of the reform and rationalization of the UN human rights protection procedures as a whole. The creation of a unified standing monitoring body instead of the now eight separate treaty bodies, and their complaint procedures, has been extensively discussed by officials[82] and academic experts.[83] But despite strong backing from the UN High Commissioner for Human Rights, for now at least such a reform appears unlikely. Some have also suggested the creation of a World Court for Human Rights.[84] Whereas in the long run such an institution may turn out to be a valuable innovation which would induce further rationalization, simplification, and enhancement of the UN human rights machinery, the necessary transition phase would inevitably be difficult. Ideally, whereas the Human Rights Council would remain a place for dialogue on human rights, notably through the universal periodic review, a future Court would be an instrument of justiciability for the individual at the international level. Some states emphasized, during the negotiations on universal

[81] As a matter of fact, this phenomenon is already afoot between some treaty bodies and the corresponding special procedures, notably between the Committee against Torture and the special rapporteur on the question of torture. See Rodley, ch 2 in this volume.

[82] See, Concept Paper on the High Commissioner's Proposal for a Unified Standing Treaty Body, HRI/MC/2006/2, 22 March 2006, and references at n 10 above.

[83] Scheinin, 'The Proposed Optional Protocol to the Covenant on Economic, Social and Cultural Rights: A Blueprint for UN Human Rights Treaty Body Reform—Without Amending the Existing Treaties', 7 Human Rights Law Review. (2006) 131 at 134; Bowman, 'Towards a Unified Treaty Body for Monitoring Compliance with UN Human Rights Conventions? Legal Mechanisms for Treaty Reform', 7 Human Rights Law Review (2007) 225 at 239–40.

[84] Nowak 'The Need for a World Court of Human Rights', 7 Human Rights Law Review (2007) 251; and Trechsel, 'A World Court for Human Rights', 1 Northwestern University Journal of International Human Rights 3 (2004) at <http://www.law.northwestern.edu/journals/JIHR/v1/3>.

periodic review, that they did not wish the Council to work as a tribunal. A World Court for Human Rights would therefore not duplicate the Council's work but complement it. However, it must be said that unfortunately the necessary state support in favour of such an ambitious project is currently lacking.

The establishment of the universal periodic review mechanism is a more modest reform. While it raises many questions, both of a substantive and procedural nature, nevertheless it is, at least potentially, a powerful tool to monitor and eventually improve human rights protection.

4

The EU Fundamental Rights Agency: Genesis and Potential

Olivier De Schutter

1. Introduction

'*On voit que l'histoire est une galerie de tableaux où il y a peu d'originaux et beaucoup de copies*'[1] ... Alexis de Toqueville, with his usual lucidity, understood that our institutional imagination was limited: whatever we call new is generally made up of bits and pieces from earlier constructions, which we assemble in ways often already familiar. The Fundamental Rights Agency of the European Union is no exception. Formally, the Agency has been in existence since 1 March 2007. Its aim is to 'provide the relevant institutions, bodies, offices and agencies of the Community and its member States when implementing Community law with assistance and expertise relating to fundamental rights in order to support them when they take measures or formulate courses of action within their respective spheres of competence to fully respect fundamental rights'.[2] It thus constitutes a pillar of expertise which the institutions of the European Union[3] and the EU member states may rely upon in order to improve compliance with fundamental rights, as part of EU law.

A brief look at the genesis of the Fundamental Rights Agency, and at the context in which it was set up, is perhaps more instructive than a description of its structure and mandate, since it allows us to identify what it replicated and which alternatives, present in the discussions in 2003–5, its creators deliberately steered away from. This contribution recalls the context in which the Agency was

[1] Alexis de Toqueville, *L'Ancien régime et la révolution* (1860) at 119.

[2] Council Regulation (EC) No 168/2007 of 15 February 2007 establishing a European Union Agency for Fundamental Rights, OJ L53, 2 February 2007, 1 (Art 2). Hereafter this Regulation shall be referred to as 'the founding Regulation'. See also Fundamental Rights Agency, Annual Work Programme 2008, April 2008, <http://www.fra.europa.eu/fra/material/pub/WP/wp08_en.pdf.>

[3] In this chapter, the expression 'European Union (EU)' will be used to denote either the EU or the European Community, although these remain, until the entry in force of the Treaty of Lisbon, two separate organizations.

established. It then examines the genesis of the Agency, highlighting in particular the two models from which it was inspired. Since the need to ensure a harmonious cooperation with the Council of Europe (rather than risk undermining the position of the latter as the primary human rights organization in Europe) constituted a decisive factor in the debates on both the definition of the mandate of the Agency and its geographical remit, a separate section is devoted to this issue. The chapter then closes with a brief epilogue. It is too early to evaluate the added value of the Fundamental Rights Agency to the promotion and protection of fundamental rights in the EU. However, it may be safely predicted that this development, although institutional in nature, will deeply affect the way in which the EU exercises its competences in order to promote fundamental rights, and may lead in time to a more proactive fundamental rights policy in the Union.

2. The Context: the Rise of Human Rights in the EU (1998–2003)

In a report prepared for the 'Comité des Sages' responsible for drafting *Leading by Example: A Human Rights Agenda for the European Union for the Year 2000,* Philip Alston and Joseph H Weiler had proposed setting up a monitoring centre for human rights within the Union, which could serve to improve the coordination of the fundamental rights policies pursued by the member states.[4] The main argument in favour of the creation of such a body, modelled on the then recently established European Union Centre on Racism and Xenophobia,[5] was that it could encourage the Union to adopt a more preventive approach to human rights. 'Systematic, reliable and focused information,' it was argued, was 'the starting point of a clear understanding of the nature, extent, and location of the problems that exist and for the identification of possible solutions.' The suggestion was retained by the Wise Persons' report. At the time though, the institutions appeared reluctant to follow the idea. In their conclusions adopted at the Cologne European Council of 3–4 June 1999, the Heads of State and Government did suggest that 'the question of the advisability of setting up a Union agency for human rights and democracy should be considered'.[6] That sentence went almost unnoticed, however, overshadowed as it was by the decision, adopted at the same meeting, to launch the work on the drafting of the Charter of

[4] See P Alston and J H H Weiler, 'An 'Ever Closer Union' in Need of a Human Rights Policy: The European Union and Human Rights', in P Alston, with M Bustelo and J Heenan (eds), *The European Union and Human Rights* (1999) 3.

[5] This Monitoring Centre, sometimes referred to as the Vienna Observatory, was created by Council Reg 1035/97 of 2 June 1997 establishing a European Monitoring Centre on Racism and Xenophobia, OJ L151 of 10 June 1997, 1 (since amended by Reg No 1652/2003, OJ L245, 29 September 2003, 33).

[6] Cologne European Council, Presidency Conclusions, para 46.

Fundamental Rights.[7] And when, in a communication of May 2001 on the EU's role in promoting human rights and democracy in third countries, the European Commission had seemed to dismiss the idea,[8] albeit at the price of misinterpreting it,[9] the idea was considered long buried.

Yet almost 10 years after their initial proposal, the regulation establishing the Fundamental Rights Agency of the European Union largely corresponds to the idea initially expressed by Alston and Weiler.[10] In the meantime however, the context had radically changed, and it is only in the light of these changed circumstances that we can understand both the apparent turn around of the institutions on this idea, and the obstacles they faced in the debate about the Agency. In 1999–2000, two developments took place which significantly transformed the role of fundamental rights in the Union. On 7 December 2000, the Charter of Fundamental Rights of the European Union was proclaimed at the Nice European Summit.[11] Inspired by the fundamental rights recognized by the European Court of Justice within the general principles of law it ensures respect for, and by the international human rights instruments binding upon the EU member states, the Charter was the single most authoritative restatement of the acquis of the Union in the field of fundamental rights. But its main impact was not as a legal document, indeed, the Charter had no binding force when it was initially proclaimed;[12] it was the transformation it brought about in the culture and the practice of the institutions. On the basis of

[7] Ibid, paras 44–5.

[8] Communication from the Commission to the Parliament and the Council, The European Union's Role in Promoting Human Rights and Democracy in Third Countries, COM(2001)252 final of 8 May 2001 at 20 (where the Commission takes the view that 'the European Union does not lack for sources of advice and information. It can draw on reports from the United Nations the Council of Europe and a variety of international NGOs. Furthermore there is no monopoly of wisdom when it comes to analysing human rights and democratization problems, or their implications for the European Union's relations with a country. The real challenge for any institution is to use the information in a productive manner, and to have the political will to take difficult decisions. An additional advisory body would not overcome this challenge. The Commission does not therefore intend to pursue this suggestion, nor the related one which has occasionally been made that the Commission should produce, or subcontract an organization to produce, a world-wide overview of the human rights situation by country, as is done by the US State Department'.)

[9] Indeed, the initial proposal was not focused on the establishment of an Observatory in order to guide the external human rights policy of the Union; instead, as the analogy to the EUMC clearly indicates, the idea was also, and perhaps mainly, to guide the EU's internal human rights policies.

[10] See the founding Reg, n 2 above.

[11] OJ C364 of 18 December 2000, 1.

[12] The Reform Treaty, signed at Lisbon on 13 December 2007 and expected to enter into force in 2009 or 2010, will contain a reference to the Charter, thus confirming its status as a legally binding instrument for the institutions of the Union and for the member states when they implement Union law. See Art 6(2) of the Treaty on European Union as amended by the Treaty of Lisbon amending the Treaty on European Union and the Treaty establishing the European Community, signed at Lisbon, 13 December 2007 (OJ C306 of 17 December 2007, 1) (referring to the EU Charter of Fundamental Rights in the revised form it has been proclaimed on 12 December 2007 (OJ C303 of 14 December 2007, 1)).

the Charter, it became possible for the European Parliament to systematically check whether the legislative proposals on which it deliberates comply with the rights, freedoms, and principles which had been proclaimed in Nice.[13] The Commission too announced its intention to verify the compatibility of its proposals with the Charter in 2001,[14] a practice which, in more recent years, it has significantly improved.[15] Invoking fundamental rights within the EU thus became routine in the work of the institutions, now that there existed a document prepared under conditions which guaranteed it a high degree of legitimacy and which listed the said rights.

The second development was the entry into force on 1 May 1999 of the Treaty of Amsterdam. This Treaty not only formulated in Article 6(1) EU the values on which the Union was founded, which include human rights and fundamental freedoms. It also backed up this affirmation by a mechanism provided for in Article 7 EU, allowing for the adoption of sanctions against a state committing a serious and persistent breach of these values. In addition, following the crisis triggered by the entry into the Austrian ruling governmental coalition of Jörg Haider's Freedom Party of Austria (FPÖ),[16] this mechanism was improved by the Treaty of Nice, which introduced the possibility of recommendations being adopted preventively where a 'clear risk of a serious breach' of those values is found to be present.[17]

[13] See Art 34 of the Rules of Procedure of the European Parliament, 16th ed, July 2006, available at <http://www.europarl.europa.eu/omk/sipade3?PUBREF=-//EP//NONSGML+RULES-EP+20060703+0+DOC+PDF+V0//EN>.

[14] SEC(2001)380/3.

[15] In 2005, the Commission adopted a Communication clarifying the methodology it would use in order to assess the compatibility with the Charter of Fundamental Rights of its legislative proposals (Communication from the Commission, Compliance with the Charter of Fundamental Rights in Commission legislative proposals. Methodology for systematic and rigorous monitoring, COM(2005) 172 final of 27 April 2005.) In addition, when they were revised in 2005, the guidelines for the preparation of impact assessments paid greater attention to the potential effects of different policy options on the guarantees in the Charter: see SEC(2005)791, 15 June 2005. Although the new guidelines are still based, just as the former impact assessments (see Communication of 5 June 2005 on Impact Assessment, COM(2002)276), on a division between economic, social and environmental impacts, in the revised set of guidelines, fundamental rights are included under these different rubrics. Indeed, a specific report was commissioned by the European Commission (DG Justice, Freedom and Security) to EPEC (European Policy Evaluation Consortium) in preparation of the revised guidelines: see EPEC, 'The Consideration of Fundamental Rights in Impact Assessment. Final Report' December 2004.

[16] On this crisis, see M Happold, 'Fourteen against One: The EU Member States' Response to Freedom Party Participation in the Austrian Government', 49 International and Comparative Law Quarterly 953 (2000); and E Bribosia, O De Schutter, T Ronse and A Weyembergh, 'Le contrôle par l'Union européenne du respect de la démocratie et des droits de l'homme par ses Etats membres: à propos de l'Autriche', Journal des tribunaux—Droit européen, March 2000, 61–5. On the insertion of Art 7(1) EU by the Treaty of Nice, see G de Búrca, 'Beyond the Charter: How Enlargement has enlarged the Human Rights Policy of the EU', in O De Schutter and S Deakin (eds), *Social Rights and Market Forces: Is the open coordination of employment and social policies the future of social Europe?* (2005) 245–78 at 259–62.

[17] This preventive mechanism is now described in Art 7(1) EU.

The inclusion of such a mechanism soon raised the question of whether these provisions of the Treaty on the European Union should lead to a permanent monitoring of the situation of fundamental rights in the member states. The European Parliament, through its Committee on Civil Liberties, Justice and Home Affairs (LIBE Committee), took the leading role in this matter. As it noted itself, the Treaty of Nice 'acknowledges Parliament's special role as an advocate for European citizens', by granting the European Parliament the right to call for a procedure to be opened in the event of a clear risk of a serious breach.[18] But even before that Treaty entered into force, the European Parliament inaugurated the practice of adopting annual reports on the situation of fundamental rights in the Union, a practice which was facilitated, by providing a clearer grid of analysis, by the adoption of the EU Charter of Fundamental Rights at the Nice Summit of 2000.[19] This practice was justified by the consideration that:

> following the proclamation of the Charter, it is [...] the responsibility of the EU institutions to take whatever initiatives will enable them to exercise their role in monitoring respect for fundamental rights in the Member States, bearing in mind the commitments they assumed in signing the Treaty of Nice on 27 February 2001, with particular reference to new Article 7(1) [and that] it is the particular responsibility of the European Parliament (by virtue of the role conferred upon it under the new Article 7(1) of the Treaty of Nice) and of its appropriate committee [the LIBE Committee] to ensure [...] that both the EU institutions and the Member States uphold the rights set out in the various sections of the Charter.[20]

[18] See the Report on the Commission communication on Art 7 of the Treaty on European Union: Respect for and promotion of the values on which the Union is based (COM(2003)606—C5-0594/2003—2003/2249(INI)) (rapp J Voggenhuber), para 6 of the proposal for a resolution; this passage has been maintained without amendment in the European Parliament legislative resolution on the Commission communication on Art 7 of the Treaty on European Union: Respect for and promotion of the values on which the Union is based (COM(2003)606—C5-0594/2003—2003/2249(INI)), adopted on 20 April 2004 (see para 6 of the operative part of the resolution).

[19] See the Report on the situation as regards fundamental rights in the European Union (2000) (rapp Th Cornillet), PE 302.216/DEF, EP Doc A5-0223/2001 (2000/2231(INI)); the Report on the human rights situation in the European Union (2001) (rapp J Swiebel), PE 311.039/DEF, EP Doc A5-0451/2002 (2001/2014(INI)) (and Resolution of 15 January 2003 on the situation concerning fundamental rights in the European Union (2001), OJ C38 E, 12 February 2004, 174); Report on the situation as regards fundamental rights in the European Union (2002) (rapp F Sylla), PE 329.881/DEF, EP Doc A5-0281/2003 (2002/2013(INI)) (and Resolution of 4 September 2003 on the situation as regards fundamental rights in the European Union (2002), P5_TA(2003)0376); Report on the situation as regards fundamental rights in the European Union (2003) (rapp A Boumediene-Thiery), PE 329.936/DEF, EP Doc A5-0207/2004 (2003/2006(INI)). The resolution proposed on the basis of the report by Ms A Boumediene-Thiery was rejected by the European Parliament. The Cornillet Report was the first to use the EU Charter of Fundamental Rights as its template. However, the practice of preparing an annual report on the situation of fundamental rights of the Union predated the adoption of the Charter: see Resolution on the annual report on human rights in the EU (1998–1999), (rapp Haarder) of 16 March 2000 (EP Doc A5-0050/2000).

[20] Res of 5 July 2001 on the situation of fundamental rights in the European Union (2000) (rapp Thierry Cornillet) (2000/2231(INI)) (OJ C65 E, 14 March 2002, 177–350), paras 2–3.

Since it soon appeared that the resources of the LIBE Committee and the expertise and time it had at its disposal were not sufficient to enable it to conduct this monitoring function in an entirely satisfactory manner, the European Parliament requested that:

> a network be set up consisting of legal experts who are authorities on human rights and jurists from each of the Member States, in order to ensure a high degree of expertise and enable Parliament to receive an assessment of the implementation of each of the rights laid down in the Charter, taking account of developments in national laws, the case law of the Luxembourg and Strasbourg Courts and any notable case law of the Member States' national and constitutional courts.[21]

That network was set up in September 2002.[22] In October 2003, the European Commission adopted a communication in which it set out its views on the implementation of Article 7 of the EU Treaty.[23] Referring to the work of the EU Network of Independent Experts on fundamental rights, it took the view that the information collected by the network:

> should make it possible to detect fundamental rights anomalies or situations where there might be breaches or the risk of breaches of these rights falling within Article 7 of the Union Treaty. Through its analyses the network can also help in finding solutions to remedy confirmed anomalies or to prevent potential breaches. Monitoring also has an essential preventive role in that it can provide ideas for achieving the area of freedom, security and justice or alerting the institutions to divergent trends in standards of protection between member states which could imperil the mutual trust on which Union policies are founded.

This language was practically borrowed from the first report of the Network, published in March 2003, which presented the situation of fundamental rights in the EU and its member states in 2002. In the report, the Network had also proposed that it should act as a clearing house for the identification and dissemination of best practices identified in the field of fundamental rights, thus inaugurating what was then fashionable to refer to as an 'open method of coordination' in that area. The Commission considered that this required a more active contribution from the member states. It wrote in its 2003 communication 'It is important for the member states to be involved in the exercise of evaluating and interpreting the results of the work of the network of independent experts. With a view to

[21] Res of 5 July 2001 on the situation of fundamental rights in the European Union (2000), cited above, para 9.

[22] The EU Network of Independent Experts on Fundamental Rights is composed of 25 experts and monitors the situation of fundamental rights in the member states and in the Union, on the basis of the EU Charter of Fundamental Rights. See the website: <http://www.ec.europa.eu/justice_home/cfr_cdf/index_en.htm> See also: Ph Alston and O De Schutter (eds), *Monitoring Fundamental Rights in the EU—The Contribution of the Fundamental Rights Agency* (2005).

[23] Communication from the Commission to the Council and the European Parliament on Art 7 of the Treaty on European Union: Respect for and promotion of the values on which the Union is based, COM(2003)606 final of 15 October 2003.

exchanging information and sharing experience, the Commission could organise regular meetings on the information gathered with the national bodies dealing with human rights.'[24]

What the Commission was in fact suggesting was that a permanent form of monitoring of compliance with fundamental rights by the EU member states should be established, both in order to contribute to the mutual trust in the establishment of an area of freedom, security, and justice, and in order, where necessary, to provide the institutions of the Union with the information they require in order to fulfil the tasks entrusted to them by Article 7 EU. It saw the EU Network of Independent Experts on fundamental rights as the laboratory of such a mechanism; the communication stated that this network might be established on a permanent basis in the future in order to perform these functions. In its response to the European Commission, the Parliament disagreed. While deploring, in other respects, the timidity of the reading proposed by the European Commission of Article 7 EU, it insisted that the use of Article 7 should be based on four principles, including the principle of confidence, which it explained thus:

> The Union looks to its Member States to take active steps to safeguard the Union's shared values and states, on this basis, that as a matter of principle it has confidence in:
> - the democratic and constitutional order of all Member States and in the ability and determination of their institutions to avert risks to fundamental freedoms and common principles,
> - the authority of the European Court of Justice and of the European Court of Human Rights.
>
> Union intervention pursuant to Article 7 of the EU Treaty must therefore be confined to instances of clear risks and persistent breaches and may not be invoked in support of any right to, or policy of, permanent monitoring of the Member States by the Union. Nevertheless, the Member States, accession countries and candidate countries must continue to develop democracy, the rule of law and respect for fundamental rights further and, where necessary, implement or continue to implement corresponding reforms.[25]

Thus, little by little, a 'fundamental rights culture' was being established within the EU institutions in the early 2000s. However, a number of different directions were being explored at the same time. First, the idea had taken root that neither the EU institutions, nor the EU member states when they implemented EU law, could afford to ignore the requirements of fundamental rights in the course of their activities. The adoption of the Charter of Fundamental Rights, by the large visibility it soon gained, essentially served that purpose: it provided guidance and legal certainty, thus facilitating self-monitoring by the institutions. Secondly, the role performed on the basis of Article 7 EU by the European Parliament and the Network of Independent Experts on fundamental rights, although the two

[24] At para 2.2. of the communication, 9–10.

[25] European Parliament legislative resolution on the Commission communication on Art 7 of the Treaty on European Union: Respect for and promotion of the values on which the Union is based (COM(2003)606—C5-0594/2003—2003/2249(INI)), adopted on 20 April 2004, para 12.

acted as a relatively inharmonious tandem,[26] gave birth to the idea that the EU might progressively develop a monitoring role, in order to identify at an early stage whether certain member states might be adopting a conduct which would threaten the mutual trust on which the area of freedom, security, and justice, was to be built. Thirdly, finally, was the idea that such a systematic comparison could constitute a condition for the development of an active 'fundamental rights policy' of the EU. This was linked to the idea that a systematic comparison of the development of fundamental rights in the member states might lead to identifying the situations where an initiative from the EU is required, or the emerging good practices which could be diffused; it was expressed most explicitly in the 'open method of coordination' proposed by the EU Network of Independent Experts on fundamental rights.

After the European Council of December 2003 had decided that the EU should establish a 'Human Rights Agency' in Vienna, and despite two particularly active presidencies of the Council of the EU on this subject,[27] three more years of discussions were necessary in order to arrive at an agreement on the tasks, structure, and relationships with other bodies or organizations of the Fundamental Rights Agency for the European Union. In large part, this is to be explained by the co-existence in the discussions of these three distinct rationales, which correspond to different tools, different degrees of independence, and different institutional balances.

3. The Birth of the Agency and the Initial Debate (2003–5)

The relatively long period of time required to find an agreement on the final Regulation may also be explained, in part, by the circumstances in which the initial decision was made to create the Agency. When the Heads of State and Government of the member states announced at the Brussels European Council

[26] During two years following the establishment of the EU Network of Independent Experts on fundamental rights in September 2002, there was relatively close cooperation between the network's activities and the LIBE Committee of the European Parliament. However, when in July 2004, the resolution proposed on the basis of the Report on the situation as regards fundamental rights in the European Union (2003) prepared by MEP A Boumediene-Thiery failed to be adopted, the LIBE Committee apparently drew the conclusion that it should not continue replicating the work of the network, whose reports in any event, thanks to the structure of the network (with one expert covering each EU member state, allowing for a detailed examination of that state and systematic comparisons of the 15, and then the 25 states), it would hardly be able to improve upon. The network pursued its activities for two further years, with the LIBE Committee using the information collected in the reports, or the opinions prepared by the network, in a more selective mode.

[27] The Austrian presidency of the first semester 2006, for obvious reasons, was particularly eager to achieve an agreement, and mostly effective in moving towards finding a consensus. Germany was due to succeed Austria in 2006 but stepped aside in favour of Finland, the next in line, as general elections were scheduled in Germany for that period. Agreement on the Fundamental Rights Agency was thus reached under the Finnish presidency of the second semester 2006, again, thanks to an effective presidency.

of 13 December 2003 their intention to extend the mandate of the EU Monitoring Centre on Racism and Xenophobia (EUMC) in order to create a 'Human Rights Agency'[28] entrusted with the mission to collect and analyse data in order to define the policy of the Union in this field, most observers were taken by surprise. The announcement was made without any feasibility study being prepared, and essentially, it would seem, to reinforce the presence of the Union in Vienna and to find a dignified solution to the need to reform the EUMC. Indeed, understandably in retrospect, the very choice of the European Council to create the Human Rights Agency by enlarging the competences of the EUMC[29] was not necessarily obvious when that option was proposed. At the time when the European Council announced its decision, the European Commission had already concluded, on the basis of an external evaluation of the activities of the EUMC between its creation in 1998 and end 2001, that 'the Centre should continue to concentrate on racism and that an extension to other fields would be an unwelcome distraction within the limits of the resources likely to be available to the Centre and that it would lead to a weakening of the emphasis on racism'.[30] The choice to broaden the mandate of the EUMC by transforming it into a Human Rights Agency seemed to go in the exact opposite direction, although that expansion was to be accompanied, obviously, by a significant increase in resources.

Thus, when the European Council requested that the European Commission make a proposal on the establishment of a 'Human Rights Agency' for the EU, the Commission had no preconceived opinion about the structure such an Agency should be given, nor about its precise mandate. Understandably, the Commission chose, prior to making a formal proposal, to organize a wide-ranging consultation in order to identify more precisely where the added value of a Fundamental Rights Agency for the European Union might reside, how it should be structured, and how its tasks should be defined. The Commission presented a public consultation document on 25 October 2004.[31] In reply to this consultation document, the Commission received contributions from a wide range of actors and, in order to discuss the modalities of the proposed institution, a public

[28] The expression 'Human Rights Agency' was also used in the Hague Programme on the strengthening of Freedom, Security and Justice in the Union appended to the conclusions of the European Council of 4–5 November 2004.

[29] This Monitoring Centre, sometimes referred to as the Vienna Observatory, was created by the Council Reg (EC) 1035/97 of 2 June 1997 establishing a European Monitoring Centre on Racism and Xenophobia, OJ L151 of 10 June 1997, 1. According to Article 2(1) of its instituting Regulation, the EUMC must 'provide the Community and its Member states (...) with objective, reliable and comparable data at European level on the phenomena of racism, xenophobia and anti-Semitism in order to help them when they take measures or formulate courses of action within their respective spheres of competence'.

[30] Communication from the Commission to the Council, the European Parliament, the European Economic and Social Committee and the Committee of the Regions on the Activities of the European Monitoring Centre on Racism and Xenophobia, together with proposals to recast Council Regulation (EC) 1035/97, COM(2003)483 final of 5 August2003.

[31] COM(2004)693 final.

hearing was held on 25 January 2005.[32] The proposals made by the Commission on 30 June 2005[33] thus reflected the result of more than a full year of debate, which involved a remarkably large number of stakeholders. As illustrated by the different positions expressed in the course of these consultations, the expectations were varied. Three basic models were proposed. The first two models were inspired by the idea of independent national human rights institutions. A third model was more in line with the classical mode of organization of EU agencies. They will be examined in turn.

A. The Relevance of the Paris Principles on National Institutions for the Promotion and Protection of Human Rights

National human rights institutions have been on the increase since the mid-1990s, following the adoption in 1991 of the so-called 'Paris Principles' defining the characteristics they should present[34] and the call made by the World Conference on Human Rights held in Vienna in June 1993, in the Declaration and Programme of Action, for the establishment of such institutions. The World Conference on Human Rights reaffirmed 'the important and constructive role played by national institutions for the promotion and protection of human rights, in particular in their advisory capacity to the competent authorities, their role in remedying human rights violations, in the dissemination of human rights information, and education in human rights'. It also encouraged 'the establishment and strengthening of national institutions, having regard to the 'Principles relating to the status of national institutions' and recognizing that it is the right of each state to choose the framework which is best suited to its particular needs

[32] The response from the academic world and from civil society organizations was remarkably high. See, for a collection of contributions submitted in the course of the consultation, <http://www.ec.europa.eu/justice_home/news/consulting_public/fundamental_rights_agency/news_contributions_fund_rights_agency_en.htm> (last consulted on 8 September 8 2008). In addition, see P Alston and O De Schutter (eds), *Monitoring Fundamental Rights in the EU. The Contribution of the Fundamental Rights Agency* (2005).

[33] Proposal for a Council Regulation establishing a European Agency for Fundamental Rights and Proposal for a Council Decision empowering the European Union Agency for Fundamental Rights to pursue its activities in areas referred to in Title VI of the Treaty on European Union, COM(2005)280, 30 June 2005.

[34] The Paris Principles on national institutions for the promotion and protection of human rights were approved by the United Nations General Assembly in 1993 in Res 48/134 of 20 December 1993 (A/RES/48/134, adopted by the 85th plenary meeting of the UN General Assembly, 'National institutions for the promotion and protection of human rights'). After having been initially adopted in 1991, at a conference convened by the French Commission nationale consultative des droits de l'homme—the earliest of such institutions to be established, in 1947—and the Office of the High Commissioner for Human Rights, these principles were approved by the Commission on Human Rights in Res 1992/54 of 3 March 1992 before being submitted to the UN General Assembly. They are further explained in *National Human Rights Institutions: a Handbook on the Establishment and Strengthening of National Institutions for the Promotion and Protection of Human Rights* (1995), see <http://www.ohchr.org/Documents/Publications/training12en.pdf>.

at the national level'.[35] The Committee of Ministers of the Council of Europe followed suit, adopting in 1997 a recommendation addressed to the Council of Europe member states requesting that they set up such institutions.[36] The same recommendation was made by a number of UN human rights treaty bodies.[37] These recommendations have been complemented by compendiums of best practices for the establishment of such institutions.[38] It was quite natural therefore for the European Commission, in the public consultation document it presented on 25 October 2004, to refer to the Paris Principles as a potential 'source of inspiration' for the establishment of the EU Fundamental Rights Agency.[39] This model was also seen as attractive because, according to its proponents, it would allow the Agency to be part of a network of existing NHRIs in the member states, and thus to rely on those NHRIs in order to prepare its reports and recommendations, following the model of 'regulation by information' which had characterized the development of EU agencies in recent years.[40]

There were two ways in which the Paris Principles could have inspired the establishment of the EU Fundamental Rights Agency, corresponding to the first two models which were explored.[41] One model was that of a Fundamental Rights Agency conceived as a 'national human rights institution' for the EU. A related yet distinct model would see the Agency as not necessarily established itself, in the definition of its mandate and in its organizational structure, on the Paris Principles, but as based on the existing network of European NHRIs, and as a forum in which the existing NHRIs (or the equivalent institutions in the member states which have no NHRI in the sense of the Paris Principles) could exchange their experiences and work together in order to contribute, through

[35] Vienna Declaration and Programme of Action of 25 June 1993, UN Doc A/CONF157/23 at para 36.

[36] Rec R(97)14 of the Committee of Ministers of the Council of Europe on the establishment of independent national institutions for the promotion and protection of human rights, adopted on 30 September 1997.

[37] See particularly General Comment No 10 of the Committee on Economic, Social and Cultural Rights of 14 December 1998: *The role of national human rights institutions in the protection of economic, social and cultural rights* (UN Doc E/C12/1998/25); General Comment No 2 of the Committee on the Rights of the Child (2002): *The role of independent national human rights institutions in the protection and promotion of the rights of the child*, HRI/GEN/1/Rev 6, 295; and General Comment No. 5 of the Committee on the Rights of the Child, of 27 November 2003: *General measures of implementation of the Convention on the Rights of the Child (arts 4, 42 and 44, para 6)*, para 65.

[38] See, apart from the United Nations *Handbook* referred to above: Council of Europe, *Non-judicial means for the protection of human rights at the national level* (1998); Commonwealth Secretariat, *National Human Rights Institutions—Best Practice* (2001).

[39] COM(2004)693 final, 25 October 2004 at p 4.

[40] See, in particular, for an excellent discussion of this form of regulation by networking, Giandomenico Majone, 'The new European agencies: regulation by information', *Journal of European Public Policy*, vol 4, no 2 (1997), 262–75.

[41] On the distinction between these two ways the Paris Principles could influence the establishment of the Fundamental Rights Agency, see Manfred Nowak, 'The Agency and National Institutions for the Promotion and Protection of Human Rights', in P Alston and O De Schutter (eds), *Monitoring Fundamental Rights in the EU*, n 32 above, ch 4.

reports, recommendations, and opinions, towards improving the protection of fundamental rights in the Union.

While analytically distinct, these two approaches could be combined to take into account the specificities of an independent human rights institution at EU level, which could also be expected to cooperate closely with actors at the member state level in monitoring the compliance with fundamental rights of the implementation of EU law by the member states. Indeed, this was the approach of the European Group of national human rights institutions.[42] Referring to the Paris Principles, which identify pluralism alongside independence as critical to the establishment of national human rights institutions, they argued that such pluralism required from the Agency that it closely cooperate 'with the already existing institutions, particularly NHRIs and other national independent bodies. The EU's subsidiarity requirement and the need for local input should guarantee the Agency's legitimacy and efficiency.'[43] They proposed, then, that the Agency's management board be composed of the representatives of the different existing NHRIs or other independent institutions of the EU member states, and that there be a formal link between the Agency and the European Group of NHRIs as a whole: 'Through the European network of NHRIs, the Agency will benefit from a solid human rights base within the member states as well as strong links with local communities.' One precedent which the European Group of National Human Rights Institutions could refer to was the 'Working Party Article 29' established under Article 29 of the 1995 Data Protection Directive.[44] This Working Party, which has an advisory role and is to act independently, is composed of a representative of the supervisory authority or authorities designated by each member state, as well as a representative of the authority or authorities established for the Community institutions and bodies, and a representative of the Commission. Essentially, the European NHRIs were proposing that such a model be replicated in the structure of the Fundamental Rights Agency, with formal representation within the Agency of each NHRI.

There is no doubt that the Paris Principles on national institutions for the promotion and protection of human rights strongly influenced the proposals made by the European Commission on 30 June 2005, when it presented to the Council draft texts for a Council Regulation establishing a European Agency for Fundamental Rights and for a Council Decision empowering the European Union Agency for Fundamental Rights to pursue its activities in areas referred to

[42] For a description of the activities of the European Coordinating Group of national institutions for the promotion and protection of human rights, see the communication submitted to the United Nations Commission on Human Rights, UN Doc E/CN4/2005/NI/2 (30 March 2005).

[43] See European Group of National Human Rights Institutions, *Common position regarding the European Commission's proposals for a Council regulation establishing a Fundamental Rights Agency for the European Union*, 17 January 2006.

[44] Dir 95/46/EC of the European Parliament and of the Council of 24 October 1995 on the protection of individuals with regard to the processing of personal data and on the free movement of such data, OJ L281, 23 November 1995, 31.

in Title VI of the Treaty on European Union.[45] Certain elements in the proposal of the Commission appeared to be influenced by the first of the two models distinguished here: for instance, the establishment of a fundamental rights forum was envisaged, the forum having to be composed in a way roughly similar to an NHRI constituted at the level of the Union;[46] it was emphasized that the Agency should be 'independent';[47] apart from the two representatives of the Commission, the other members of the management board were to be 'independent persons' appointed by each member state (27 members thus, or more if third countries participate), by the European Parliament (1), by the Council of Europe (1); and the Agency was encouraged to undertake a close cooperation with civil society, non-governmental organizations, and social partners.[48]

Other elements however may be related to the second model: in particular, the 'independent persons' the member states should appoint to the management board of the Agency were to be persons 'with high level responsibilities in the management of an independent national human rights institution or with thorough expertise in the field of fundamental rights gathered in the context of other independent institutions or bodies',[49] which suggested a vision of the management board as a network of NHRIs and equivalent institutions which may exist in the member states; the two representatives of the Commission on the management board were to have a right to vote on the decisions adopted by the board, which was not in conformity with the requirement under the Paris Principles that if the government is represented, its representatives should have only a consultative voice; furthermore, the executive board was to comprise not only the chairperson and the vice-chairperson of the management board, but also the two representatives of the Commission, which again would not be compatible with an understanding of the EU Fundamental Rights Agency conceived as a national institution for the promotion and protection of human rights for the legal order of the Union.

Thus, while there were many nods to the Paris Principles in the proposals of the Commission, and while the composition of the management board seemed to reflect the idea of an Agency built as a network of the representatives of the NHRIs or equivalent bodies established within the member states, the proposals did not espouse any of the two models distinguished above in their pure form; nor did they entirely follow the lines suggested by the European Group of NHRIs, which were a combination of both. Indeed, the discussions revealed a number of objections made to each of these two models or to any compromise between them which would adhere firmly to the Paris Principles. Some considered that the Paris

[45] COM(2005)280, 30 June 2005.

[46] Art 14 of the proposal for a Reg.

[47] Art 15(1) of the proposal for a Reg: 'The Agency shall fulfil its tasks in complete independence'.

[48] Art 4(1)(i) of the proposal for a Reg.

[49] Art 11(1), al. 2, of the proposal for a Reg.

Principles could not be reconciled with the specificities of EU law and the role of agencies in the EU institutional construction. It was said, in particular, that the fact that the EU has limited competences—it may only exercise the competences which it has been attributed by the member states—would not be reconcilable with the tasks normally entrusted to an NHRI. Secondly, it was added, the institutions of the Union should preserve their entire freedom of appreciation concerning what initiatives to take in the exercise of their competences to develop fundamental rights, and such appreciation—especially where it might involve the very delicate appreciation of the situation of fundamental rights in the member states—could not be left to an Agency. Thirdly, the agencies as they exist under the framework of European Community law[50] would not be reconcilable with the kind of organization required from an independent institution for the promotion and protection of human rights.

None of those arguments were really conclusive, of course. In particular, even if organized as an NHRI in conformity with the Paris Principles, it was clear that the Agency would have had to take into account the principle of conferral, and that its conclusions and opinions should not contain recommendations to the Union institutions that they exercise powers beyond those attributed to them. It was equally clear, and quite compatible with the Paris Principles themselves, that any conclusions or opinions adopted by the Agency would not be binding upon the institutions, who were to be left entirely free either to take them into account or to disregard them, in the exercise of their powers: indeed, NHRIs are normally conceived as acting on an advisory basis, ie as bodies with purely consultative powers. Finally, despite the apparent novelty of introducing the Paris Principles into the legal order of the EU, there were many similarities between a Fundamental Rights Agency and other agencies set up in order to provide the necessary expertise collected through independent means to the institutions in order to facilitate their work, many of which have a decentralized and 'networked' structure linking them to national bodies, so that the classical model of Community agencies was in fact transposable to the setting up of an EU Fundamental Rights Agency conceived along the lines of an NHRI for the Union.

The conception of the EU Fundamental Rights Agency as a network of NHRIs or equivalent institutions existing in the EU member states faced an important obstacle, however, which is the lack of uniformity among the member states. At the time when the debate was held about the future structure of the Agency, only 13 out of 25 member states had NHRIs deemed in compliance with the Paris Principles, and even among those states, strikingly different types of institutions could be identified; while in a few of the other member states institutions performing functions relatively similar to those of NHRIs do exist, seven member states still had no institution even vaguely similar to an NHRI, and in certain

[50] See, in particular, European Commission, *Meta-Evaluation on the Community Agency System*, Final Report of the Budget DG—Evaluation Unit, 15 September 2003.

cases, for example in the Netherlands, the government had explicitly rejected the idea of creating such an institution.[51] In addition, establishing the EU Fundamental Rights Agency as a network of existing NHRIs, with each NHRI (or equivalent institution) being represented as such within the structure of the Agency, would have left open one important matter: whereas each NHRI deals with national questions (ie with the promotion and protection of human rights at national level), the Agency would require expertise on specifically European questions (ie which concern the development of Union legislation and policies), which are potentially very different and have their own specificities. Finally, this model could have led to some confusion as to the actual role of the EU Fundamental Rights Agency: while the Agency would in principle be entrusted with contributing to the promotion and protection of human rights within the legal order of the EU, it might be perceived, with such a structure, as a forum where the member states' performances in the field of human rights are compared with one another, and where national institutions meet in order to share concerns they have about human rights developments at the national level.

On these various issues, the differences should not be underestimated with the Working Party created under Article 29 of the Data Protection Directive, which the European Group of NHRIs had referred to in its contributions to the consultation on the future shape of the Fundamental Rights Agency for the EU.[52] This Working Party, which has an advisory role and is to act independently, is composed of a representative of the supervisory authority or authorities designated by each member state, as well as a representative of the authority or authorities established for the Community institutions and bodies, and a representative of the Commission. However, under this Directive, each member state has to set up an independent supervisory authority responsible for monitoring the application within its territory of the provisions adopted pursuant to the Directive.[53] It would probably have been unrealistic for the Commission to suggest, as part of its proposals for the establishment of the EU Fundamental Rights Agency, that all the member states be obliged to create an independent institution for the promotion and protection of human rights, thus ensuring an equivalent uniformity. Even apart from questions of subsidiarity and proportionality, this would have entailed budgetary consequences and raised political issues, which almost certainly would have led the states to reject any such suggestion. Moreover, while the rules on which both the national supervisory authorities and the Working Party created under Article 29 of the Data Protection Directive have been harmonized throughout the member states (so that the Working Party may ensure that the

[51] The EU Network of Independent Experts on Fundamental Rights prepared a comparative table of NHRIs within the EU member states in March 2004. Opinion No 1-2004. The documents of the Network may be consulted on: <http://www.europa.eu.int/comm/justice_home/cfr_cdf/index_en.htm>

[52] n 43 above.

[53] See ch VI of the Data Protection Directive, n 44 above.

interpretations converge and that problems of interpretation are clarified in its opinions) certainly no such harmonization can be said to have taken place in the vast fields related to the protection of fundamental rights. Indeed, fundamental rights are not as such a 'field': they are a set of requirements that have to be complied with in all the fields in which the public authorities act, and they cannot be circumscribed to any particular domain of activity.

B. The Relevance of the Community Framework for the Establishment of Agencies

The decision to establish a Fundamental Rights Agency happened at a time when such agencies had been growing significantly in the EU.[54] There were four such agencies in 1993; in 2003, their number had grown to 15, and three further agencies were proposed in that year alone.[55] Since the early days of European integration, the European Court of Justice has imposed strict limitations on the delegation of powers to agencies. Whether for reasons of 'institutional balance' or because of the limited enumeration of powers of the Commission in Article 211 of the EC Treaty,[56] the Court considered that such delegation could only concern 'clearly defined executive powers the exercise of which can, therefore, be subject to strict review in the light of criteria determined by the delegating authority'.[57] Indeed, the Commission itself has traditionally adopted quite a strict reading of this case law,[58] notwithstanding the critiques addressed in scientific literature to the approach followed by the Court.[59] Both in its 2002 contribution to the

[54] This sparked a growth of the literature on the subject. See Renaud Dehousse, 'Regulation by networks in the European Community: the role of European agencies', Journal of European Public Policy, vol 4, No 2 (1997), 246–61; Michelle Everson, 'Independent Agencies : Hierarchy Beaters?' European Law Journal, vol 1 (1995), 180–204; A Kreher, 'Agencies in the European Community—a step towards administrative integration in Europe', Journal of European Public Policy, vol 4, no 2 (1997), 93–118; Giandomenico Majone and Michelle Everson, 'Institutional Reform: Independent Agencies, Oversight, Coordination, and Procedural Control', in O De Schutter, Notis Lebessis and John Paterson (eds), *Governance in the European Union*, OOPEC (2001); Mark Thatcher, 'Regulation after delegation : independent regulatory agencies in Europe', *Journal of European Public Policy*, vol 9, no 6 (2002), 954–72; Ellen Vos, 'Reforming the European Commission: What Role to Play for EU Agencies ?', Common Market Law Review vol 37 (2000), 1113–34; Ellen Vos, 'Agencies and the European Union', in L Verhey and T Zwart (eds), *Agencies in European and Comparative Law* (2003).

[55] D Geradin and N Petit, 'The Development of Agencies at EU and National Levels: Conceptual Analysis and Proposals for Reform', *Yearbook of European Law*, 137–97 at 137.

[56] Case 98/80, *Giuseppe Romano v Institut national d'assurance maladie-invalidité* [1981] ECR 1241.

[57] Case 9/56, *Meroni v High Authority* [1957–8] ECR 133.

[58] See Commission of the European Communities, *European Governance. A White Paper*, COM(2001)428 final, 25 July 2001 at 24 (defining the conditions for the creation of regulatory agencies at EU level).

[59] See, in particular, Ellen Vos, 'Reforming the European Commission: What Role to Play for EU Agencies ?'(n 54 above), who considers that under the current Treaty provisions, 'agencies could be delegated discretionary powers provided that this is accompanied by a reinforcement of re-balancing of the existing institutions' (at 1124); or D Geradin and N Petit, 'The Development of

Convention on the Future of Europe and in the so-called 'Penelope' project prepared as a contribution to the debate on the Constitutional Treaty, the European Commission advocated inserting into the Treaty establishing a Constitution for Europe a provision allowing for the establishment of regulatory agencies, but along the lines suggested by the 'Meroni' doctrine of the Court.[60] Despite this, the model was considered attractive to the Commission for a number of reasons.[61] First, the delegation to agencies of certain well-defined tasks allows the Commission to focus on its core missions, and to face the increasingly important workload the expansion of EU policies entails. Secondly, such delegation ensures a relative insulation of the applicable policy fields from political pressure, including pressure from the member states in favour of their national interests, thus also improving policy consistency across time. Thirdly, since the agencies are to develop a highly specialized technical expertise, their creation contributes to 'reducing asymmetries of information between the operators and the administration'.[62] The risk is, of course, that the specialized nature of the agencies' functions will facilitate regulatory capture by the sectors concerned.

Although few would contest the reality of these advantages, it is probably no exaggeration to say that the attempts of the Commission to provide a coherent framework for the development of agencies within the EU, each of which has been set up to respond to needs identified, at a particular moment, in a specific sector, were a complete failure. In December 2002, the Commission adopted a Communication on the Operating Framework for the European Regulatory Agencies.[63] This document aimed to offer a typology of the different agencies operating at EU level. It resulted, however, in a bizarre distinction between two categories of agencies: 'executive' agencies on the one hand, which were delegated purely managerial tasks and which were to assist the Commission in the implementation of certain programmes; and 'regulatory' agencies on the other hand, who were 'required to be actively involved in exercising the executive function by enacting instruments which contribute to regulating a specific sector'.[64] But this second category itself was sub-divided into 'decision-making' agencies and 'executive' agencies, with only the former being given the power to adopt legal acts binding upon third parties. The reintroduction of the sub-category of

Agencies at EU and National Levels: Conceptual Analysis and Proposals for Reform' (n 55 above at 148–9).

[60] See Communication from the Commission to the European Convention on the Institutional Architecture, 'For the European Union, Peace, Freedom, Solidarity', COM(2002)728 final of 11 December 2002 (proposing a clause to the effect that 'agencies cannot be given either the responsibilities which the Treaty assigns directly to the Commission, nor decision-making powers in areas in which they would be required to arbitrate in conflicts between public interests, nor can they exercise political appraisal powers or make complex economic assessments').

[61] On these arguments, see in particular the report commissioned by the European Commission, M Everson, G Majone, L Metcalfe, and A Schout, *The Role of Specialised Agencies in Decentralising Governance*, (1999).

[62] D Geradin and N Petit, n 55 above, 170.

[63] COM(2002)718 final, of 11 December 2002.

[64] Ibid at 4.

'executive' agencies within the category of 'regulatory' (ie 'non-executive') agencies (a choice deemed 'simply absurd' by Geradin and Petit[65]) created, in the end, even more confusion than existed beforehand.

The absence of a coherent framework or typology for the establishment of agencies at EU level did not constitute a serious handicap in the discussions on the Fundamental Rights Agency, however. It was indeed clear from the outset that, since the new agency was to be built on the existing EUMC, it would constitute an agency entrusted mainly with information-gathering tasks, like the European Environment Agency or the European Monitoring Centre for Drugs and Drug Addiction. As already noted, the main task of the EUMC was to provide the Community and its member states with 'objective, reliable and comparable data at European level on the phenomena of racism, xenophobia and anti-Semitism in order to help them when they take measures or formulate courses of action within their respective spheres of competence'.[66] At the same time, this was not necessarily incompatible with an understanding of the Fundamental Rights Agency inspired by the Paris Principles on national institutions for the promotion and protection of human rights, since the EUMC was already authorized in its founding regulation to 'formulate conclusions and opinions for the Community and its member states'[67]—a power it had used only sparingly and with great caution, but which a Fundamental Rights Agency, conceivably, could have developed to a much greater extent.

In the end, continuity prevailed. Most of the structural features of the Fundamental Rights Agency, both in the proposals put forward by the Commission in June 2005 and in the final Regulation adopted in February 2007, closely link it to the EUMC. Although some form of monitoring the situation of fundamental rights in the EU member states had developed in the period 2000–6, through the combined and partly overlapping practices of the European Parliament's LIBE Committee and the EU Network of Independent Experts on Fundamental Rights,[68] this task clearly was not entrusted to the Agency. The founding Regulation does not confer upon the Agency the mandate to supervise compliance with fundamental rights in the Union, even as regards the activities of the institutions or bodies of the Union or of the member states when they implement Union law. Rather, the Agency is to be seen as a pillar of expertise in human rights, which will provide advice to the institutions and the member states, in order to improve their understanding of the requirements of fundamental rights and to better inform any initiatives they adopt in this field.[69]

[65] n 55 at 181.

[66] Art 2(1) of the Council Reg (EC) No 1035/97 of 2 June 1997 establishing a European Monitoring Centre on Racism and Xenophobia, OJ L151, 10 June 1997.

[67] Art 2(2)(e), of the Council Regulation (EC) No 1035/97 of 2 June 1997 establishing a European Monitoring Centre on Racism and Xenophobia, cited above.

[68] n 22 above.

[69] See Art 2 of Reg 168/2007: 'The objective of the Agency shall be to provide the relevant institutions, bodies, offices and agencies of the Community and its member states when implementing

The Paris Principles on national institutions for the promotion and protection of human rights recommend that such institutions choose freely which issues to take up, provided they relate to their role in the promotion and protection of human rights. However the Paris Principles failed to influence the proposals of the European Commission on this point. Neither the initial proposals of the Commission, nor the final Regulation, authorized the Agency to decide for itself what issues it should focus on, and whether it should address recommendations to the institutions on pending legislative discussions. Instead, it was agreed that the annual work programme of the Agency would be based on a Multi-Annual Framework adopted by the Council on a proposal of the Commission.[70] And the possibility for the Agency to intervene in the legislative process was severely constrained by Article 4(2) of the founding Regulation, which stated that the conclusions, opinion, and reports the Agency could adopt:

> may concern proposals from the Commission (...) or positions taken by the institutions in the course of legislative procedures *only where a request by the respective institution has been made* (...). They shall not deal with the legality of acts within the meaning of Article 230 of the Treaty [concerning actions for annulment of Community acts] or with the question of whether a Member State has failed to fulfil an obligation under the Treaty within the meaning of Article 226 of the Treaty [concerning infringement proceedings against member States for failure to comply with their obligations under EC law].

The latter restrictions imposed on the Agency were the combined result of a faithful replication and consolidation of what had been the practice of the EUMC during its nine years of operation, and of a desire of the institutions not to see their legislative work disrupted by interferences by the Agency. However it is clear that the European Parliament will be tempted to rely on the Agency in all cases where serious doubts are expressed about the compatibility of a legislative proposal with the requirements of fundamental rights. As to the exclusion of any role of the Agency in the monitoring of the member states, it may be explained by two other factors. One was the desire to preserve the purely political character of the sanctions' mechanism of Article 7 of the EU Treaty. Another was the very active role of the Council of Europe in the debate on the establishment of the Fundamental Rights Agency. These two factors combined with one another. Through various channels, the Council of Europe expressed the fear that it would risk being marginalized if the EU Fundamental Rights Agency were to duplicate the monitoring performed by the Council of Europe bodies. Those concerns were well received by the EU member states within the Council of the EU, since it provided the Council with a welcome pretext for narrowing down the competences

Community law with assistance and expertise relating to fundamental rights in order to support them when they take measures or formulate courses of action within their respective spheres of competence to fully respect fundamental rights.'

[70] See Art 5 of the founding Reg, n 2 above.

of the Agency, and severely restricting, in particular, its ability to examine the situation of fundamental rights in individual countries.

4. The Role of the Council of Europe in the Debate on the Fundamental Rights Agency (2003–6)

A. The Reactions of the Council of Europe to the Proposal to Establish an EU Fundamental Rights Agency

The initial reaction of the Council of Europe to the decision by the European Council to create a 'Human Rights Agency' for the European Union was not openly hostile; but it was clearly defensive. In her intervention at the public hearing organized by the European Commission on 25 January 2005 the Deputy Secretary General of the Council of Europe Ms de Boer-Buquicchio sought to distinguish the function the EU Fundamental Rights Agency could fulfil—crafted along the lines of a national institution for the promotion and protection of human rights for the Union—from the tasks entrusted to the Council of Europe monitoring bodies, by emphasizing the difference between monitoring as *collection and analysis of data* on the one hand (what might be called 'advisory monitoring'), and monitoring as *evaluation of compliance* with certain standards on the other (or 'normative monitoring').[71] Although to deny the EU Fundamental Rights Agency any role in 'normative monitoring' thus understood might seem contradictory with the idea that it should be an independent institution for the promotion and protection of human rights for the EU—indeed, under the Paris Principles, NHRIs should, amongst other matters, adopt opinions on 'situation of violation of human rights which it decides to take up'.[72] The preoccupation behind this distinction was clear enough: the Agency should not duplicate the work of the monitoring bodies of the Council of Europe, since this might undermine their efforts and diminish their authority. It was suggested, since this might undermine their efforts and diminish their authority; it should constitute a think tank, a pole of expertise on human rights issues for the EU institutions, but not some appeals tribunal for the evaluation performed by the Council of Europe.

[71] Monitoring 'can also be understood as comprising the verification of actual compliance, identifying violations, shortcomings and best practices as well as addressing recommendations to individual states. It is in this latter sense that monitoring is understood and carried out within the Council of Europe' (Public Hearing on the Agency on Fundamental Rights of 25 January 2005, statement by Ms de Boer-Buquicchio, Deputy Secretary General of the Council of Europe, available on <http://www.ec.europa.eu/justice_home/fsj/rights/fsj_rights_agency_en.htm>.

[72] See para 3(a)(ii), of the Paris Principles (Principles Relating to the Status of National Institutions, annexed to UNGA Res 48/134, 'National institutions for the promotion and protection of human rights', 20 December 1993).

This roughly corresponded to the views adopted simultaneously by the Parliamentary Assembly of the Council of Europe (PACE).[73] Acting on the basis of the McNamara report prepared within the Committee on Legal Affairs and Human Rights,[74] the Parliamentary Assembly adopted on 18 March 2005 a resolution in which it recalled the human rights acquis developed by the Council of Europe through intergovernmental cooperation, the monitoring by the Council of Europe of compliance with these standards by its member states,[75] and the practical assistance work by the Council of Europe designed to facilitate attainment of the requisite standards, as well as its activities in the field of human rights education and awareness-raising. While welcoming the establishment of a Fundamental Rights Agency of the EU, the PACE insisted that 'there is no point in reinventing the wheel by giving the agency a role which is already performed by existing human rights institutions and mechanisms in Europe. That would simply be a waste of taxpayers' money.'[76] Similar to the Council of Europe Deputy Secretary-General, the PACE concluded that the role of the agency should be limited to 'collect[ing] and provid[ing] to the EU institutions information about fundamental rights that is relevant to their activities, and thus contribut[ing] to mainstreaming human rights standards in the EU decision-making processes'.[77]

In the view of the Parliamentary Assembly, this understanding of the role of the EU Fundamental Rights Agency had three implications. First, it should have a mandate limited to the scope of application of Union law, including the implementation by EU member states of Union law, but should not intervene

[73] It should be noted however that the president of the Parliamentary Assembly, the Dutch René Van der Linden, seemed to adopt a rather more radical attitude of opposition towards the very establishment of a Fundamental Rights Agency of the EU. As a result of his opposition, which he saw as a means of defending the monitoring bodies of the Council of Europe against the risk of marginalization, the Dutch Senate (of which Mr Van der Linden is a member) adopted by unanimity a motion in March 2006 in which it took the view that, since an agreement could be concluded between the EU and the Council of Europe in order for the EU to benefit from the monitoring systems already established in the framework of the Council of Europe, the proposal to establish a Fundamental Rights Agency for the EU did not pass the test of subsidiarity. On 31 March 2006, the President of the Dutch Senate, Ms Yvonne Timmermann-Buck, wrote to the speakers of the national parliaments of the other EU member states as well as to the speaker of the European Parliament urging them to use the tools of 'parliamentary diplomacy' in order to oppose the establishment of the Fundamental Rights Agency.

[74] 'Plans to set up a Fundamental Rights Agency of the European Union', Doc 10241, Draft resolution and draft recommendation adopted unanimously by the Committee on Legal Affairs and Human Rights of the Parliamentary Assembly of the Council of Europe on 27 January 2005.

[75] Res 1427 (2005) notes in this regard: 'Such monitoring is carried out by several well-established independent human rights bodies with recognised expertise and professionalism, both on a country-by-country basis (including through country visits and on-the-spot investigations) and, increasingly, also thematically. Through these mechanisms, the Council of Europe monitors compliance with all the human rights obligations of its member states (including the twenty-five member states of the European Union), identifies issues of non-compliance, addresses recommendations to member states and, in the case of the European Court of Human Rights, issues judgments binding on states parties whenever these standards are not respected' (at para 4).

[76] At para 10. [77] At para 13.

in areas outside EC/EU competence, where member states act autonomously. In other terms, although the mutual trust on which mutual recognition mechanisms within the Union are built presupposes that the EU member states comply with fundamental rights in general, rather than only with the implementation of Union law,[78] the Agency should not monitor fundamental rights beyond the situations to which the fundamental rights recognized as general principles of Union law already apply under the supervision of the European Court of Justice, and which define the scope of application of the EU Charter of Fundamental Rights.[79] Secondly, the Agency should work on a thematic, not a country-by-country basis, focusing on certain specified themes with a special connection to EC/EU policies. While this restriction does not follow from the definition of the Fundamental Rights Agency as a 'national institution for the promotion and the protection of human rights' for the Union, it was put forward, presumably, to limit any risk of the Agency competing with the monitoring bodies of the Council of Europe, and in particular of the Agency arriving at different conclusions than those of these bodies as regards specific situations arising in the member states. Indeed, in a later recommendation, the PACE stated very clearly that 'the agency should be explicitly excluded, in its mandate, from engaging in activities that involve assessing the general human rights situation in specific countries, in particular those that are members of the Council of Europe'.[80] Thirdly, the PACE considered that the future Agency should include within its reference instruments not only the European Convention on Human Rights, but also the other human rights instruments of the Council of Europe.[81] The PACE also recommended that the Council of Europe be included in the management

[78] See below, pt V.

[79] On the precise delineation of the situations in which the member states are bound by fundamental rights as general principles of EC or EU law, see esp J H H Weiler, 'The European Court at a Crossroads: Community Human Rights and Member State Action', in: *Du droit international au droit de l'intégration. Liber amicorum Pierre Pescatore* (1987) 821; J. Temple Lang, 'The Sphere in Which Member States are Obliged to Comply with the General Principles of Law and Community Fundamental Rights Principles', Legal Issues of European Integration, 1991/2, 23; J H H Weiler, 'Fundamental Rights and Fundamental Boundaries: On Standards and Values in the Protection of Human Rights', in N Neuwahl and A Rosas, *The European Union and Human Rights* (1995) 56; and K Lenaerts, 'Le respect des droits fondamentaux en tant que principe constitutionnel de l'Union européenne', *Mélanges en hommage à Michel Waelbroeck* (1999) 423. The wording of the Charter of Fundamental Rights is more restrictive than what the caselaw of the European Court of Justice would suggest, since it refers not in general to the scope of application of Union law (which would include situations where the member states act under exceptions provided by EC/EU law (see eg Case C-368/95 *Familiapress* [1997] ECR I-3689 (para 24); Case C-112/00 *Schmidberger* [2003] ECR I-5659 (para 81))) but only to situations where the EU member states *implement* Union law (see Art 51 of the Charter).

[80] PACE Recommendation 1744 (2006), *Follow-up to the 3rd Summit: the Council of Europe and the proposed fundamental rights agency of the European Union*, adopted on 13 April 2006 on the basis of the report prepared within the Committee on Legal Affairs and Human Rights (Doc 10894, rapp Mr Jurgens) (see para 11.4 of the recommendation).

[81] PACE Res 1427 (2005) para 14(ii).

structures of the Agency, and that a cooperation agreement be concluded to that effect between the Council of Europe and the Union.[82]

There were two reactions by the governments of the member states of the Council of Europe to the position thus expressed by the Parliamentary Assembly. At their Third Summit held in Warsaw on 16–7 May 2005, the Heads of State or Government of the member states of the Council of Europe adopted a Declaration on the future relationship between the EU and the Council of Europe,[83] and they agreed on a set of guidelines on the relations between the two, which stated in particular that: 'The future Human Rights Agency of the European Union, once established, should constitute an opportunity to further increase cooperation with the Council of Europe, and contribute to greater coherence and enhanced complementarity.'[84] The Heads of State or Government also requested Prime Minister of Luxembourg, Jean-Claude Juncker, that he prepare, in his personal capacity, a report on the relationship between the Council of Europe and the European Union, on the basis of the decisions adopted at the Summit and taking into account the importance of the human dimension of European construction.[85]

Secondly, the Committee of Ministers of the Council of Europe replied on 13 October 2005 to Recommendation 1696 (2005) of the Parliamentary Assembly.[86] After recalling the results of the Warsaw Summit, the Committee of Ministers referred to the proposals made in the meantime by the European Commission on the establishment of a Fundamental Rights Agency,[87] which (it considered)

> take several of the recommendations made by the [Parliamentary Assembly of the Council of Europe] and the Secretary General into account. Many of the tasks foreseen for the agency would indeed be complementary to the activities carried out by the Council of Europe. As regards co-operation with the Council of Europe, the Committee of Ministers acknowledges that the draft regulation [establishing the EU Fundamental Rights Agency] provides for a close institutional relationship, including provisions that the agency shall co-ordinate its activities with those of the Council, that a bilateral co-operation agreement shall be concluded and that an independent person shall be appointed by the Council to the management board of the agency.

[82] Ibid, para 14(iii). These elements are summarized in Recommendation 1696 (2005) adopted by the Parliamentary Assembly on the same day.

[83] See the Declaration adopted at the Warsaw Summit (Third Summit of the Heads of State and Government of the Member States of the Council of Europe), <http://www.Assembly.coe.int/Sessions/2006/speeches/20060411_report_JCJuncker_EN.pdf>.

[84] Para 8 of the guidelines.

[85] 'Council of Europe—European Union; a sole ambition for the European continent', report by Jean-Claude Juncker to the Heads of State and government of the Member states of the Council of Europe, 11 April 2006, available at <http://www.Assembly.coe.int/Sessions/2006/speeches/20060411_report_JCJuncker_EN.pdf> (hereafter referred to as the 'Juncker report').

[86] CM/AS(2005)Rec1696 final, adopted at the 939th meeting of the Ministers' Deputies.

[87] n 33 above.

It also stated, in paragraph 4 of its reply, that it 'agrees with the Assembly that the agency's mandate should focus on human rights issues within the framework of the European Union, address its advice to the EU institutions and ensure that unnecessary duplication with the Council of Europe is avoided'; and it expressed its hope 'that these points will be fully reflected in the future Community regulation'.

It is doubtful that these statements have fully reassured the Secretariat and the Parliamentary Assembly of the Council of Europe. On the contrary, after his meeting in July 2005 with Vice-President F Frattini, in charge of the Commission of Justice, Freedom and Security, the Secretary General of the Council of Europe, Mr Terry Davis, agreed to provide the Commission with an analysis, by the Secretariat of the Council of Europe, of the proposals on the establishment of the EU Fundamental Rights Agency. This memorandum was finalized on 8 September 2005.[88] Many of the themes evoked above are reiterated, in particular the idea that, in order to avoid duplication with the missions of the Council of Europe, the Agency should not systematically monitor the human rights performance of non-EU member states who are member states of the Council of Europe. These concerns were again reiterated by the Parliamentary Assembly of the Council of Europe in April 2006.[89]

How justified were these concerns? The question of whether the establishment of the Fundamental Rights Agency risks undermining the efforts of the Council of Europe monitoring bodies should be put into proper perspective. The primary task of the Agency will be to provide advice to the institutions of the Union in the field of fundamental rights. This task is not fulfilled, for the moment, by the Council of Europe bodies.[90] This is an important lacuna which the establishment of the Agency, in part, will help to fill. That alone would justify setting up the Agency, in order to ensure that fundamental rights are taken into account *ex ante* on a systematic basis in the legislative procedure of the European Union, rather than only *ex post*, through judicial review mechanisms.[91] However, leaving

[88] This document is on file with the author. It will be referred to hereafter as the 'Council of Europe Memorandum of 8 September 2005'.

[89] PACE, Recommendation 1744 (2006), *Follow-up to the 3rd Summit: the Council of Europe and the proposed fundamental rights agency of the European Union*, cited at n 8 above.

[90] Of course, the international responsibility of the EU member states may be engaged if they fail to ensure that human rights are respected within their jurisdiction, even in situations where the alleged violation has its source in European Union law. See eg Eur Ct HR (GC), *Matthews v the United Kingdom* (Appl No 24833/94) judgment of 18 February 1999, para 32 Eur Ct HR (GC), *Bosphorus Hava Yollari Turizm ve Ticaret Anonim Şirketi v Ireland* (Appl No 45036/98) judgment of 30 June 2005, para 154.

[91] However, as a result of Art 4(2) of the Regulation establishing the Agency, the review by the Agency of the instruments or policies adopted by the Union will not be systematic. In addition, while both the European Commission and the European Parliament have currently included mechanisms ensuring that they will take into account the EU Charter of Fundamental Rights in making legislative proposals or in contributing to the legislative procedures, no such mechanism exists as regards legislative proposals made by the member states according to Art 34(2) EU, which provides that the Council may, in the field of police cooperation and judicial cooperation in

aside this important function of the Agency, the focus here will be on the role of the Agency vis-à-vis the national authorities of the member states of the Council of Europe, since it is here, of course, that the risk of overlap with the tasks fulfilled by the Council of Europe bodies is greatest. The Agency shall 'monitor' the situation of fundamental rights both in relation to the EU member states as they implement Community law, and in relation to certain non-EU member states. Does this create a risk of overlap, and of undermining the kind of supervision of the EU member states' human rights obligations performed by Council of Europe monitoring bodies?

B. The Reality of the Duplication of Tasks between the EU Fundamental Rights Agency and the Council of Europe Bodies

The question of duplication cannot be answered without keeping in mind the strict limits imposed on the Fundamental Rights Agency by its founding regulation. First, as already mentioned,[92] the Fundamental Rights Agency is not conceived of as entrusted mainly with a monitoring mission, in the sense of 'normative monitoring'—evaluation of compliance on the basis of a preexisting normative grid;[93] rather, it is to provide technical advice on the basis of its collection and analysis of information pertaining to the situation of fundamental rights in the member states. Whether it will be possible, in practice, to maintain a watertight division between these two functions remains to be seen: even mere fact-finding, after all, necessarily consists in highlighting certain situations, and thus putting pressure on the actors concerned to remedy any deficiencies found to exist. In addition, even though the emphasis or formulations may differ—with expert bodies of the Council of Europe explicitly evaluating certain situations for their compliance with the relevant standards, and the Fundamental Rights Agency more cautiously reporting about what it has found to occur and making certain recommendations of a general nature about trends—it remains the case that the same situations may be considered under both mechanisms. The EU Fundamental Rights Agency will publish annual reports and

criminal matters (Title VI EU) adopt common positions, framework decisions, or decisions, acting unanimously on the initiative of any member state or of the Commission. Ironically, it is precisely this field, which the current safeguards are most clearly lacking, that the Council has decided not to include among the fields to which the mandate of the Agency should extend, at least for the time being. The exclusion of Title VI EU from the fields falling under the remit of the Agency was the single most fundamental change made to the original proposals of the European Commission in the course of the discussions within the Council. A 'rendez-vous' clause is provided in a declaration attached to the Regulation, providing that the mandate of the Agency could be extended to judicial cooperation in criminal matters and police cooperation in 2009.

[92] See pt IV 2.

[93] On this distinction, see M Scheinin, 'The Relationship between the Agency and the Network of Independent Experts', in P Alston and O De Schutter (eds), *Monitoring Fundamental Rights in the EU. The Contribution of the Fundamental Rights Agency* (2005) at 73–90.

formulate conclusions and opinions on fundamental rights dimensions of the implementation of Community law by the member states, although the adoption of reports or recommendations on *individual member states* is not defined as one of the tasks of the Agency in Article 4 of the Regulation establishing the Agency. On the contrary, Article 4(1)(d) specifically mentions that the Agency shall 'formulate and publish conclusions and opinions *on specific thematic topics*, for the Union institutions and the member states when implementing Community law', a formulation which seems to be calculated to exclude conclusions and opinions on individual member states or on specific events or measures.[94] It is doubtful that the Agency will fully abstain from even naming, in its thematic reports or annual reports, specific member states when describing the situation of fundamental rights in the Union. Nevertheless, the tasks of the Agency remain distinct from those of a monitoring body in the classic meaning of the expression, such as those established under Council of Europe instruments.

Another limitation on the tasks entrusted to the Agency may play an equally decisive role. The EU member states will only be provided assistance by the Agency and be 'monitored' through the opinions and reports of the Agency *in the implementation of EC Law*. The original proposals of the Commission also envisaged that the Agency could be invited to provide its 'technical expertise' in the context of Article 7 EU which, as we have seen, allows the Council of the EU to react to serious and persistent breaches by one member state of the values on which the Union is founded, or to a 'clear risk' that such serious breaches will occur.[95] However, the Legal Service of the Council of the Union[96] took the view that such a possibility would 'go beyond Community competence', and that, moreover, it would be incompatible with Article 7 EU itself, insofar as this provision would not allow for the adoption of implementation measures and was, in this sense, self-sufficient. The Commission answered that the draft Article 4(1)(e) it proposed 'should be seen not as an autonomous exercise of Community competence needing a proper legal basis in the EC Treaty, but rather as a largely declaratory opening clause, admitting a possibility that the Council would arguably have anyway, while clarifying modalities and limits'.[97] Indeed, Article 7(1) EU itself refers to the possibility to 'call on independent persons to submit within a reasonable time limit a report on the situation in the Member State in question' in order to determine whether there exists a 'clear risk of a serious breach

[94] In the original proposal of the Commission, this provision read: '[the Agency shall] formulate conclusions and opinions *on general subjects*, for the Union institutions and the Member States when implementing Community law, either on its own initiative or at the request of the European Parliament, the Council of the Commission' (emphasis added).

[95] See Art 4(1)(e) of the Draft Reg (n 45 above). On Art 7 of the EU Treaty, see above, text corresponding to nn 16–17.

[96] Doc 13588/05JUR 425 JAI 363 COHOM 36 (26 October 2005).

[97] Note from the Commission to the Council *Ad hoc* Working Party on Fundamental Rights and Citizenship, Council Doc 14702/05, JAI 437, CATS 75, COHOM 38 COEST 202 (18 November 2005) paras 46–52.

by a Member State of principles mentioned in Article 6(1)', among which principles are human rights and fundamental freedoms. The implicit view of the Commission was that the Agency could either be an 'independent person' for the purposes of this provision, or contribute to identifying such independent persons, in accordance with the broad margin of appreciation which Article 7(1) EU intended to leave to the Council. In the view of the Commission therefore, including Article 4(1)(e) in the proposed Regulation added nothing to Article 7 EU itself.[98] Referring to the possibility of the Agency contributing its technical expertise upon request of the Council, in particular, 'should be distinguished from any further reaching provision that would enable other institutions to seize the [...] Agency or even an own initiative power of the latter to analyse possible Article 7 EU situations. Any such provision might indeed exceed Community competence and conflict with the exhaustive institutional setting in Article 7 EU.' The Commission was taken at its word. Within the Council *Ad hoc* Working Party on Fundamental Rights and Citizenship in charge of examining the proposal of the Commission on the Fundamental Rights Agency, a number of delegations expressed doubts as to the need to include a reference to Article 7 EU in the text of the Regulation establishing the Agency, as such a reference would, according to the Commission's own admission, serve no useful purpose and, going beyond Community law, could moreover lack a legal basis. The compromise solution consisted therefore in appending to the Regulation establishing the Agency a Declaration of the Council confirming this possibility, without any reference being made to Article 7 EU in the text of the Regulation itself.[99] This solution also preserved the purely political character of Article 7 EU, in the sense that the mechanisms it provides for should allow for a political appreciation by the Council of the European Union and the European Parliament, without, in particular, the question of whether a state is in serious and persistent breach of the values listed in Article 6(1) EU or whether there exists a clear risk of a serious breach, being determined by the European Court of Justice, as was suggested by the European Commission on a number of occasions, or by any other independent instance such as a Fundamental Rights Agency.

But the question of any potential role the Agency might have to play under Article 7 EU remains of marginal importance, in any event, in comparison with its role in providing the member states when implementing Community law with 'assistance and expertise relating to fundamental rights', as provided

[98] Already in a Communication where it clarified its understanding of Art 7 EU, the Commission has mentioned the possibility that the Council draw up a list of independent personalities which could be called upon the assist the Council in exercising its functions under Art 7(1) EU (see COM(2003)606 final of 15 October 2003 at para 1.3).

[99] This Declaration states: 'The Council considers that neither the Treaties nor the Regulation establishing the European Union Agency for Fundamental Rights preclude the possibility for the Council to seek the assistance of the future European Union Agency for Fundamental Rights when deciding to obtain from independent persons a report on the situation in a Member State within the meaning of Article 7 TEU when the Council decides that the conditions of Article 7 TEU are met.'

under Article 2 of the Regulation. This may overlap with the activities of the Council of Europe bodies. Indeed, even when they implement Union law, the member states remain fully bound to respect their other international obligations as defined, in particular, by instruments adopted within the framework of the Council of Europe.[100] Therefore, the Council of Europe bodies (in particular, the European Court of Human Rights, the European Committee of Social Rights, the Advisory Committee of the Framework Convention for the Protection of National Minorities, or the Commissioner for Human Rights) routinely examine whether the states parties to Council of Europe instruments comply with their obligations under these instruments, even where the states concerned act in fulfilling their obligations under Union law. Whether this overlap may prove problematic depends therefore on the nature of the relationship established between the Council of Europe and the EU Agency for Fundamental Rights, and even more decisively, on the status which the findings made by the Council of Europe monitoring bodies will have in the opinions, conclusions, and reports of the Agency.

C. Third Countries

It is on the question of the geographical remit of the Fundamental Rights Agency that the influence of the Council of Europe was perhaps most felt in the course of the discussions held in 2003–2006. The initial proposals of the Commission included a possibility for the Agency to provide, at the request of the Commission, information and analysis on fundamental rights issues concerning third countries with which the Community has concluded association agreements or agreements containing provisions on respect for human rights, or has opened or is planning to open negotiations for such agreements in particular countries covered by the European Neighbourhood Policy (ENP).[101] The ENP was developed in the context of the EU's 2004 enlargement, with the objective of avoiding the emergence of new dividing lines between the enlarged EU and neighbouring countries, instead strengthening stability, security, and well-being for all in the countries bordering the EU.[102] While the ENP does not offer an accession prospect, it does offer the countries concerned a privileged relationship, building upon a mutual commitment to common values (democracy and human rights, rule of law, good governance, market economy principles, and sustainable development). Originally, the ENP was intended to apply to the immediate neighbours of the European Union (Algeria, Belarus, Egypt, Israel, Jordan, Lebanon, Libya, Moldova, Morocco, the Palestinian Authority, Syria, Tunisia, and Ukraine). In 2004, it was extended to

[100] See above, n 90.

[101] Art 3(4) of the Proposal for a Regulation (see n 45 above).

[102] See generally the Communication of the Commission, *European Neighbourhood Policy: Strategy Paper*, COM(2004)373 final of 12 May 2004.

also include the countries of the Southern Caucasus with whom the then candidate countries Bulgaria, Romania, and Turkey share either a maritime or land border (Armenia, Azerbaijan, and Georgia).[103]

It was also envisaged that the Agency would collect information on the situation of fundamental rights in countries which have concluded an association agreement with the Community and which are recognized as candidate or potential candidate countries, where the relevant Association Council decides on the participation of these countries in the Agency.[104] The Agency would then extend the remit of its activities to the concerned countries, *mutatis mutandis*. In principle, the Agency would concern itself only with the respect for fundamental rights in the implementation of the acquis of Union law, rather than in all fields or with respect to a situation presenting no link to Union law. However, the precise modalities of such an extension to these countries of the activities of the Agency remained vaguely defined in the draft Regulation, not only because the relevant Association Council is to determine the precise modalities of such participation, but also because under Articles 6(1) and 49 EU, respect for human rights and fundamental freedoms is a condition for accession,[105] which may justify that, vis-à-vis acceding countries, the Agency's remit would be broader than vis-à-vis the EU member states.

At the time, when the Commission presented its proposal for the establishment of the Agency for Fundamental Rights, 14 member states of the Council of Europe belonged to either of these two categories of non-EU countries to which the geographical remit of the Agency could extend. These were four candidate countries: Bulgaria and Romania (which now, of course, have become full members of the EU), Croatia and Turkey; four potential candidate countries: Albania, Bosnia and Herzegovina, Serbia and Montenegro (which then still constituted one single State), the former Yugoslav Republic of Macedonia; and six countries either covered by the ENP or with which the EU has an agreement containing a human rights clause: Armenia, Azerbaijan, Georgia, Moldova, Russia, and Ukraine.

This raised the concern, within the Council of Europe, that the Fundamental Rights Agency for the European Union would be duplicating the work performed by the monitoring bodies of the Council of Europe, without this being justified by a sufficiently close link to the activities of the European Union. In the Recommendation it adopted on 13 April 2006 on this question, for instance, the Parliamentary Assembly of the Council of Europe took the view that 'the agency should have no mandate to undertake activities concerning non-European Union member states. Should such a mandate nevertheless be considered absolutely

[103] Although Russia is also a neighbour of the EU, the relations between the EU and Russia are instead developed through a Strategic Partnership covering four 'common spaces'.
[104] Art 27 of the Proposal for a Regulation.
[105] n 120 below.

necessary, it should be strictly confined to candidate countries and limited to issues arising from the accession process.'[106]

Partly as a reaction to such concerns, the discussions within the *Ad hoc* Working Group of the Council gradually led to the narrowing down of the geographical remit of the Agency. This led to dissociating the modalities of the possible participation as observers of candidate countries on the one hand, and of potential candidate countries with which a Stabilization and Association Agreement has been concluded on the other. In the former group are Croatia and Turkey, which started negotiations on accession on 3 October 2005, and the former Yugoslav Republic of Macedonia, which was granted candidate status at the latest in December 2005, but with whom accession negotiations have not started. The latter group comprises the countries of the Western Balkans whose natural vocation it is, in the future, to accede to the European Union, and for whom Stabilization and Association Agreements are seen as an instrument to prepare themselves as candidate countries.[107] These countries are Albania, Bosnia and Herzegovina, Montenegro, and Serbia, all of which are considered potential candidates.[108] For none of these countries will the extension of the remit of the Agency be automatic, since it will depend in all cases on a decision of the respective Association Council. But following the final compromise put forward by the Finnish presidency of the Council of the EU for the second semester 2006 and agreed by the Council, any potential candidate country with which a Stabilization and Association Agreement has been concluded can only participate in the Agency as an observer following a unanimous decision by the Council inviting it to do so, a condition not imposed as regards the participation of candidate countries.[109]

We may therefore expect that, in the immediate future at least, participation in the Agency will be envisaged only for only a limited number of third countries with candidate or pre-candidate status, and that the geographical remit of the Agency therefore will almost completely be restricted to the member states of the European Union. In part, this choice was justified by the need to avoid an overlapping of tasks with those performed by the Council of Europe: while it does make sense to facilitate the implementation of the acquis of Union law by candidate countries, or by the Western Balkan countries preparing for candidate status, by ensuring that the fundamental rights dimension is taken into account in that preparation—indeed, this is the purpose of the participation of these countries in

[106] PACE, Rec 1744 (2006), *Follow-up to the 3rd Summit: the Council of Europe and the proposed fundamental rights agency of the European Union*, cited above at para 11.3.

[107] See, in particular, the Declaration adopted in Thessaloniki on 21 June 2003, following the EU-Western Balkans Summit (Doc 10229/03 (Presse 163)) and the *Thessaloniki agenda for the Western Balkans: Moving towards European Integration*, General Affairs and External Relations Council, 2518th Council session, External Relations, Luxembourg, 16 June 2003, adopted by the European Council on 20 June 2003.

[108] Albania signed a Stabilization and Association Agreement with the EU in 2006, Montenegro and Bosnia-Herzegovina in 2007.

[109] See Art 28(3) of the Council Reg (EC) 168/2007.

the work of the Agency, as the Regulation makes explicit[110]—it would go beyond the objective of the Agency as defined in Article 2 of the Regulation (to provide member states when implementing Community law with assistance and expertise relating to fundamental rights) to extend its tasks beyond this; the situation of other countries may be ascertained through other means, and concerning the Council of Europe member states in particular, by consulting the findings of the monitoring bodies of the Council of Europe.

D. An Evaluation

To the extent that the implementation of Community law includes an obligation for the States concerned to take into account the requirements of fundamental rights, the Agency will have a role in providing them advice. Such 'monitoring' of individual States through the Agency will bear scant resemblance to the normative monitoring performed by the Council of Europe bodies.[111] Nevertheless, in the course of the discussions leading to the establishment of the Agency, the risk of 'duplicating' the work of the Council of Europe bodies was often referred to. Three arguments were generally put forward.[112]

First, it was said that 'the existence of such parallel mechanisms (one for the twenty-five [now twenty-seven] member states of the Union and one for the forty-six [now forty-seven] member states of the Council of Europe) would be a serious blow to the principle that there should be no dividing lines in Europe'.[113] This is a powerful rhetorical argument, but unconvincing when examined carefully. The instruments of the Council of Europe impose *minimum* standards on the states parties, and they contain provisions which allow these states to go beyond those

[110] See Art 28(2) of Council Reg (EC) 168/2007, (mentioning that, as regards countries participating as observers, the Agency may deal with 'the fundamental rights issues within the scope of [European Community law] in the respective country, to the extent necessary for the gradual alignment to Community Law of the country concerned'). It will be noted that, under the new framework for the conduct of accession negotiations with candidate countries agreed upon by the Brussels European Council of 16 and 17 December 2004, the Commission may recommend, and the Council decide by qualified majority, the suspension of future negotiations in the presence of a serious and persistent breach by a candidate state of the principles enshrined in Art 6(1) EU (para 23 of the Presidency conclusions). Although it would be natural for the analysis of the Agency to contribute to such an evaluation as may be required for such a recommendation to be made by the Commission and for such a decision to be taken by the Council, this would go beyond the wording of Arts 2 and 28(2) of the Reg, if read literally. Perhaps a reasoning by analogy with that which presided to the compromise on Art 7 EU (text corresponding to n 97 above) could be justified here: to the extent that the member states may entrust the Commission to perform, in their name, tasks lying outside Community competence, a practice accepted by the Court (see Joined Cases C-181/91 and C-248/91, *European Parliament v Council and Commission* [1993] ECR I-3685 (concerning aid to Bangladesh), para 20), it should be allowable for the Council to call upon the Agency to provide them with such an analysis.

[111] See text corresponding to n 71 above.

[112] These arguments are explicitly stated in Res 1427(2005) adopted by the Parliamentary Assembly of the Council of Europe.

[113] PACE Res 1427(2005), para 12.

minimal requirements either by the adoption of internal legislation, or by the conclusion of international agreements affording more favourable protection to the individual.[114] It is no more a problem for the European Union to ensure a guarantee of fundamental rights under the jurisdiction of its member states which goes beyond the requirements of the Council of Europe instruments concluded by those states, than it would be for any individual state to go beyond those requirements in its national constitutional or legislative framework. Indeed, when the European Community adopted directives on the basis of Article 13 EC,[115] or when it adopted Directive 95/46/EC on the basis of Article 95 EC (then Article 100A of the EC Treaty),[116] going beyond the protection from discrimination and the protection of private life in the processing of personal data as provided under Council of Europe instruments, this did not lead to 'dividing lines in Europe' in the field of fundamental rights. Quite the contrary, it contributed to the overall progress of the protection of human rights in Europe and inspired, in turn, developments within the framework of the Council of Europe itself.[117] Indeed, the risk of 'dividing lines' in Europe was also invoked when the EU Charter of Fundamental Rights was negotiated between October 1999 and October 2000, since this was perceived as an attempt by the EU, through the adoption of its own human rights charter, to dissociate itself from the instruments of the Council of Europe.[118] But the answer made then to this objection—that nothing in the Council of Europe instruments imposes a prohibition on the EU member states

[114] See eg Art 53 of the European Convention on Human Rights; Art 32 of the 1961 European Social Charter; Art H of the Revised European Social Charter; Art 11 of the Convention for the Protection of Individuals with regard to Automatic Processing of Personal Data; Art 22 of the Framework Convention for the Protection of National Minorities; Art 27 of the Convention on Human Rights and Biomedicine.

[115] Council Dir 2000/43/EC of 29 June 2000 implementing the principle of equal treatment between persons irrespective of racial or ethnic origin, OJ L180 of 19 July 2000, 22; Council Directive 2000/78/EC of 27 November 2000 establishing a general framework for equal treatment in employment and occupation, OJ L303 of 2 December 2000, 16.

[116] Dir 95/46/EC of 24 October 1995 on the protection of individuals with regard to the processing of personal data and on the free movement of such data, OJ L281 of 23 November 1995, 31.

[117] For instance, the Additional Protocol to the Convention for the Protection of Individuals with regard to Automatic Processing of Personal Data, regarding Supervisory Authorities and Transborder Dataflow (CETS No 181, opened for signature on 8 November 2001), was inspired by the chapter relating to the establishment of such supervisory authorities in the field of data protection in Dir 95/46/EC of 24 October 1995 on the protection of individuals with regard to the processing of personal data and on the free movement of such data (OJ L281 of 23 November 1995, 31). In the same vein, a number of provisions both in the 1988 Additional Protocol (CETS No 128) to the 1961 European Social Charter (CETS No 35) and in the 1996 Revised European Social Charter (CETS No 163) were inspired by provisions from European Community directives adopted in the field of social rights. It may also be noted that the Racial Equality and Employment Equality Directives have influenced the case law of the European Court of Human Rights in the interpretation of Art 14 of the European Convention on Human Rights (eg Eur Ct HR (GC), *Nachova and Others v Bulgaria* (Appl Nos 43577/98 and 43579/98), judgment of 6 July 2005, para 80).

[118] See PACE Res 1210 (2000), *Charter of fundamental rights of the European Union*, para 5 (in which the Parliamentary Assembly 'draws attention to the risks of having two sets of fundamental rights which would weaken the European Court of Human Rights').

or on the Union itself to further improve the protection of human rights in their respective spheres of competence—is the same which should be made to the fears raised by the establishment of a Fundamental Rights Agency for the EU.

A second argument put forward against any duplication of tasks between the Council of Europe bodies and the EU Agency was that such a duplication would constitute a waste of resources.[119] What this argument is missing however, is that to the extent the 'monitoring' of individual states by the EU Fundamental Rights Agency is envisaged, this monitoring is performed for reasons specific to the needs of the Union. In particular, in order to assist the EU member states in their implementation of Union law, which should better take into account the requirements of fundamental rights, and in order to facilitate the progress of candidate countries to the EU towards meeting the accession criteria. While the findings by the Council of Europe bodies should fully be made use of in these different contexts, they nevertheless will be relied upon with these very different aims in mind, which do not correspond to the aims pursued by the bodies of the Council of Europe under their specific mandates. Indeed, it would unthinkable to entrust those bodies, for instance, with the task of evaluating whether a country complies with the criteria laid down for accession to the Union.[120] And it would be incompatible with the principle of autonomy of the legal order of the Union,[121] moreover, to have such bodies decide authoritatively whether a member state has implemented Union law in conformity with the obligation (as imposed under Union law itself) to ensure that this implementation is in conformity with the requirements of fundamental rights.[122] The principle of autonomy of the Union legal order implies that 'only the institutions of the particular legal order are competent to interpret the constitutional and legal rules of that order'.[123] It would

[119] PACE Res 1427(2005), para 10.

[120] See Art 49 EU, which, since it was amended by the 1997 Treaty of Amsterdam, includes a reference to the fact that the European State seeking to apply for membership of the EU must respect the principles set out in Art 6(1) EU (comp. with Article O of the Treaty on the European Union signed in Maastricht, which did not contain a similar reference); and the so-called 'political criterion' included among the criteria defined for accession by the Copenhagen European Council of 21–2 June 1993 (Conclusions of the Presidency, 44), referring to the stability of institutions guaranteeing democracy, the rule of law, human rights, and respect for and protection of minorities. On the use of the Copenhagen criteria, see C Hillion, 'The Copenhagen criteria and their progecy', in C Hillion (ed), *EU enlargement: a legal approach* (2004) 13.

[121] The principle of autonomy is derived from Arts 220 EC and 292 EC. See Opinion 1/91, Draft agreement between the Community, on the one hand, and the countries of the European Free Trade Association, on the other, relating to the creation of the European Economic Area, [1991] ECR I-6079 (14 December 1991); Opinion 1/92, (Second) Draft agreement between the Community, on the one hand, and the countries of the European Free Trade Association, on the other, relating to the creation of the European Economic Area [1992] ECR I-2821 (10 April 1992).

[122] It would also be in violation of the principle of autonomy of the legal order of the Union to entrust bodies of the Council of Europe with the task of deciding whether there exists in a member state a clear risk of a serious breach of the values on which the Union is based, or whether a member state has been persistently in serious breach of those values, under Art 7 EU.

[123] Th Schelling, 'The Autonomy of the Community Legal Order: An Analysis of Possible Foundations', Harvard International Law Journal, vol 37, no 2, 1996, 389. In addition, the principle

thus not be compatible with this principle to attribute to Council of Europe bodies tasks which would imply that they interpret and apply Union law, with results binding on the EU institutions. On the other hand, it may perfectly be envisaged that the Council of Europe bodies be entrusted with fact-finding tasks, on the basis of which the Agency could report back to the Union institutions.[124] Such a delegation to the Council of Europe mechanisms of fact-finding tasks, not implying authoritative interpretation and application of Union law, may be seen as contributing to a more rational use of the available resources. But it does not constitute an obstacle to the Fundamental Rights Agency reporting on the situation of fundamental rights in specific countries, provided it uses any such findings as may be available from the Council of Europe monitoring bodies.

A third argument put forward by the Council of Europe institutions against the risk of duplication of tasks deserves more careful attention. This argument was best expressed by the Parliamentary Assembly of the Council of Europe when it voiced its concern that any monitoring performed by the EU Fundamental Rights Agency could result in 'the dilution and weakening of [the] individual authority [of the findings made by the Council of Europe monitoring bodies], which in turn will mean weaker, not stronger, protection of human rights, to the detriment of the individual'.[125] The Council of Europe Memorandum of 8 September 2005 explained that any duplication of the role of the Council of Europe bodies by a general monitoring of the EU member states or even, under the circumstances described above, of non-member countries, would 'entail a real risk of undermining legal certainty. A situation where assessments made by the Agency would diverge from, or even contradict, assessments made by Council of Europe monitoring bodies would result in considerable confusion for individuals and member states. It would also be highly detrimental to the overall coherence and effectiveness of human rights protection in Europe.'[126]

It is already the case of course that the member states of the Council of Europe are subjected to different forms of monitoring, under different human rights

of autonomy of the EU legal order is only one implication of the monopoly which Arts 220 and 292 EC reserve to the European Court of Justice in the final interpretation of the EC Treaty: attributing to the Agency for Fundamental Rights the task of deciding whether a member state complies with its human rights obligations under EU or EC law would not be compatible with this monopoly. Consistent with this requirement, Art 4(2) of the Reg establishing the Agency states that the conclusions, opinions, and reports adopted by the Agency 'shall not deal with the legality of acts within the meaning of Art 230 or with the question whether a member state has failed to fulfil an obligation under the Treaty within the meaning of Art 226 of the Treaty'.

[124] Indeed, in its Memorandum of 8 September 2005, the Secretariat of the Council of Europe proposed that, 'instead of multiplying monitoring mechanisms', we should 'build on the successful experience regarding the preparation of candidate countries for EU accession. Findings of the Council of Europe human rights mechanisms have been central elements in the Commission's assessment of the human rights situation in the candidate countries. If necessary, such findings could be presented in a more targeted way, and the details of such co-operation could be specified in an exchange of letters': Council of Europe Memorandum of 8 September 2005 at para 9.

[125] PACE Res 1427(2005), para 11.

[126] n 88.

instruments which have set up a wide array of monitoring bodies. The clearest example is the duplication which exists between the United Nations human rights treaties and the instruments of the Council of Europe. For instance, the Human Rights Committee monitors the member states of the Council of Europe under the International Covenant on Civil and Political Rights,[127] which contains essentially the same guarantees as the European Convention on Human Rights, which clearly entails a risk of contradictory conclusions being adopted by the respective supervisory bodies;[128] the UN Committee on Economic, Social and Cultural Rights monitors them under the International Covenant on Economic, Social and Cultural Rights,[129] the substantive guarantees of which largely intersect with those of the 1961 and 1996 European Social Charters; many other examples could be given. Similarly, the European Court of Justice, which has included fundamental rights among the general principles of law which it ensures respect for in application of Union law, routinely bases itself on the European Convention on Human Rights in situations where the European Court of Human Rights may also have to exercise its jurisdiction.[130] Indeed, even within the Council of Europe such 'overlapping' takes place: the European Committee for the Prevention of Torture and Inhuman and Degrading Treatments and Punishments (CPT), in its country reports following its visits to the States parties' places of detention, makes recommendations which contribute to the implementation of Article 3 of the European Convention on Human Rights; the Advisory Committee created under the Framework Convention for the Protection of National Minorities has interpreted this instrument in its opinions on the States parties, although the European Court of Human Rights has read Article 8 of the European Convention on Human Rights, as well as, with respect to religious minorities, Article 9, in combination or not with Article 14, as protecting similar rights to those listed in the Framework Convention. In general, far from this 'duplication' resulting in a lowering of the overall level of protection of human rights, it has been beneficial. These different bodies have sought inspiration from one another. By regularly referring to one another's interpretation of the respective instruments which they seek to ensure the compliance with by the states parties, they have ensured the progressive development of a 'ius commune'

[127] Opened for signature on 16 December 1966, 999 UNTS 171.

[128] See Human Rights Committee, *Correia de Matos v Portugal*, Communication 1123/02, decision of 28 March 2006; CCPR/C/86/D/1123/2002 (2006); 13 IHRR 949 (2006), which offers a reading of Art 14(3)(d) of the International Covenant on Civil and Political Rights which differs from the reading offered of Art 6(3)(c) ECHR by the European Court of Human Rights (Eur Ct HR (3d sect.), *Correia de Matos v Portugal*, appl 48188/99, decision (inadmissibility) of 15 November 2001, ECHR 2001-XII 161.

[129] Opened for signature on 16 December 1966, 999 UNTS 3.

[130] See O De Schutter, 'L'influence de la Cour européenne des droits de l'homme sur la Cour de justice des Communautés européennes', in G Cohen-Jonathan and J-Fr Flauss (dir), *Le rayonnement international de la jurisprudence de la Cour européenne des droits de l'homme* (2005) 189–242.

of international human rights as the outcome of such dialogue between different jurisdictions.[131]

Yet, should the 'monitoring' by the EU Agency for Fundamental Rights lead to conclusions which, in specific cases (for example, with respect to the compatibility of a particular legislative measure or policy with the requirements of fundamental rights), and although based on identically formulated standards, would differ from the appreciation of any competent body of the Council of Europe,[132] that might be problematic. This would create confusion, be detrimental to legal certainty, and indeed would risk diminishing the authority of each individual organ, as feared by the Parliamentary Assembly of the Council of Europe. This however is not the consequence of an overlapping of monitoring functions as such. Rather, it would result from such an overlapping taking place when not combined with an explicit and systematic reference to the findings of the Council of Europe bodies, in the interpretation of the different provisions which together constitute the acquis of European human rights law. If, on the other hand, in exercising its tasks, the EU Agency for Fundamental Rights were to refer systematically to the findings of the Council of Europe bodies, this might strengthen, rather than weaken, the authority given to the interpretation by those bodies of the instruments they apply, and contribute to an improved follow-up of the recommendations they address to the states parties.[133]

Thus, whether or not the fears about the work of the Fundamental Rights Agency undermining the authority of the Council of Europe bodies were well-founded would seem to depend on the strength of the links between the EU Fundamental Rights Agency and the Council of Europe, considered both in its standard-setting and in its fact-finding functions. It is important to note, in this respect, that the debate on the EU Fundamental Rights Agency ran

[131] See further on this theme C McCrudden, 'A Common Law of Human Rights?: Transnational Judicial Conversations on Constitutional Rights', 20 OJLS 499 (2000); A-M Slaughter, 'A Typology of Transjudicial Communication', 29 University of Richmond Law Review 99 (1994); A-M Slaughter, 'A Global Community of Courts', 44 Harvard International Law Journal 191 (2003).

[132] Perhaps ironically, the risk of confusion stems from the fact that the normative sources relied upon by the Fundamental Rights Agency (Art 6(1) EU and, in practice, the EU Charter of Fundamental Rights) include the European Convention on Human Rights which Art 6(1) EU refers to, thus leading to a situation where different bodies might arrive at different evaluations *on the basis of the same normative texts*. The risk would have been much less present if the EU had opted for an entirely different text, corresponding, for instance, to the specificities of the EU or based on the rights of the EU citizen.

[133] As noted by the Council of Europe Commissioner for Human Rights in his first annual activity report, there is therefore no reason to fear that the EU Fundamental Rights Agency will undermine the monitoring exercised by the Council of Europe bodies: 'the primary task of the Agency will be to provide advice to the institutions of the European Union in the field of human rights, a task which is not within the Council of Europe's remit. If the Agency systematically refers to findings of Council of Europe bodies within its work, this may strengthen and not weaken the Council of Europe's authority' (Annual Activity Report 2006 of Mr. Thomas Hammarberg, Council of Europe Commissioner for Human Rights, presented to the Committee of Ministers and the Parliamentary Assembly, 1 April 2007, CommDH(2007)3, para 3.2).

parallel to another debate concerning the organization of the future relationship between the European Union and the Council of Europe. This question was central to the Third Summit of the Heads of State or government of the member states of the Council of Europe, held in Warsaw in May 2005.[134] The Summit reaffirmed the determination of the Council of Europe member states to 'ensure complementarity of the Council of Europe and the other organizations involved in building a democratic and secure Europe', and resolved to 'create a new framework for enhanced co-operation and interaction between the Council of Europe and the European Union in areas of common concern, in particular human rights, democracy and the rule of law'.[135] In an Annex to the Declaration, the Heads of State and Government called upon the Council of Europe to 'strengthen its relations with the European Union so that the Council of Europe's and the European Union's achievements and future standard-setting work are taken into account, as appropriate, in each other's activities'; they also emphasized that the new framework of enhanced cooperation and political dialogue between the Council of Europe and the European Union should focus especially on 'how the European Union and its member states could make better use of available Council of Europe instruments and institutions, and on how all Council of Europe members could benefit from closer links with the European Union'.[136] Finally, they agreed on a set of guidelines on the relations between the Council of Europe and the European Union, which state in particular that the Council of Europe 'will, on the basis of its expertise and through its various organs, continue to provide support and advice to the European Union in particular in the fields of Human Rights and fundamental freedoms, democracy and the rule of law', and that '[c]ooperation between the European Union and specialised Council of Europe bodies should be reinforced'.[137] The EU Fundamental Rights Agency, as already mentioned, was described as a body where such cooperation could further develop.

The outcome of this process was the conclusion between the Council of Europe and the EU of a Memorandum of Understanding on 23 May 2007, providing that reference should be made by the EU to case law elaborated in the context of the Council of Europe when developing human rights standards,[138] and encouraging consultation and cooperation between the EU and the Council of Europe, including the Commissioner for Human Rights, in order to ensure that EU law is coherent with human rights guarantees stemming from Council of Europe

[134] Third Summit of the Heads of State and Government of the Member states of the Council of Europe, <http://www.coe.int/t/dcr/summit/20050517_decl_varsovie_en.asp>.

[135] See para 10 of the Declaration adopted at the Warsaw Summit.

[136] Annex IV, 1, to the Warsaw Declaration.

[137] Paras 6–7.

[138] Memorandum of Understanding between the Council of Europe and the European Union, adopted at the 117th Session of the Committee of Ministers held in Strasbourg on 10–11 May 2007, CM(2007)74 (10 May 2007) (hereinafter referred to a 'Memorandum of Understanding').

treaties.[139] The Memorandum of Understanding also stipulates that the EU's institutions should take into account 'decisions and conclusions of its monitoring structures…where relevant'. This follows a proposal made in the Juncker report on the future of the relationships between the European Union and the Council of Europe, released on 11 April 2006,[140] and immediately endorsed by the Parliamentary Assembly of the Council of Europe.[141] In this report, Prime Minister Jean-Claude Juncker proposed that a working rule be established, according to which 'the decisions, reports, conclusions, recommendations and opinions of [the Council of Europe] monitoring bodies: 1. will be systematically taken as the first Europe-wide reference source for human rights; 2. will be expressly cited as a reference in documents which they produce'. As noted by the report, this:

> merely confirms existing practice. But it does mean taking something which today is simply a practice, and turning it into a rule for EU institutions on all levels. This explicit formula will enhance the status of the Council of Europe's human rights instruments and monitoring machinery in all its member states, both EU members and others. It will also make for more effective co-operation between the two organisations.

Consistent with this understanding of the relationship between the two organizations, the EU Fundamental Rights Agency shall take into account, in its interpretation of fundamental rights, the human rights instruments adopted within the Council of Europe, but also the findings of the Council of Europe bodies in any monitoring of individual member states by the EU Fundamental Rights Agency. This is provided for by the Regulation establishing the Fundamental Rights Agency, which—anticipating the Memorandum of Understanding, concluded formally in May 2007 but under negotiation since the Spring of 2006—refers to 'the findings and activities of the Council of Europe's monitoring and control mechanisms, as well as of the Council of Europe Commissioner for Human Rights'; in addition, a reference to the activities of the Organization of Security and Co-operation in Europe (OSCE), the United Nations, and

139 Memorandum of Understanding, paras 17–19.

140 'Council of Europe—European Union; a sole ambition for the European continent', report by Jean-Claude Juncker to the Heads of State and government of the member states of the Council of Europe, 11 April 2006, available at <http://www.Assembly.coe.int/Sessions/2006/speeches/20060411_report_JCJuncker_EN.pdf> (hereafter referred to as the 'Juncker report').

141 See PACE, Rec 1743 (2006), *Memorandum of understanding between the Council of Europe and the European Union*, in which the PACE recommends to the Committee of Ministers to propose to the European Union to formally acknowledge in the Memorandum of Understanding between the two organizations that 'the Council of Europe must remain the benchmark for human rights, the rule of law and democracy in Europe, in particular ensuring that the European Union bodies recognise the Council of Europe as the Europe-wide reference in terms of human rights and that they systematically act in accordance with the findings of the relevant monitoring structures'. This Recommendation was adopted on 13 April 2006, immediately following the presentation by Mr Juncker of his report before the Parliamentary Assembly of the Council of Europe. It was based on a report prepared within the Political Affairs Committee by Mr Kosachev (rapp).

unspecified 'other international organizations' has been included.[142] It is difficult to be more explicit.

Once the principle is agreed upon that the EU Fundamental Rights Agency should base itself on the findings of the Council of Europe bodies, what becomes crucial for the implementation of this provision is that the Council of Europe is adequately represented within the management structure of the Agency in order to ensure that all the findings of the Council of Europe are carefully considered and that any risks of diverging approaches or duplication in fact-finding are avoided.[143] In this regard, the draft Regulation proposed by the Commission on 30 June 2005 provided that the Council of Europe shall appoint an independent person to the Management Board of the Agency, but that, in contrast to the current situation existing within the EUMC,[144] that person shall not necessarily be a member of the Executive Board. As correctly pointed out by the Council of Europe Secretariat,[145] this was not satisfactory. The day-to-day business of the Agency, as well as the definition of the position of the Agency on what may be politically highly sensitive points, will be defined within the Executive Board, rather than by the Board of Management. Therefore, it was felt necessary to widen the composition of the Executive Board, in order to ensure that the independent person appointed by the Council of Europe will be in a position to contribute effectively to the coherence of the approaches adopted by the EU Fundamental Rights Agency on the one hand, and by the Council of Europe bodies on the other. Following the compromise solution proposed by the Austrian presidency of the Council on 9 June 2006 and agreed to by the Council, the Regulation now stipulates that, although not formally a member of the Executive Board, the person appointed by the Council of Europe in the Management Board 'may participate in the meetings of the Executive Board'.[146]

[142] See Art 6(2)(b) and (c) of the Regulation establishing the Agency n 2 above; Art 6(2)(c) of the initial draft Regulation proposed by the Commission (n 33 above) stated that the Agency shall, 'in order to avoid duplication and guarantee the best possible use of resources, take account of existing information from whatever source, and in particular of activities already carried out by (...) the Council of Europe and other international organisations'. In the final text of the Regulation, the language has thus been strengthened and made more precise.

[143] As already mentioned, while the duplication of monitoring is not in principle problematic, as any monitoring performed by the EU Agency would be for other purposes than the monitoring performed by the Council of Europe bodies, duplication in fact-finding and in the evaluation of specific situations should be avoided as it may be seen as an unnecessary waste of resources and as creating a risk of divergent conclusions. The EU Agency should systematically refer to the findings made within the Council of Europe, but it should then process this information, collected by the Council of Europe bodies, in order to draw the necessary conclusions which are relevant to the fundamental rights policies of the European Union.

[144] Art 9(1) of Reg 1035/97 establishing the EUMC (n 66 above).

[145] Council of Europe Memorandum of 8 September 2005 (n 88 above).

[146] Art 12(1) of the draft Reg, Council of the European Union, Doc. 10289/06, 9 June 2006; and, now, Art 13(1) of Council Reg (EC) 168/2007.

Finally, on the basis of Article 9 of the Regulation establishing the Fundamental Rights Agency,[147] an agreement will be concluded between the EU and the Council of Europe on the cooperation of both organizations within the EU Fundamental Rights Agency. At the time of writing, the European Commission has put forward a proposal for such an agreement, which it negotiated with the Council of Europe on the basis of negotiating directives from the Council.[148] The draft agreement, which the Council should in principle approve provides, amongst other issues, that the Agency shall 'take due account of the judgments and decisions of the European Court of Human Rights concerning the areas of activity of the Agency and, where relevant, of findings, reports and activities in the human rights field of the Council of Europe's monitoring and intergovernmental committees, as well as those of the Council of Europe's Commissioner for Human Rights'.[149] The 'monitoring committees' in question include the European Committee of Social Rights, the European Committee for the Prevention of Torture, the European Commission against Racism and Intolerance, the Committee of Experts of the European Charter for Regional or Minority Languages, the Advisory Committee of the Framework Convention for the Protection of National Minorities, as well as 'any other such independent bodies that the Council of Europe might set up in the future'; the intergovernmental committees are those set up by the Committee of Ministers of the Council of Europe. The draft Agreement also provides, again consistent with the Memorandum of Understanding of May 2007, that 'whenever the Agency uses information taken from Council of Europe sources, it shall indicate the origin and reference thereof. The Council of Europe shall proceed in the same way when using information taken from Agency sources'.[150]

It is clear, therefore, that the activism of the Council of Europe exercised a profound influence on the final shape of the EU Fundamental Rights Agency. This activism explains in part why the Regulation establishing the Agency does not define the mandate of the Agency as including any 'monitoring' in the classic meaning of the expression, of either the EU member states or of the institutions. It

[147] This provides that: 'In order to avoid duplication and in order to ensure complementarity and added value, the Agency shall coordinate its activities with those of the Council of Europe, particularly with regard to its Annual Work Programme [...] and cooperation with civil society [...]. To that end, the Community shall, in accordance with the procedure provided for in Article 300 of the [EC] Treaty, enter into an agreement with the Council of Europe for the purpose of establishing close cooperation between the latter and the Agency. This agreement shall include the appointment of an independent person by the Council of Europe, to sit on the Agency's Management Board and on its Executive Board [...].'

[148] Proposal for a Council Decision relating to the conclusion of an Agreement between the European Community and the Council of Europe on cooperation between the European Union Agency for Fundamental Rights and the Council of Europe, COM(2007)478 final, of 21 August 2007. For the negotiation guidelines, see Document of the Council 6150/07 JAI66 CATS11 COHOM14 COEST37 FIN46 (RESTREINT UE).

[149] Draft Agreement, para 8.

[150] Draft Agreement, para 9.

explains why the emphasis is on thematic studies, rather than on country-specific reports. It explains why the competences of the Agency do not extend to the EU member states beyond the implementation of EU law. And, finally, it explains why third countries, particularly Council of Europe member states, in principle do not fall under the territorial scope of the activities of the Agency, with the exception of candidate and pre-candidate countries, to the extent that fundamental rights are to be taken into account in the absorption by these countries of the EU acquis. However, the insistence of the Council of Europe on restricting the definition of the mandate of the Agency would not have been as effective if it had not been echoing certain fears of the EU member states themselves, that they were going to be subjected to yet another form of scrutiny, and that findings by the Agency identifying certain lacunae in their domestic legal systems or policies could have endangered, rather than facilitated, cooperation within the Area of freedom, security, and justice.

5. Epilogue

The final issue that was raised in the negotiations leading to the establishment of the Fundamental Rights Agency concerned the extension of its mandate to 'third pillar' issues, ie the issues of police cooperation and judicial cooperation in criminal matters which are covered by Title VI EU. Despite the fact that these fields are highly sensitive from the point of view of civil liberties, certain member states opposed the proposal made by the Commission to allow the Agency to also analyse the situation of fundamental rights under this Title of the EU Treaty. Instead, a political declaration was attached to the regulation adopted containing a 'rendez-vous' clause allowing the mandate to be re-examined in 2009, 'with a view to the possibility of extending it to cover the areas of police and judicial cooperation in criminal matters'. In addition, according to another declaration by the Council appended to the Regulation:

> the Union institutions may, within the framework of the legislative process and with due regard to each others' powers, each benefit, as appropriate and on a voluntary basis, from [the expertise gained by the Agency in the field of fundamental rights] also within the areas of police and judicial cooperation in criminal matters.... [this expertise] may also be of use to the Member states that wish to avail themselves thereof when they are implementing legislative acts of the Union in that area.

Therefore, although the remit of the Agency does not extend beyond Community law, to the domains of police cooperation and judicial cooperation in criminal matters covered by Title VI EU, the future is preserved. Indeed, it can be expected that any sensitive instrument proposed under Title VI EU will be presented to the Agency for it to deliver an opinion, since it might be politically difficult to justify circumventing the Agency, once it will have gained sufficient credibility by being truly independent and, especially, by the quality of its reports. Finally, although the Agency will not be tasked with the preparation of regular reports on third pillar issues, the evaluation of the policies pursued by the Union and the member states in this field might be conducted through other techniques—in particular peer review mechanisms, coordinated and facilitated by the Commission, on the basis of the information provided by the member states—as was proposed by the Commission in June 2006.[151]

Even taking into account all the limitations referred to above, the establishment of the Fundamental Rights Agency does not merely constitute an institutional development. It would be surprising if this institutional innovation did not produce a powerful rejuvenating effect on the exercise by the Union of the competences it has been attributed, in a number of fields, to contribute to the implementation of the values enshrined in the EU Charter of Fundamental Rights. The establishment of the Fundamental Rights Agency was not intended, explicitly at least, as a means to promote a more active fundamental rights policy in the Union. The objective pursued in creating such an agency was to evaluate better, from the point of view of the fundamental rights recognized in the EU Charter of Fundamental Rights, the measures adopted by the Union and by the member states in the implementation of Union law, and to promote mutual learning in this field. It was not to bring about a more dynamic exercise by the Union of its legal competences in this field; nor, of course, was it to lead to a transferral of supplementary powers to the Union. At the same time, it seems almost unavoidable that, just as the adoption of the EU Charter of Fundamental Rights is already influencing the exercise by the Union of the competences it shares with the member states, the creation of the Agency will lead the Union to move from a reactive approach to fundamental rights (focused on the obligation to avoid violating them) to a proactive approach—asking instead how it may contribute to promoting them.[152] This is all the more necessary in the current context, at a time when harmonization has become difficult to achieve due to enlargement and the diverse sensibilities that coexist within the Council, and when, as a result, mutual recognition (under its many incarnations) appears as a potential substitute. Not only compliance with the minimum standards imposed by fundamental rights but also the absence of too important divergences between the member states in the implementation of fundamental

[151] Communication from the Commission to the Council and the European Parliament, *Evaluation of EU Policies on Freedom, Security and Justice*, COM(2006)332 final, of 28 June 2006.

[152] In favour of such a development see O De Schutter, 'Les droits fondamentaux dans le projet européen. Des limites à l'action des institutions à une politique des droits fondamentaux' in O De Schutter and P Nihoul (eds) *Une Constitution pour l'Europe. Réflexions sur les transformations du droit de l'Union européenne* (2004) 81; and O De Schutter, 'Fundamental Rights and the Transformation of Governance in the European Union', Cambridge Yearbook on European Legal Studies (2007) 133–75. For an excellent discussion of the relationship between the protection of fundamental rights and the question of competences, see Piet Eeckhout, 'The EU Charter of Fundamental Rights and the Federal Question' (2002) 39 Common Market Law Review 945.

rights should define the limit, or the precondition, for such mutual recognition techniques to be authorized to develop, and to function without strains. There are signs that the need for the Union to actively promote a high level of protection of fundamental rights in the Union is being recognized. The Agency, whose added value was put in doubt by many during the lengthy negotiations leading to its establishment, could in the future constitute the primary lever through which such a development might occur.

5

A Comparative and European Examination of National Institutions in the Field of Racism and Discrimination

Isabelle Rorive

1. Introduction

The twenty first century is far from marking the end of inequality. Discrimination remains a widespread phenomenon across Europe and stereotypes are hard to overcome. In March 2007, the Deputy Prime Minister and Minister for Education of the former Polish Government, with the public support of the Prime Minister, announced a draft law punishing 'homosexual propaganda' in schools, which was to provide for dismissal, fines, or imprisonment for school heads, teachers, and pupils. They also expressed a desire to promote the adoption of similar laws at European level.[1] During the communist government period and the 1990s, numerous Roma women were sterilized without consent in public Slovak hospitals. In 2003, Amnesty International and other Non-Governmental Organizations (NGOs) denounced the fact that investigation into the allegations was not being conducted independently, thoroughly, and impartially as required by international law.[2] And this is but one instance of many concerning Roma, whose place is described by the United Nations Committee on the Elimination of All Forms of Racial Discrimination as being 'among those most disadvantaged and most subject to discrimination in the contemporary world'.[3] In the UK, a 2001 research study on religious discrimination showed that Muslims, Sikhs, and Hindus frequently experience unfair treatment in

[1] See the reaction of the European Parliament in a Resolution on homophobia in Europe, 26 April 2007, P6TA-PROV(2007)0167. See also the European Parliament Resolution on the increase in racist and homophobic violence in Europe, 15 June 2006, P6TA(2006)0273.

[2] Amnesty International, *Slovakia: Failing to Ensure an Impartial and Thorough Investigation into Allegations of Illegal Sterilization of Romani Women* (2003), AI Index: EUR 72/002/2003.

[3] General Recommendation No 27, Discrimination against Roma (57th session, 16 August 2000), UN Doc A/55/18. In the EU, see the policy documents and the various declarations available on the website of the European Commission, DG Employments, Social Affairs and Equal Opportunities, under the heading 'the EU and Roma' (<http://ec.europa.eu/employment_social/fundamental_rights/roma/rpub_en.htm>).

education, employment, housing, criminal justice, and local government.[4] In 2008, the European Commission stressed that many gender gaps remain: 'The indicators for pay, labour market segregation and the number of women in decision-making jobs have not shown any significant increase for several years.'[5] And these are only random examples illustrating specific cases of discrimination or structural discriminatory practices, as the number of cases seems infinite.[6]

Creating stronger legal instruments is one solution to tackling these issues and to achieving more equality. Bearing this in mind, EU non-discrimination law has developed tremendously in recent years, with a focus on efficiency and the establishment of bodies to promote equality of treatment at national level. The first part of this chapter aims at giving a succinct account of how the general principle of equality, which is deeply embedded within EU law, has received new applications in order to go far beyond the primary concern of removing barriers to free movement within the internal market. However, despite the supranational character of EU law, one cannot grasp its impact on national laws through a top-down model of regulation. Implementation of EU law is often entangled in national traditions and always anchored in national legal cultures. This is particularly the case when member states are required to set up institutions which, by definition, have to fit within the national legal system. Accordingly, the second part of this chapter seeks to show the broad range of equality bodies now in place in European countries, with an emphasis on models that have been of significant influence.[7] Part 3 addresses the various missions that equality bodies are undertaking and tries to provide some insight into the paths that might be considered to achieve effective enforcement of the principle of non-discrimination in day-to-day life. Finally, the key question of independence of such bodies will be discussed taking into account international standards, such as the 'Paris Principles',[8] to fill the gaps of EU law in this respect.

2. A Glimpse at EU Anti-Discrimination Law

From the outset, anti-discrimination has been a key element of European integration.[9] On the one hand, a common market relying on free movement could not be consistent with discrimination based on nationality. In line with this, the primary

[4] P Weller, A Feldman and K Purdam, *Religious Discrimination in England and Wales* Home Office Research Study 220 (2001). See also *Fairness and Freedom: the Final Report of the Equalities Review: A Summary*, Equalities Review Panel (2007).

[5] 'Report on Equality Between Women and Men' (2008), at 8.

[6] See *Discrimination in the European Union*, (Special Eurobarometer 263, 2007) and the Gallup Organization's analytical report (2008).

[7] The national 'Country Reports on Measures to Combat Discrimination' issued by the European Network of Legal Experts in the Non-discrimination Field were a crucial source of information to account for the national situations (available on the website of the European Commission, DG Employment, Social Affairs and Equal Opportunities).

[8] See pt 2 below, especially n 33.

[9] See, for instance, M Bell, *Anti-discrimination Law and the European Union* (2002); D Martin, *Egalité et non-discrimination dans la jurisprudence communautaire* (2006); Bribosia, 'La lutte contre les discriminations dans l'Union européenne: une mosaïque de sources dessinant une approche

EEC Treaty included a number of provisions forbidding discrimination against EU nationals living or working in another member state. On the other hand, the principle that men and women should receive equal pay for equal work was considered necessary to avoid distortions of competition between member states. Over the years, discrimination in payment, and more generally discrimination against women, was also recognized as a social problem and as a breach of fundamental human rights.[10]

Despite the solitary nature of the provision governing discrimination based on gender in the 1957 Treaty of Rome[11] and its market-oriented background, a body of law on gender equality has progressively grown within the EU to constitute a 'separate citadel in the fortress of Community law', as Lord Wedderburn put it.[12] The movement started in the early 1970s and over the years, a significant body of European legislation has been put in place. At the same time, the European Court of Justice has refined and strengthened this legal framework tackling gender discrimination related to pay, working conditions, and social security.

The emergence of EU citizenship and the need for more popular legitimacy of the EU called for broader equal opportunities policies. Since the early 1990s, civil society organizations have been eager to drive the debate forward: they have pressed the European Community to tackle discrimination on a number of additional grounds, notably race and ethnicity.[13] The result of this process was the inclusion of Article 13 in the EC Treaty, following the entry into force of the 1997 Amsterdam Treaty. This provision is the cornerstone of potentially wide-ranging European anti-discrimination laws, as it empowered the Community 'to take appropriate action to combat discrimination based on sex, racial or ethnic origin, religion or belief, disability, age or sexual orientation'. The adoption of Article 13 suggests a growing recognition of the need to develop an integrated approach towards the fight against discrimination and to benefit from exchanges of experience and good practice across the various grounds.

Although Article 13 represents a fundamental step forward in the implementation of the principle of equal treatment within Europe, this provision lacks direct effect and, as such, does not oblige the European institutions to act.[14] The approval of

différenciée', in C Bayart, S Sottiaux, and S Van Drooghenbroeck (eds), *Les nouvelles lois luttant contre la discrimination* (die Keure-La Charte, Brugges-Brussels, 2008) 31–62.

[10] See the landmark decisions of the European Court of Justice: Case 43/75 *Defrenne II* [1976] ECR 455; Case 149/77 *Defrenne III* [1978] ECR 1365.

[11] Art 119, pt 1 of the EEC Treaty (now embodied in Art 141.1 of the EC Treaty) states that 'Each Member State shall . . . ensure . . . the application of the principle that men and women should receive equal pay for equal work.'

[12] *Labour Law on Freedom: Further Essays in Labour Law* (1995) at 265.

[13] For instance, the Starting Line Group, a coalition, created in 1991, of more than 400 non-governmental actors active in the anti-discrimination field and originating from all across Europe. On the Starting Line Group's activities, see, for instance, Chopin, 'The Starting Line: A Harmonised Approach to the Fight against Racism and to Promote Equal Treatment', 1 European Journal of Migration and Law (1999) 111–29.

[14] See, for instance, E. Dubout, *L'article 13 du traité CE. La clause communautaire de lutte contre les discriminations* (2006). For recent applications of Art 13 EC as a guide for interpreting secondary EC law, see, Advocate General Maduro in Case C-303/06 *Coleman*, opinion delivered on

appropriate legal measures to combat discrimination entails unanimity within the Council on a proposal from the Commission, after consultation with the Parliament. Because of the unanimity requirement, many shared the view that nothing was likely to happen within years, if ever. Two directives were, however, adopted in 2000, the year following the entry into force of the Amsterdam Treaty: Directive 2000/43/EC implementing the principle of equal treatment between persons irrespective of racial or ethnic origin (Racial Equality Directive)[15] and Directive 2000/78/EC establishing a general framework for equal treatment in employment and occupation with respect to religion or belief, disability, age and sexual orientation (Employment Equality Directive).[16] Such a speedy achievement was the result of years of civil society campaigning which prepared the ground for broad support for legislative measures. Exceptional political circumstances also played a decisive role. Oddly enough, Jörg Haider, the leader of the FPÖ (an Austrian extremist right wing political party), boosted the process. His participation in the Schüssel Government in 2000 caused deep concern in other EU member states at the time. Implementing concrete measures against racial discrimination was considered to be a priority in Europe and Austria, facing political confinement, could not afford to vote against the adoption of anti-discrimination legislation.

The Racial Equality Directive and the Employment Equality Directive significantly raise the level of legal protection against discrimination across the EU. They prohibit four forms of unlawful discrimination: direct and indirect discrimination, harassment, and instructions to discriminate. Direct discrimination deals with situations where 'one person is treated less favourably than another is, has been or would be treated in a comparable situation' because of a prohibited ground of discrimination.[17] This is, for instance, the case when an advertisement for renting a flat bluntly says 'foreigners not welcome'.[18] Conversely, indirect discrimination is not necessarily linked to any discriminatory intent.[19] It occurs where 'an apparently neutral provision, criterion or practice' would put persons of a particular racial or ethnic origin, religion or belief, age, disability, or sexual orientation at a particular disadvantage, unless it can be 'objectively justified by a legitimate aim and the means of achieving that aim are appropriate and necessary'.[20] A company dress code could amount to indirect discrimination based on religion when it is incompatible with the wearing of the headscarf, the kippa, or the turban without proper justification (ie safety for jobs requiring wearing of a helmet,

31 January 2008, especially points 7–14 and Case C-54/07 *Feryn*, opinion delivered on 12 March 2008, especially point 14.

[15] OJ 2000 L180/22. [16] OJ 2000 L303/16.

[17] Art 2(2)(a) of the Racial Equality and the Employment Equality Directives.

[18] Difference of treatment based on race or ethnicity can never be justified except when it constitutes 'a genuine and determining occupational requirement' (Racial Equality Directive, Art 4). The classical instance concerns a film maker who intends to hire an actor playing Martin Luther King or Muhammad Ali.

[19] In EU law, the concept of indirect discrimination was originally built by the European Court of Justice in equal payment cases. See the following landmark decisions: Case 96/80 *Jenkins* [1981] ECR 911; Case 170/84 *Bilka-Kaufhaus* [1986] ECR 1607.

[20] Art 2(2)(b) of the Racial Equality and the Employment Equality Directives.

public health for jobs in the food industry, etc). Compared to direct and indirect discrimination, harassment entails unwanted conduct which lasts for a certain period of time. The behaviour amounts to harassment where it has the purpose or effect of violating the dignity of a person and creates an intimidating, hostile, degrading, humiliating, or offensive environment.[21] An employee in a same sex couple partnership is, for instance, being harassed when he has to face recurring homophobic remarks from his boss or colleagues. Finally, the ban on instructions to discriminate means that the mere act of enjoining a third party to discriminate on prohibited ground equals unlawful discrimination.[22] Accordingly, an employer giving instruction to a temping agency only to hire 'white people' is in breach of EU anti-discrimination law as is the temping agency.

It should be stressed that the Racial Equality Directive and the Employment Equality Directive do not have the same material scope. With respect to race and ethnic origin, employment, training, education, social security, healthcare, housing, and access to goods and services are covered. As to religion or belief, disability, age, or sexual orientation, the protected area is confined to employment and occupation, as well as vocational training.[23] However, concerning the level of protection, EU law lays down minimum standards, thus giving the member states the option of introducing or maintaining more favourable provisions.[24] This has been the case in a number of member states where provisions were beyond the requirements of the Employment Equality Directive.[25]

The Racial Equality Directive and the Employment Equality Directives were built on the gender experience and the case law of the European Court of Justice. In contrast to the 1976 Gender Equal Treatment Directive[26] which mainly focused on forbidding discrimination between women and men in all aspects of the employment relationship, the 2000 Directives also pay particular attention to issues related to remedies and enforcement, mainly defence of rights, burden of proof, and sanctions. EU practice with gender discrimination has clearly shed light on the need to put emphasis on an effective mechanism for enforcement, to allow successful litigation and operative implementation of the principle of equal treatment.[27] Recent directives that strengthen and expand the legal framework

[21] Art 2(2)(3) of the Racial Equality and the Employment Equality Directives.

[22] Art 2(2)(4) of the Racial Equality and the Employment Equality Directives.

[23] Human European Consultancy and Migration Policy Group (eds), in Reports VT/2005/062 prepared for the use of the European Commission, 'Comparative analyses on national measures to combat discrimination outside employment and occupation: Mapping study' (2006).

[24] Recital 25 of the Preamble to the Racial Equality Directive; Recital 28 of the Preamble to the Employment Equality Directive.

[25] M Bell, I Chopins, and F Palmer, in Report prepared for the European Commission, *Developing Anti-Discrimination Law in Europe* (2007) at 38.

[26] Council Dir 76/207/EEC of 9 February 1976 on the implementation of the principle of equal treatment for men and women as regards access to employment, vocational training and promotion, and working conditions, OJ 1976 L39/40.

[27] On the wide range of obstacles women faced in bringing successful litigation, see, for instance, J Blom and ors in Report V/782/96-EN prepared for the use of the European Commission, *The Utilisation of Sex Equality Litigation in the Member States of the European Community: A Comparative Study* (1995).

implementing the principle of equal treatment between women and men follow this approach.[28]

The establishment of 'bodies for the promotion of equal treatment'[29] is undoubtedly one of the measures designed to improve the implementation of equality norms. In many member states, experience from anti-racist and gender laws has shown that too often the latter remain only on paper. According to the European Commission, 'it is clear that legislation alone is not sufficient to tackle discrimination. Take for example the experience from the gender equality field, where there is still a gender pay gap of some 20 per cent despite legislation on equal pay since the 1970s.'[30] As the Preamble of the Racial Equality Directive puts it: '[p]rotection against discrimination based on racial or ethnic origin would itself be strengthened by the existence of a body or bodies in each Member State, with competence to analyse the problems involved, to study possible solutions and to provide concrete assistance for the victims.'[31] This is in line with General Policy Recommendation No 2 that the European Commission against Racism and Intolerance of the Council of Europe (ECRI) issued in 2001.[32] In turn, the latter invokes the United Nations 'Paris Principles' which underline 'the significant role that institutions at the national level can play in promoting and protecting human rights and fundamental freedoms and in developing and enhancing public awareness of those rights and freedoms'.[33] Even though these principles were originally set out to provide a basic framework for Commissions on Human Rights, they are, as we shall see, widely referred to as setting the standards for equality bodies.

[28] See Council Dir 2004/113/EC of 13 December 2004 implementing the principle of equal treatment between men and women in the access to and supply of goods and services, OJ 2004 L373/37 ('Gender Goods and Services Directive'); Dir 2006/54/EC of the European Parliament and of the Council of 5 July 2006 on the implementation of the principle of equal opportunities and equal treatment of men and women in matters of employment and occupation (recast), OJ 2006 L204/203 ('Recast Gender Employment Directive').

[29] Expression used in the title of chs III of the Racial Equality Directive and the Gender Goods and Services Directive. The Recast Gender Employment Directive speaks of 'equality bodies' (Art 20). In the literature 'equality bodies', 'specialized bodies', 'independent bodies', or 'enforcement bodies' are all used to describe those institutions.

[30] Nolan, 'EU Anti-Discrimination Policy', in J Cormack (ed), Report of the sixth experts' meeting—Towards the Uniform and Dynamic Implementation of EU Anti-Discrimination Legislation: The Role of Specialised Bodies, *Strategic Enforcement and the EC Equal Treatment Directives* (2004) 58 at 60.

[31] Recital 24. To the same effect, see Recital 25 of the Preamble to the Gender Goods and Services Directive.

[32] General Policy Recommendation No 2 on Specialised Bodies to Combat Racism, Xenophobia, Antisemitism and Intolerance at National Level, Council of Europe, 13 June 1997, ECRI(97)36.

[33] In 1992, the United Nations Commission on Human Rights determined the first substantial set of principles for human rights bodies, known as the 'Paris Principles'. They enshrine guidelines on the status, powers, and modes of operation of national human rights institutions. These recommendations were endorsed by the UN General Assembly in its resolution A/RES/48/134 of 20 December 1993. See McCrudden, 'International and European Norms Regarding National Legal Remedies for Racial Inequality', in S Fredman (ed), *Discrimination and Human Rights. The Case of Racism* (2001) 251 at 282–5.

The paramount importance of equality bodies for the implementation of non-discrimination legislation whatever the grounds concerned is well documented 'given the role they can play in supporting victims of discrimination, giving guidance to Government and other public and private bodies on how to work towards equality, providing other stakeholders and the public with information on anti-discrimination rights, and conducting specialized surveys and research into discrimination and ways of eradicating it.'[34]

However, at present EU laws only require the designation of bodies for the promotion of equal treatment in relation to *race or ethnicity* and *gender*. In this respect, the Racial Equality Directive states that:

1. Member States shall designate a body or bodies for the promotion of equal treatment of all persons without discrimination on the grounds of racial or ethnic origin. These bodies may form part of agencies charged at national level with the defence of human rights or the safeguard of individuals' rights.
2. Member States shall ensure that the competences of these bodies include:
   - ... providing independent assistance to victims of discrimination in pursuing their complaints about discrimination,
   - conducting independent surveys concerning discrimination, publishing independent reports and making recommendations on any issue relating to such discrimination.[35]

Equivalent provisions are enshrined in the Gender Equality Directives which cover employment and occupation as well as goods and services.[36] On this matter, the Racial Equality Directive had a 'snowball effect' on EC gender law, where the equality body requirement only appeared in 2002.[37] Conversely, the Employment Equality Directive does not require member states to set up any equality body competent to tackle discrimination based on religion or belief, disability, sexual orientation, or age. This fact is often pinpointed as regrettable and as 'a disappointing perpetuation of hierarchy among discrimination grounds'.[38] However, a significant number of states have chosen to go beyond the EU law

[34] Niessen and Cormack, 'National Specialised Equality Bodies in the Wake of the EC Anti-Discrimination Directives', in J Cormack (ed), Report of the seventh experts' meeting—Towards the Uniform and Dynamic Implementation of EU Anti-Discrimination Legislation: The Role of Specialised Bodies, *Considerations for Establishing Single Equality Bodies and Integrated Equality Legislation* (2004) 20 at 21.

[35] Racial Equality Directive, Art 13.

[36] Gender Goods and Services Directive, Art 12(1), Recast Gender Employment Directive, Art 20.

[37] Dir 2002/73/EC of 23 September 2002 amending Council Dir 76/207/EEC on the implementation of the principle of equal treatment for men and women as regards access to employment, vocational training and promotion, and working conditions, OJ 2002 L269/15 (new Art 8a inserted in Dir 76/207/EEC).

[38] Niessen and Cormack, 'National Specialised Equality Bodies', n 34 above, at 25, See, however, the Commission's Proposal for a Council Directive on implementing the principle of equal treatment between persons irrespective of religion or belief, disability, age or sexual orientation, 2 July 2008, COM (2008) 426 final.

requirement and have empowered equality bodies to monitor additional grounds of discrimination other than ethnicity and gender.[39]

3. An Equality Body Model at National Level?

A. A Broad Range of Practices

As Rikki Holmaat put it, '[t]he spread of equality bodies throughout the European Union has been rapid, like a field of mushrooms appearing on the ground overnight.'[40] In this respect, the EU law requirement is certainly innovative and many national authorities had to start from scratch. Across Europe, less than one third of states appointed existing institutions with a renewed mandate and the others established new institutions. Today, most member states have designated a specialized body for the promotion of equal treatment irrespective of racial or ethnic origin and one for gender. Even though such a designation relies on EU directives, one can only be puzzled by the variety of national practices and the differences in the form, mandate, competences, functions, size, and effectiveness of these equality bodies. As a matter of fact, equality bodies are intrinsically linked to their individual national context and are the result of differing political, historical, and legal circumstances. The lack of one single format for an equality body should not necessarily mean that no general trends or possible classifications can be identified. Any attempt at rationalization, however, has its difficulties. A possible division could be made between *ombuds-type bodies* and *commissions* in the sense that Ombudsmen traditionally tend to be more complaint-focused while commissions, which are constituted by a plurality of members often representing particular interests or components of society, are usually eager to develop equality promotion work. However, such a division occurs to be unsatisfactory as these are far from being unwavering categories and 'many of the roles undertaken by bodies which fall within the two broad categories will overlap'.[41]

Another possible division rests on the various *models* of equality bodies. Sophie Latraverse of the French High Authority against Discrimination and for Equality (HALDE) identifies four.[42] The *Scandinavian model* of the Ombudsman relies

[39] See the examples given in Bell, Chopin, and Palmer, n 25 above, at 66.

[40] In the report of the European Network of Legal Experts in the Non-discrimination Field for the European Commission, *Catalysts for Change? Equality Bodies According to Directive 2000/43/EC—Existence, Independence and Effectiveness* (2006) at 28. For a systematic survey on equality bodies, see Network of Legal Experts on the Application of Community Law on Equal Treatment Between Women and Men (European Commission), *Report on Gender Equality Bodies* (2004); ECRI, *Examples of Good Practices: Specialised Bodies to Combat Racism, Xenophobia, Antisemitism and Intolerance at National Level* (2006), CRI(2006)5. See also the country-by-country details provided on the website of the DG Employment, Social Affairs and Equal Opportunities of the European Commission.

[41] Moon, 'Enforcement Bodies', in D Schiek, L Waddington, and M Bell (eds), *Cases, Materials and Texts on National, Supranational and International Non-Discrimination Law* (2006) 871 at 880.

[42] 'Organismes nationaux de lutte contre les discriminations: les défis posés aux organismes nationaux', paper presented in *The Fight Against Discrimination in Practice*, Seminar organized by

on an approach based on individual requests, mediation, and recommendations. It favours a culture of consensus. The *Dutch model* of a quasi-judicial body focuses on the need for alleged victims of discrimination to have access to law. To a large extent, it has recourse to the moral weight of non-binding rulings and on the building of precedents. The *Belgian model* of a public agency (Centre) seeks a balance between the promotion of equality and strategic litigation. A substantial amount of its resources is allocated to providing assistance to individuals and to reaching informal settlements. The *British model* of a Commission is the oldest in Europe in the field of anti-discrimination. It dedicates a large amount of effort towards the promotion of equality, the monitoring of practices of public authorities as well as those of private stakeholders. Support for litigation is strategically oriented to enhance substantial changes in society.

Beyond the difficulties in categorizing equality bodies, it is clear that those which were established prior to the adoption of the Racial Equality Directive in 2000 have had a profound influence in member states lacking such an equivalent institution. In this respect, the European Network of Equality, Equinet,[43] has played a decisive role, enhancing the exchange of experience, information, and best practices.[44] As Niall Crowley, the former CEO of the Irish Equality Authority, put it, '[T]he key element is that we face similar challenges. There are persistent inequalities across the grounds covered by European Directives. We need to be a part of the solution to that problem. To do that, we look at how we use our powers and, increasingly, how we can support changes in attitudes.'[45] Cooperation through Equinet is still fruitful for European equality bodies. In practical terms, it is mainly based on working groups focusing on specific issues. These include groups working on 'strategic enforcement' and 'dynamic interpretation' of equality laws, 'policy formation' with a view to developing equality mainstreaming and 'promotion of equality'.

B. Influential Models of Equality Bodies

Five models of equality bodies have mostly retained the attention of policy makers: the British Commission for Racial Equality and its counterparts for gender and disability equality, now brought together in the Commission for Equality and Human Rights; the various Swedish Ombudsmen, currently in the process of merging

the Academy of European Law (ERA), Trier 18–19 June 2007.

[43] See Equinet's website <http://www.equineteurope.org>.

[44] Equinet began as a cooperation between a few equality bodies. The cooperation became formalized in a 2003–4 project funded under the EU's Community Action Programme to combat discrimination: 'Towards the Uniform and Dynamic Implementation of EU Anti-discrimination Legislation: the Role of Specialised Bodies'. This led to the 'Equinet' trans-national project, bringing together 20 EU equality bodies. The network now comprises 27 equality bodies, in addition to the Migration Policy Group, an international NGO based in Brussels, which acts as a partner of the network and as its Secretariat.

[45] Cited in 'October 2007 spotlight: Equinet', the European Commission's website, DG Employment, Social Affairs and Equal Opportunities: <http://ec.europa.eu/employment_social/fundamental_rights/spot/oct07_en.htm>.

within one ombuds-institution; the Belgian Centre for Equal Opportunities and Opposition to Racism; the Dutch Equal Treatment Commission, and the Irish Equal Authority. All of them (or the bodies they were replacing) had at least several years of experience handling individual complaints and working on equality law enforcement at the time of the adoption of the directives implementing Article 13 of the Amsterdam Treaty. It is worth noting that, apart from the Irish Equal Authority which came into being in 1999, they all went through substantial changes in their institutional set-up or mandate as a result of the development of EC equality law.

1. *The British Commission for Equality and Human Rights*

In Great Britain, bodies promoting equality had already been established in the 1970s and their long expertise made them very influential in Europe. Until recently, the institutional set-up of equality bodies was made up of three commissions: the Equal Opportunities Commission (EOC, competent for gender, established in 1975), the Commission for Racial Equality (CRE, competent for colour, race, nationality, citizenship, and ethnic or national origin, established in 1976), and the Disability Rights Commission (DRC, established in 1999). On 30 October 2003, the Government announced its intention to set up a single Commission for Equality and Human Rights (CEHR). The 'vision' behind this process was based on the belief 'that fairness for all is the basis for a healthy democracy, economic prosperity and the effective delivery of... public services. Equality and human rights therefore matter to all..., not just those who experience discrimination and unfair treatment.'[46] While paying tribute to the three Commissions for having contributed to challenging discrimination and promoting equality, the Government stressed that 'change is not happening quickly enough' and that a substantial step forward is necessary in how equality and human rights are promoted, enforced, and delivered.[47]

After two years of a wide consultation process, a new single equality and human rights body for Great Britain[48] was established in the Equality Act 2006. From 1 October 2007, the CEHR[49] has taken on the role and functions of the EOC, CRE, and DRC. Additional grounds of discrimination have been added to the mandate of the new Commission, namely sexual orientation, religion and belief, and age.

[46] White paper: 'Fairness for All: A New Commission for Equality and Human Rights' (2004) at 11, point 1.2.

[47] Ibid at 12, point 1.4.

[48] The Commission's mandate extends to England, Scotland, and Wales but not Northern Ireland which has separate institutions. The Equality Commission for Northern Ireland (ECNI) is also the result of a process of integration. In 1999, the four bodies that existed at that time (the Commission for Racial Equality for Northern Ireland, the Equal Opportunities Commission for Northern Ireland, the Fair Employment Commission, and the Northern Ireland Disability Council) merged. In 2003, sexual orientation was added to the grounds of race, religious belief or political opinion, sex, marital status, and disability when the 2003 Employment Equality (Sexual Orientation) Regulations (Northern Ireland) entered into force. See <http://www.equalityni.org>.

[49] See the website of the CEHR at <http://www.equalityhumanrights.com/en>.

The Equality Act 2006 gives the CEHR a wide range of powers and functions similar to those that were exercised by the former Commissions, but broader in certain areas. The CEHR has a duty to consider applications by victims of discrimination seeking legal redress and power to provide such assistance in a variety of forms, including legal representation in court. It may conduct formal investigations for any purpose connected with its duties. In the case of investigation based on a suspicion of unlawful discrimination, it can use statutory powers to obtain documents and information. It is also entitled to institute proceedings in relation to discriminatory advertisements and instructions to discriminate. The CEHR has the general responsibility of advising the Government on the working of the anti-discrimination law. It organizes training sessions for public authorities and private stakeholders on how to avoid discrimination and promote equal opportunities. More generally, it gives advice and guidance to businesses, the voluntary and public sectors, and also to individuals. It may issue codes of practice which enter into force after approval by Parliament and the Secretary of State. One of the new powers available to the CEHR under the Equality Act 2006 is to seek injunctive relief to prevent discriminatory acts and to bring judicial review proceedings in its own name in relation to human rights.

As with the members of the equality bodies it is replacing, the 17 Commissioners of the CEHR are appointed by the Secretary of State to serve for a fixed term. The CEHR is a non-departmental public body and receives funding out of the Secretary of State's departmental budget, to whom it reports annually. To conform with the 'Paris Principles', which stress the importance of guaranteed funding to national human rights institutions,[50] the Equality Act 2006 provides that the CEHR should have funding which is '*reasonably sufficient* for the purpose of enabling [it] to perform its functions'.[51]

The three previous Commissions were, in general, perceived as being largely independent of government interference. As the remit of the CEHR also includes human rights, there was concern during the consultation process that real independence might be more difficult to achieve and that the new body should report directly to Parliament instead of to the executive. To provide reassurance on the Commission's independence, the following provision was inserted into the Equality Act 2006: 'The Secretary of State shall have regard to the desirability of ensuring that the Commission is under a few constraints as reasonably possible in determining (a) its activities, (b) its timetables, and (c) its priorities.'[52] The drafting of this duty by parliamentary counsel should have relevance for other statutory bodies.

[50] See pt 5 below.

[51] Equality Act 2006, para 38, sched 1, (author's emphasis). Initially the Bill stated that the Secretary of State shall pay to the Commission such sums as appear to the Secretary of State appropriate for the purpose of enabling the Commission to perform its functions.

[52] Equality Act 2006, para 42(3), sched 1. See B Cohen, *United Kingdom Country Report on Measures to Combat Discrimination* (2007) at 86.

2. The Swedish Ombudsmen

At present, there are still four single ground Ombudsmen in Sweden: the Ombudsman against Ethnic Discrimination (DO, established in 1986, competent for ethnicity and religion or other beliefs),[53] the Equal Opportunities Ombudsman (JämO, established in 1991, competent for gender),[54] the Disability Ombudsman (HO, established in 1994)[55] and the Ombudsman against Discrimination on grounds of Sexual Orientation (HomO, established in 1999).[56]

For the last several years, a parliamentary enquiry has been looking into the benefits of an integrated anti-discrimination Act to replace the seven pieces of current legislation[57] as well as into the advantages of an integrated equality body combining the existing Ombudsmen and adding age discrimination. A Bill to this effect is currently pending in Parliament and the proposed reform enjoys wide support from the political parties. It should lead to the establishment of an integrated equality body on 1 January 2009, the Ombudsman against Discrimination.

Each of the current Ombudsmen has the power to investigate complaints concerning discrimination and to represent individuals in settlement proceedings or, ultimately, before a court.[58] This last course of action is only open if no settlement can be reached. Usually, the Ombudsman initiates the process of settlement by contacting the alleged discriminator. As a matter of policy, the Ombudsmen represent individuals in court mostly in cases with broad social impact or with potentially important value as precedents. More generally, the Ombudsmen have duties to give advice and support to individuals or institutions, to supervise employers' compliance with legislation, to raise awareness through training and campaigning, to carry out independent surveys, to make recommendations to the Government in order to keep the law under review, and to monitor international developments.

Though accountable to the Ministry of Justice, the Ombudsmen have an independent status. The Government is precluded from giving directions on how the law should be applied or on how individual cases should be handled.[59]

[53] See the website of DO at <http://www.do.se>.

[54] See the website of JämO at <http://www.jamombud.se>.

[55] See the website of HO at <http://www.ho.se>.

[56] See the website of HomO at <http://www.homo.se>.

[57] The Equal Opportunities Act (1991), the Act on Measures against Discrimination in Working Life on Grounds of Ethnic Origin, Religion or other Belief (1999), the Prohibition of Discrimination in Working Life on Grounds of Disability Act (1999), the Act on a Ban against Discrimination in Working Life on Grounds of Sexual Orientation (1999), the Equal Treatment of Students at Universities Act (2001), the Act Prohibiting Discriminatory and Other Degrading Treatment of Children and Pupils (2006), and the Prohibition of Discrimination Act (2005).

[58] Note that the competence of the Ombudsman is subsidiary. In employment cases, when the person making a complaint is a trade union member, the competent Ombudsman is entitled to investigate the complaint only if the union is not willing to take the case. This should be put in perspective with the very high degree of affiliation in Sweden (roughly 85% of the workers).

[59] A Numhauser-Henning, *Sweden Country Report on Measures to Combat Discrimination* (2007) at 57.

3. *The Belgian Centre for Equal Opportunities and Opposition to Racism*

The Centre for Equal Opportunities and Opposition to Racism[60] was set up by an Act of Parliament in 1993[61] replacing the Royal Commissariat for Immigration Policy.[62] To start with, the Centre had two fields of action: promoting equal opportunities (preventive mission) and combating racism on the basis of criminal law and punishing discrimination based on so-called race, colour, descent, ethnic origin, or nationality (repressive mission). In the course of time, its remit was extended to embody genocide denial (a criminal offence in Belgium), human trafficking, poverty, aliens law and, finally, 'non-racial' discrimination. The latter covers sexual orientation, marital status, birth, fortune, age, religion or philosophical convictions, current and future state of health, physical disability traits or genetic characteristics, or political opinion.[63] These grounds of discrimination were introduced in Belgian law in the process of transposing the Employment Equality Directive.

According to its mandate, the Centre is in charge of producing studies and reports, making recommendations to public authorities and private individuals or institutions, helping any person seeking advice on his or her rights and obligations, taking legal action, collecting and analysing statistics and case law relating to its fields of competence, and obtaining information in order to make enquiries when it has reasons to believe that discrimination may have occurred.

The Centre is responsible to the Prime Minister of the Belgian federal Government and the 21 members of its administrative board are nominated by the Council of Ministers. At the same time, statutory law provides that it fulfils its duties in all independence which seems to be largely the case in practice. For example, the Centre publicly defended a different position than the Flemish Minister for Housing and Home Affairs on a recent controversial issue. That concerned regional legislation adopted on 15 December 2006 restricting access to social housing to persons who speak or make the commitment to learn Dutch.[64]

4. *The Dutch Equal Treatment Commission*

The Equal Treatment Commission (CGB)[65] was established in 1994 to deal with unequal treatment on the grounds of gender, race, religion, belief, political opinion,

[60] *Centre pour l'égalité des chances et la lutte contre le racisme/Centrum voor Gelijkheid van Kansen en Racismebestrijding*—see <http://www.diversite.be>.

[61] Act of 15 February 1993 pertaining to the foundation of a Centre for Equal Opportunities and Opposition to Racism, as subsequently amended.

[62] The Royal Commissariat for Immigration Policy was established in 1989 following the rise of extreme right-wing parties in Belgium.

[63] Federal Act of 25 February 2003 against discrimination, now replaced by the Federal Act of 10 May 2007 against certain forms of discrimination.

[64] On this issue known as the '*Wooncode*' question (ie Flemish Code of Housing), see the Committee on the Elimination of Racial Discrimination (72nd session), *Considerations of Reports Submitted by States Parties under Article 9 of the ICERD. Concluding Observations: Belgium* (7 March 2008), point 16 (CERD/C/BEL/CO/15).

[65] *Commissie Gelijke Behandeling*—see <http://www.cgb.nl>.

nationality, sexual orientation, civil status, full and part-time work, and the permanent or temporary nature of a labour relationship. In 2003 and 2004, disability, chronic illness and age were added as protected grounds to its mandate. The CGB is a *quasi-judicial body*. Its principal function is to investigate alleged cases of discrimination and to issue non-legally binding opinions.[66] In addition, it may investigate structural instances of discrimination in its own right. It may also provide advice to public authorities or private stakeholders who wish to know whether their policies are in accordance with the law. Additionally, it may make recommendations to the Government on discrimination issues, including legislative proposals.

The Commission receives funding from several departments of the Government and is accountable to the executive. The nine Commissioners are appointed by the Government and have an independent status.

5. The Irish Equality Authority and the Irish Equality Tribunal

In 1999, two independent bodies were established in Ireland under the Employment Equality Act 1998:[67] the Equality Authority and the Equality Tribunal. They are involved in the promotion of equal treatment irrespective or racial or ethnic origin (including membership of the Traveller Community), gender, disability, age, sexual orientation, religion, marital status, and family status.

The Equality Authority replaced the Employment Equality Agency and has a greatly expanded role and functions. It is an independent statutory body in charge of a dual mandate: to combat discrimination and to promote equality and opportunity. The legislation provides the Equality Authority with a large range of powers. At its discretion, it may assist those who consider that they have been discriminated against. Its other means of action include research and awareness-raising, review of legislation and drafting of statutory codes of practice. It also carries out independent reports on thematic issues and may conduct inquiries.[68] The Equality Authority is headed by a Board of Directors consisting of 12 members appointed by the Minister for Justice, Equality and Law Reform. Each year, the Chief Executive Officer of the Equality Authority submits estimates of income and expenditure to that Minister.

The Equality Tribunal (formerly the Office of the Director of Equality Investigations) is a statutory body as well as an independent and impartial forum for hearing or mediating alleged discrimination. Equality Officers investigate complaints and issue a legally reasoned and public decision. This decision is *binding*, but is also subject to appeal. A mediation process comes before the investigation providing there is consent from both parties. A mediated settlement agreed by the parties is also binding.[69] For a couple of years, there have been clear

[66] For more details, see pt 4.B.3 below.

[67] The Equal Status Act 2000 extended the material scope of their remit.

[68] S Quinlivan, *Ireland Country Report on Measures to Combat Discrimination* (2007) at 71.

[69] See pt 4.B.2 below.

concerns about the funding of the Equality Tribunal. These concerns relate to the extension of its mandate, the increase in its workload, leading to a significant backlog of cases without any significant extension to its budget.[70]

C. Single or Multiple Equality Bodies?

There has been substantial discussion in Europe about whether it is more *effective* to have separate specialized equality bodies for each type of discrimination or to set up one comprehensive equality body at national level covering multiple grounds. The arguments for a 'horizontal approach' to discrimination take into account the experience of all-encompassing commissions present mainly in common law jurisdictions such as Australia, Canada, Ireland, Northern Ireland, or New Zealand.[71] These are several, depending on the point of view considered.[72]

As to *victims*, it appears more straightforward to approach one equality body (a 'one-stop shop') and more acceptable to have, when relevant, the various aspects of their identity recognized. Any individual is likely to present a combination of protected characteristics (ie an Islamic woman, a homosexual black man, a disabled and elderly worker, a young Rom) and it is well known that concrete cases of unequal treatment could be based on a combination of grounds. When different equality bodies are competent for each protected ground, they are only entitled to deal with one aspect of the case, leaving aside the special issues of social stereotyping disclosed by such a situation.[73]

Accordingly, the issue of multiple discrimination[74] shows that, from *practitioners' point of view*, a single equality body allows an integrated method of work

[70] Quinlivan, n 68 above, at 74.

[71] See, for instance, C O'Cinneide, in EOC Working Paper Series No 4, *Single Equality Bodies: Lessons from Abroad* (2003).

[72] This account of the arguments is based, in part, on PLS Ramboll Management A/S, in Report prepared for the European Commission, *Specialised Bodies to Promote Equality and/or Combat Discrimination* (2002) at 8 and 59–67; Niessen and Cormack, 'National Specialised Equality Bodies', n 34 above, at 27–8; McCrudden, 'The Contribution of the EU Fundamental Rights Agency to Combating Discrimination and Promoting Equality', in P Alston and O De Schutter (eds), *Monitoring Fundamental Rights in the EU. The Contribution of the Fundamental Rights Agency* (2005) 148–51; Jacobsen and Rosenberg Khawaja, 'Legal Assistance to Individuals. Powers and Procedures of Effective and Strategic Individual Enforcement', in Report by Equinet Working Group 2 on Strategic Enforcement, *Strategic Enforcement: Powers and Competences of Equality Bodies* (2006) 9 at 11–12. See also the UK Government's justifications for its decision to amalgamate the different equality Commissions into the Commission for Equality and Human Rights, which are summed up in the White Paper: 'Fairness for All: A New Commission for Equality and Human Rights' (2004).

[73] Gerards, 'Discrimination Grounds', in D Schiek, L Waddington, and M Bell (eds), *Cases, Materials and Texts on National, Supranational and International Non-Discrimination Law* (2006) 33 at 172. For instances of multiple discriminations addressed by a comprehensive equality body, see: in Ireland, *Maughan v The Glimmer Man*, Equality Tribunal, 18 December 2001, DEC-S2001–020; in the Netherlands, the opinion 1998–48 of the Equal Treatment Commission.

[74] Within the category of multiple discrimination, two subcategories can be distinguished. First, 'cumulative' or 'additive' discrimination which refers to situations where adverse treatment is

which appears necessary to achieve consistency in policy and legal construction. A cross-grounds approach enables a more efficient handling of multiple discrimination cases[75] as long as the internal organization of the institution avoids compartmentalization based on discrimination grounds. In this respect, the Dutch Equal Treatment Commission's experience is worthy of note. It abandoned a division into several chambers competent to deal with specific grounds of discrimination for the reason that such a sharing out of tasks was inappropriate to address the increasing number of intersectional cases of discrimination.[76] Furthermore, in a comprehensive equality body, cross-fertilization, transfer of knowledge, and good practices among sectors seem easier. Consider, for instance, the issue of 'reasonable accommodation' which is only addressed with respect to disability in European law[77] although its application in other fields seems promising and actually, to a certain extent, unavoidable.[78] Could indirect discrimination based on religion, (eg a regulation in a laboratory preventing a Muslim woman from wearing the *hidjab*), be justified on the basis of safety when a reasonable accommodation is suggested and could easily be implemented (ie wearing a fireproof headscarf)?[79]

based on a *concurrence* of grounds. Second, 'intersectional discrimination' where adverse treatment is based on a *unique combination of factors* (ie black women can be stereotyped as such and be discriminated against because they are *black women*, not because, one the one hand, they are women and, on the other, they are black). See Gerards, n 73 above, at 171. See also Hannett, 'Equality at the Intersections: The Legislative and Judicial Failure to Tackle Multiple Discrimination', 23 Oxford Journal of Legal Studies (2003) 68; Fredman, 'Double Trouble': Multiple Discrimination and EU Law', 2 European Anti-Discrimination Law Review (2005) 13; Danish Institute for Human Rights, in Report prepared for the use of the European Commission, *Tackling Multiple Discrimination: Practices, Policies and Laws* (2007).

[75] O'Cinneide, 'The Racial Equality Directive as a Basis for Strategic Enforcement', in J Cormack (ed), Report of the sixth experts' meeting—Towards the Uniform and Dynamic Implementation of EU Anti-Discrimination Legislation: The Role of Specialised Bodies, *Strategic Enforcement and the EC Equal Treatment Directives* (2004) 48 at 50.

[76] PLS Ramboll Management A/S, n 72 above, at 6. For other instances of equality bodies which are organizing their work by function rather than according to the field of discrimination, see, among others, the Equality Authority in Ireland and the High Authority against Discrimination and for Equality in France. Both organizations have integrated more grounds of discriminations than those listed in Art 13 EC.

[77] Employment Equality Directive, Art 5.

[78] For instance, the Irish Equality Tribunal has applied the interpretation of reasonable accommodation normally only used in relation to disability to migrant workers. See J Cormack (ed), Report of the seventh experts' meeting—Towards the Uniform and Dynamic Implementation of EU Anti-Discrimination Legislation: The Role of Specialised Bodies, *Considerations for Establishing Single Equality Bodies and Integrated Equality Legislation* (2004) at 31.

[79] On the use of 'reasonable accommodation' in religious cases in Europe, see, for instance, L Vickers, in Report prepared for the European Commission, *Religion, and Belief Discrimination in Employment—The EU Law* (2006) at 19–23; Bribosia, Ringelheim and Rorive, 'Aménager la diversité : le droit de l'égalité face à la pluralité religieuse', *Revue trimestrielle des droits de l'homme* (2009) 319–73. In Canada, see, J Woehrling, 'L'obligation d'accommodement raisonnable et l'adaptation de la société à la diversité religieuse', 43 (1998) McGill Law Journal 325–401; 'Neutralité de l'Etat et Accommodements : Convergence ou Divergence' (2007) Options Politiques 20–7.

In its relations with *other equality stakeholders* and decision-makers, a single equality body is likely to have a stronger impact as it is a larger organization representing the interests of more people. More specifically, particular equality agendas may gain in strength from being associated with those which have the political priority. According to Christopher McCrudden, in some jurisdictions 'the movement against disability discrimination might have stronger political weight if it were associated with gender equality, which is perceived to be given greater political priority at the present time, and therefore benefit from greater financial resources'.[80] Generally speaking, a cross-grounds approach is considered more suited to 'educate people at large as to the common principle of equality that underlies all forms of equality legislation, and may increase popular support and understanding'.[81] In addition, in the search for renewed approaches to tackle racism, it has been stressed that '[e]xploring the common links as well as the overlap between different forms of group discrimination may help to release the subject of racism and racial discrimination from its historical and politicized past.'[82] Finally, as to the use of *resources*, a comprehensive equality body is cost-saving as it allows economies of scale.[83] This is not insignificant in an area where resources are limited, both in terms of expertise and finances.

The arguments favouring a single equality body have, however, to be assessed in light of the challenges and pitfalls facing such an institution.[84] First, the danger of establishing a hierarchy of interests raises a major concern, the risk being that one or two discrimination grounds (usually race and gender) attract the most attention to the detriment of other issues. Conversely, those opposing the merging of equality bodies consider that there is a hierarchy of inequalities and that some types of discrimination require special attention.[85] In EU law, they rest

[80] 'The Contribution of the EU Fundamental Rights Agency', n 72 above, at 148.

[81] O'Cinneide, 'The Racial Equality Directive', n 75 above, at 50.

[82] Boyle and Baldaccini, 'A Critical Evaluation of International Human Rights Approaches to Racism', in S Fredman (ed), *Discrimination and Human Rights. The Case of Racism* (2001) 135 at 189.

[83] In Great Britain, according to the White Paper: 'Fairness for all: A New Commission for Equality and Human Rights' (2004), a comprehensive body is estimated to cost 15–25% less than six separate commissions (app B, para 19).

[84] This account is based, in part, on Moon, n 41 above, at 876; McCrudden, 'The Contribution of the EU Fundamental Rights Agency', n 72 above, at 150–1; Niessen and Cormack, 'National Specialised Equality Bodies', n 34 above, at 28–9; Collins, 'Challenges and Choices—Establishing a Single Equality Commission in Northern Ireland', in J Cormack (ed), Report of the seventh experts' meeting—Towards the Uniform and Dynamic Implementation of EU Anti-Discrimination Legislation: The Role of Specialised Bodies, *Considerations for Establishing Single Equality Bodies and Integrated Equality Legislation* (2004) 4 at 6–9; Choudhury, 'The Commission for Equality and Human Rights: Designing the Big Tent', 13 Maastricht Journal of European and Comparative Law (2006) 311–22.

[85] In 1998, Michael Head, the Vice Chairman of the European Commission against Racism and Intolerance (ECRI) of the Council of Europe stated that 'it seems inconceivable to us in ECRI that any national body, irrespective of its precise form and remit, should not have within it at least a section dedicated to dealing with problems of discrimination on the grounds of race' (in *The Place and Role of National Specialised Bodies in Combating Racism*, Lausanne, Switzerland 22–4 October 1998, Summary of the Proceedings, CRI(98)85 at 8, quoted by McCrudden, 'The Contribution of

their position on the more far-reaching protection of race equality in the Racial Equality Directive and on the long-standing place of gender equality in the main body of the EC Treaty.[86] Outside the EU, they also rely on specific UN instruments fighting racism and inequalities between women and men.[87] Behind these debates lies the practical issue of the allocation of resources between the grounds of discrimination. Secondly, the necessary balance between the horizontal implementation of the principle of equality and the characteristics of each ground of discrimination is not an easy one to achieve. For instance, the approach of indirect discrimination in terms of 'disproportionate impact' largely depends on the availability of statistics although the latter raises different issues when it concerns sensitive data (eg race or ethnicity, disability, religion) or non-sensitive data (eg gender, age).[88] Thirdly, in a single equality body, instances of grounds of discrimination working against each other (eg religion versus sexual orientation) are more likely to be accounted for. In this respect, the limits of 'genuine and determining occupational requirements' as well as 'ethos-based organizations' are still to be thought through and will not be easy to handle.[89] Fourthly, many countries have several pieces of legislation implementing the principle of equal treatment and often the protection varies (in scope and/or level) according to the grounds of discrimination considered. On the whole, the benefits of a single equality body appear illusory if the statutory provisions differ widely when dealing with gender, race, religion, disability, or other grounds.[90] Building an integrated equal treatment statute (a 'Single Equality Act') seems to be the more effective answer. In Great Britain, Northern Ireland, the Netherlands, and Sweden, such a step forward, nevertheless, has given rise to much political debate.

In addition, there are special pitfalls to overcome when merging single ground equality bodies together. As it involves major reorganization and numerous adjustments (new staff, increased workload, decrease in resources allocated to the original

the EU Fundamental Rights Agency', n 72 above, at 150). With respect to gender, where equality bodies deal with multiple grounds of discrimination, there are fears that this might lead to gender discrimination being marginalized. See *Report on Gender Equality Bodies*, n 40 above, at 4.

86 This debate should be widened in the light of the recent case law of the European Court of Justice searching for a proper implementation of the general principle of equality. See Case C-144/04 *Mangold* [2005] ECR I-9981; Case C-411/05 *Palacios de la Villa*, judgment of 16 October 2007, and the opinion of Advocate General Mazak not yet published in the ECR; Advocate General Colomer, in Cases C-55/07 and C-56/07, *Subito*, opinion of 24 January 2008; Advocate General Sharpston, in Case C-427/06, *Bartsch*, 22 May 2008. See also the Commission's Proposal adopted on 2 July 2008, n 38 above.

87 International Convention on the Elimination of all Forms of Racial Discrimination (1969); International Convention on the Elimination of all Forms of Discrimination against Women (1981).

88 See, for instance, J Ringelheim, in J Monnet Working Paper 08/06, *Processing Data on Racial or Ethnic Origin for Antidiscrimination Policies: How to Reconcile the Promotion of Equality with the Right to Privacy* (2006).

89 Employment Equality Directive, Art 4.

90 For an example in Sweden, see PLS Ramboll Management A/S, n 72 above, at 37.

discrimination grounds, etc), the process could lead to dissatisfaction.[91] From a strategic point of view, it could also appear counter-productive. As a matter of fact, the strength of separate agencies could be intrinsically linked to the identification of a specific group with the organization and be diluted as a result of the merging.

Nowadays, there is a clear tendency for European states to go for one comprehensive equality body over several bodies in charge of specific discriminatory grounds. The UK and Sweden are examples of countries familiar with multiple equality bodies which are currently in the process of merging. Amongst the institutions prior to the EU directives, it is striking to note that the integrated model is often favoured.[92] However, political considerations and pressure from lobbies can lead to the reverse situation. Thus in Belgium, whereas the mandate of the Centre for Equal Opportunities and Opposition to Racism was enlarged with numerous grounds of discrimination in 2003,[93] no agreement could be reached on the issue of gender and a separate Institute for the Equality of Women and Men was created.[94] One of the major justifications for this outcome was that the situation of women is entirely different as they do not represent a *minority* group of the society which is stigmatized. Neither practitioners nor academics found the argument convincing and the effectiveness of this Institute is still much doubted.[95] It is striking to note that in Sweden, the only institution which has voiced strong concerns against the amalgamation of the four Ombudsmen, is JÄmO, the Equal Opportunities Ombudsman which fears that gender discrimination issues might be marginalized as a result of the process.

4. What Do Equality Bodies Do?

A. EU Requirements

To meet EU standards, national equality bodies in the field of race and ethnicity, as well as gender, should play a triple role:

1. to provide 'independent assistance to victims of discrimination in pursuing their complaints about discrimination';

[91] For an account of the history of the Equality Commission for Northern Ireland which came to existence in 1999 from the merging of four equality bodies, see Collins, n 84 above, at 5–9.

[92] Consider, for instance, the Bulgarian Protection against Discrimination Commission, the French High Authority against Discrimination and for Equality, the Hungarian Authority of Equal Treatment, and the Romanian National Council for Combating Discrimination.

[93] See pt 3.B.3 above.

[94] Federal Act of 16 December 2002 establishing the Institute for the Equality of Women and Men.

[95] See, for instance, van der Plancke, 'Organismes indépendants: une exigence européenne', 470/471 *Après-demain* (2005) 38 at 39. During the parliamentary debates which led to the establishment of the Institute for the Equality of Women and Men, there were voices strongly advocating the conclusion of an agreement protocol between the two federal equality bodies. Such a formal step has not yet been taken, but in practice the two institutions seem to work together. In light of this, the Director of the Centre for Equal Opportunities and Opposition to Racism is entrusted with a deliberative vote in the administrative board of the Institute for the Equality of Women and Men.

2. to conduct 'independent surveys concerning discrimination';
3. to issue 'independent reports' and make 'recommendations on any issue relating to such discrimination'.[96]

The Recast Gender Employment Directive also requires from the member states that the competences of these bodies include 'at the appropriate level exchanging available information with corresponding European bodies such as any future European Institute for Gender Equality.'[97] This fourth competence seems to reflect in part the work done by the network Equinet[98] to encourage information exchange between equality bodies.

These provisions are of considerable importance as they anchor already established national equality bodies in EU law and compel the setting up of such agencies in member states where they were lacking. Compliance with the Directives requires that these bodies should carry out their tasks in an *independent* manner.[99] It also implies that equality bodies are given *formal powers* to perform their functions and the *necessary resources* to enable them to carry out these functions effectively. The language and wording of the directives in outlining the mandate of equality bodies has been criticized as excessively vague.[100] Many questions are left open. For instance, what precisely does 'assisting victims' involve? Does it include representing them in court or is the provision of advice sufficient? What kind of 'surveys' should be done? To whom should 'reports and recommendations' be issued?[101] What seems to be at stake is a combination of two objectives: *enforcing* anti-discrimination law and *promoting* equality.

As Colm O'Cinneide emphasizes :

> complex questions of tactics and strategy arise in trying to combat discrimination, especially when it is deep-rooted and systematic in nature. Equality bodies will inevitably have to struggle with limited resources and questions of how best to deploy these resources.... Comparative experience from different countries as to which strategies work will be of great value in identifying appropriate approaches to combating inequality.[102]

[96] Racial Equality Directive, Art 13(2); Gender Goods and Services Directive, Art 12(2); Recast Gender Employment Directive, Art 20(2).

[97] Art 20(2)(d). See Parliament and Council Reg 1922/2006 on establishing a European Institute for Gender Equality, OJ 2006 L403/9. Art 2 of this Regulation provides that '[t]he overall objectives of the Institute shall be to contribute to and strengthen the promotion of gender equality, including gender mainstreaming in all Community policies and the resulting national policies, and the fight against discrimination based on sex, and to raise EU citizens' awareness of gender equality by providing technical assistance to the Community institutions, in particular the Commission, and the authorities of the Member States'. The Institute was formally set up on 20 December 2006. It will be located in Vilnius. See <http://europa.eu/scadplus/leg/en/cha/c10938.htm>.

[98] See nn 43 and 44 above.

[99] On the independence requirement, see pt 5 below.

[100] O'Cinneide, 'The Racial Equality Directive', n 75 above, at 49.

[101] R Holtmaat, 'Netherlands Country Report on Measures to Combat Discrimination' (2007), in *Catalysts for Change? Equality Bodies According to Directive 2000/43/EC—Existence, Independence and Effectiveness* (2006) at 16.

[102] O'Cinneide, 'The Racial Equality Directive', n 75 above, at 49.

To the extent that there is no single model of how an equality body should assist victims, conduct surveys, or make recommendations on any issue relating to race and gender discrimination, a comparative approach is undoubtedly useful to identify good practices in strategic enforcement of equality law and to provide some insight on the pitfalls that could be avoided.

B. Assistance to Victims and Legal Casework

Whilst requiring equality bodies to provide 'independent assistance to victims of discrimination in pursuing their complaints about discrimination',[103] the Racial and Gender Equality Directives do not define the nature or form of this assistance. Their Preamble speaks of 'concrete assistance'[104] and most equality bodies provide some kind of *legal* support. Once again, their mandates are very diverse and span a broad range of activities which go beyond assistance to victims as such, while falling under the larger heading of 'legal casework'.[105] These activities include providing information about the existence of anti-discrimination legislation and the possibility of taking legal action; referring the victim to an organization (trade union, NGO, anti-discrimination bureau, etc) that could assist with formulating an official complaint; helping the victim and the perpetrator to come to an amicable settlement (eg mediation); hearing and investigating complaints; issuing opinions (advisory rulings) or binding decisions; going to court either on behalf of a victim, or in the name of the equality body, or even as an *amicus curiae*. With the support of some examples and good practices, this section aims to examine how equality bodies are using legal actions to work towards a more inclusive society.

1. Strategic Litigation

In handling their tasks when assisting victims of discrimination, equality bodies should be eager to find a good balance between two objectives. On the one hand, they should bear in mind that assistance in discrimination cases is a precondition for effective enforcement of anti-discrimination law. 'Experience has shown that few individuals who feel they have been discriminated against take their claims to court themselves—presumably because legal action is too strenuous, expensive and time-consuming a process to embark on.'[106] On the other hand, equality bodies should take care not to engulf themselves in individual cases to the extent that they are left with no resources to carry out other functions. In this respect, 'it has [also] been the experience of equality bodies that handling

[103] nn 35 and 36 above.

[104] Recital 24 of the Preamble to the Racial Equality Directive; Recital 25 of the Preamble to the Gender Goods and Services Directive.

[105] Moon, n 41 above, at 891–914. PLS Ramboll Management A/S, n 72 above, at 69–94.

[106] Jacobsen and Rosenberg Khawaja, n 72 above, at 10.

individual complaints is a resource-intensive process that is not always in proportion to the results achieved on a larger scale. [In addition] some types of discrimination, e.g. systemic discrimination, cannot be combated effectively solely by individual enforcement'.[107] Finding the right balance between the two objectives is not an easy task.[108]

Strategic litigation seems particularly useful for equality bodies that are competent to represent complainants in courts, acting as advocates for them.[109] This approach focuses on cases that have a wider impact than those of just one individual. Classically, they are cases that could lead to sustainable changes in various respects. First, they may contribute to the stabilization and clarification of a point of law; secondly, they may relate to an area concerning a large number of people; thirdly, they may have a strong likelihood of success and are valuable in order to set up a precedent and/or to change public attitudes; fourthly, even when the lawsuit is unlikely to succeed, they may contribute to documenting institutionalized injustices.[110]

With the raising of public awareness about the existence of anti-discrimination laws and the establishment of organizations to promote equality, the challenge of an increasing caseload is one that should be seriously considered. In order to avoid a backlog of cases which would result in significant delay and could discredit the institution,[111] some well-established equality bodies have developed a policy of strategic litigation which involves *triaging complaints*. A policy of triaging complaints complies with EU directives which do not require that 'the equality body assist all cases where discrimination is alleged to have occurred'.[112] In national legal systems, the scale of assistance to be given in each single case is often left to the discretion of the equality body.

In Ireland, for instance, much emphasis is put on developing a clear and coherent policy of strategic litigation.[113] According to its mandate, the Equality

[107] Ibid.

[108] The policy of the UK Commission for Racial Equality was to finance racial equality councils or complainant aid organizations. It faced criticism for not taking on enough individual cases of discrimination. See Cohen, n 52 above, at 84.

[109] This is not the case for all equality bodies (eg the French Authority against Discrimination and for Equality). For other instances, see Jacobsen and Rosenberg Khawaja, n 72 above, at 22 fn 61.

[110] European Roma Rights Center, Interights, Migration Policy Group (eds), *Strategic Litigation of Race Discrimination in Europe: From Principle to Practice. A Manual on the Theory and Practice of Strategic Litigation with Particular Reference to the EC Race Directive* (2004), at 34–65, especially 37. For examples of the strategy changing legislation or current practice through lost cases, see PLS Ramboll Management A/S, n 72 above, at 84–5.

[111] The experiences of the US Equal Employment Opportunity Commission and, from time to time, that of the Canadian Human Rights Commissions are classical examples of institutions substantially overloaded.

[112] Moon, n 41 above, at 892.

[113] See also the new UK Commission for Equality and Human Rights, n 48 above. On its website, one can read: 'Our priorities for 2008/2009 . . . Prioritise legal cases in new areas of equality in order to build case law. Address gaps in our knowledge base including pay gaps across all equality groups.'

Authority grants assistance, at its discretion, if it is convinced that the case raises an important point of principle or if it is unreasonable to leave the person without assistance to present the case.[114] In practice, the Equality Authority provides assistance only in a small percentage of cases on the basis of criteria set down by its Board.[115] These criteria include :

1. The capacity of the individual to represent himself/herself.
2. The complexity of the issues involved.
3. The availability of material which would assist the individual in bringing the case.
4. The availability of trade union, legal, or advocacy assistance.
5. The possibility of alternative remedies.
6. The extent to which serious injustice has been perpetrated.
7. The impact/effect of the discrimination on the individual.
8. The potential beneficial impact:
   - for others
   - for change in practice by employers or service providers
   - for development of equality practices.
9. The geographical spread of claims.
10. Whether the issue applies to:
    - areas such as health, education, welfare, accommodation, and transport
    - multiple discrimination.
11. Whether a substantial body of precedent has been developed.
12. Whether the claim is reasonably likely to succeed.
13. The resources available to the Equality Authority.[116]

A recent example of the importance of test case litigation, and the role of equality bodies in this respect, is provided by the reference for a preliminary ruling to the European Court of Justice in the case *Centre for Equal Opportunities and Opposition to Racism v Feryn*.[117] It began in April 2005 when a journalist contacted the Feryn company about massive advertisements placed along a

[114] Barry, 'Strategic Enforcement—From Concept to Practice' in J Cormack (ed), Report of the sixth experts' meeting—Towards the Uniform and Dynamic Implementation of EU Anti-Discrimination Legislation: The Role of Specialised Bodies, *Strategic Enforcement and the EC Equal Treatment Directives* (2004) 4 at 13. For the experience of the Commission for Racial Equality in Great Britain, see Karim, 'A Legal Strategy to Combine and Coordinate Different Tools Available', ibid at 30–2; as to the Equality Commission for Northern Ireland, see O'Neill, 'Positive Duties and Strategic Enforcement', ibid at 19–21.

[115] Quinlivan, n 68 above, at 70. Note that the Irish Equality Authority has overtly acknowledged that such a policy comes from a lack of resources (Holtmaat, *Catalysts for Change?*, n 101 above, at 48).

[116] Barry, 'Strategic Enforcement', n 114 above, at 14. In its strategic plan for 2006–8, *Embedding Equality*, the Irish Equality Authority gives as one of its major objectives 'to maintain and further develop a culture of compliance with the equality legislation'.

[117] Case C-54/07.

motorway to find garage door fitters. After the publication of articles in several newspapers where Mr Feryn, the director of the company, was reported to have said that his firm would not recruit persons of Moroccan origin, he participated in an interview on Belgian national television where he publicly stated :

> [W]e have many of our representatives visiting customers... Everyone is installing alarm systems and these days everyone is obviously very scared. It is not just immigrants who break in. I won't say that, I'm not a racist. Belgians break into people's houses just as much. But people are obviously scared. So people often say: 'no immigrants'.... I must comply with my customers' requirements. If you say 'I want a particular product or I want it like this and like that', and I say 'I'm not doing it, I'll send these people', then you say 'I don't need that door.' Then I'm putting myself out of business. We must meet the customers' requirements. This isn't my problem. I didn't create this problem in Belgium. I want the firm to do well and I want us to achieve our turnover at the end of the year, and how do I do that? I must do it the way the customer wants it done![118]

Following mediation with the Centre for Equal Opportunities and Opposition to Racism, the Feryn company committed itself to change its discriminatory recruitment policy but failed to do so. Consequently, the Centre launched a civil action in emergency proceedings to obtain a judge's order according to which Mr Feryn should end his discriminatory recruitment policy. On appeal, important issues were raised and the Centre asked the Employment Court to bring the case before the European Court of Justice. The reference for preliminary ruling brought up crucial questions on how the shift of the burden of proof should operate in practice.[119] Furthermore, one of the key questions addressed to the European Court of Justice was whether it constitutes direct discrimination for the purposes of the Racial Equality Directive if an employer publicly states, in the context of a recruitment drive, that applications from persons of a certain ethnic origin will be turned down. In short, *can words amount to discrimination*? Is the principle of equal treatment violated when the *victim* is only *hypothetical*? On 10 July 2008, the European Court of Justice gave a decision of great significance in construing EU equality law.[120] It followed the core of the opinion of Advocate General Maduro:

> [A]n interpretation that would limit the scope of the Directive to cases of identifiable complainants who have applied for a particular job would risk undermining the effectiveness of the principle of equal treatment in the employment sector. In any recruitment process, the greatest 'selection' takes place between those who apply, and those who do not.

[118] Advocate General Maduro, opinion delivered on 12 March 2008, point 4. See para 25 of the decision of the Court.

[119] Racial Equality Directive, Art 8; Framework Equality Directive Art 10; Gender Goods and Services Directive Art 9; Recast Gender Employment Directive, Art 19. On the issue of the burden of proof in discrimination cases, see among others, I Rorive, *Proving Discrimination Cases. The Role of Situation Testing* (Migration Policy Group, Centre for Equal Rights, 2008); Rorive and van der Plancke, 'Quels dispositifs pour prouver la discrimination?', in C Bayart, S Sottiaux, and S Van Drooghenbroeck (eds), *Les nouvelles lois luttant contre la discrimination* (die Keure-La Charte, Brugges-Brussels, 2008) 415–61.

[120] Case C-54/07 *Feryn* 10 July 2008.

Nobody can reasonably be expected to apply for a position if they know in advance that, because of their racial or ethnic origin, they stand no chance of being hired. Therefore, a public statement from an employer that persons of a certain racial or ethnic origin need not apply has an effect that is anything but hypothetical. To ignore that as an act of discrimination would be to ignore the social reality that such statements are bound to have a humiliating and demoralising impact on persons of that origin who want to participate in the labour market and, in particular, on those who would have been interested in working for the employer at issue.[121]

The *Feryn* case also illustrates another competence granted to some equality bodies, ie *taking action in the absence of individual litigants*. The competence of the Centre for Equal Opportunities and Opposition to Racism is, however, dependent on the *consent* of the victim where the alleged violation has an identifiable victim.[122] Such a condition does not circumscribe the power of the Irish Equality Authority to bring a case in its own right before the Equality Tribunal.[123] For those equality bodies that have no explicit powers to take action in their own name, it remains to be assessed against relevant national procedural law whether a *locus standi* could not be inferred from their general mandate.[124]

Finally, *interventions* and *amicus curiae* applications are other paths that equality bodies may consider in pursuing strategic litigation. Classically, parties apply to intervene in a case in protection of their own interest, while an *amicus curiae* ('friend of the court') exclusively intends to assist the court in its determination of a particular point of law. Nowadays, the *amicus curiae* is rarely wholly disinterested in the outcome of the litigation.[125] This is well-illustrated in the case law of the US Supreme Court and, more recently, of the European Court of Human Rights.[126] While the practice of 'interventions' is more familiar in common law jurisdictions, it is facing a growing success in civil law countries and this capacity has been expressly granted to some equality bodies.[127] Generally speaking,

[121] Opinion delivered on 12 March 2008, point 15.

[122] Art 31 of the Belgian Federal Act of 15 February 1993 pertaining to the foundation of a Centre for Equal Opportunities and Opposition to Racism, as subsequently amended.

[123] Irish Employment Equality Acts 1998–2004, ss 85–6.

[124] See *R v Secretary of State for Employment ex parte Equal Opportunities Commission and anor* [1994] ICR 317 (HL), commented on in Moon, n 41 above, at 902–3.

[125] Note that in some countries, as in Ireland or the UK, interventions are distinguished from *amicus curiae*. See Moon, n 41 above, at 904. Barry, 'Interventions and Amicus Curiae Applications. Making Individual Enforcement More Effective', in Report by Equinet Working Group 2 on Strategic Enforcement, *Strategic Enforcement: Powers and Competences of Equality Bodies* (2006) 31 at 36–8. In England and Wales, the court may ask for a barrister to assist it with research and to offer an independent legal point of view. See, for instance, on the issue of prospective overruling before the House of Lords, *National Westminster Bank plc v Spectrum Plus Ltd* [2005] UKHL 41.

[126] In the field of discrimination, two recent decisions of the European Court of Human Rights are emblematic of the increasing weight of *amicus curiae* briefs on the case law of the court: *DH v The Czech Republic*, ECHR (Grand Chamber), 13 November 2007; *EB v France*, ECHR (Grand Chamber), 22 January 2008.

[127] For instance, the Belgian Centre for Equal Opportunities and Opposition to Racism, the Hungarian Equal Treatment Authority, and the French High Authority against Discrimination

equality bodies' intervention in key cases is not a widespread phenomenon in Europe, although there are voices to suggest that this is a strategic role that these institutions ought to pursue.[128]

In Great Britain, *Igen Ltd v Wong*[129] is an influential case where the Commissions for Equal Opportunities, Racial Equality and Disability Rights made a joint intervention before the Court of Appeal for England and Wales. There were actually three cases of alleged discrimination in the workplace (on the ground of sex for two of them and on the ground of ethnicity for one of them)[130] concerning the application of the shift of the burden of proof provisions[131] introduced into domestic law as a result of the implementation of the EU directives. The Court of Appeal took the opportunity to examine earlier guidance provided in a judicial precedent and to set it out again with the amendments suggested by the Commissions.[132] This ruling has had a widespread impact in the UK and is referred to in other national jurisdictions across Europe.

2. *Settling Cases Outside Court*

Alternative dispute resolution mechanisms, such as conciliation or mediation, have well-known advantages over classical litigation. Chiefly, they are considered less time-consuming, much less costly, and they should ideally lead to solutions which have no winner or loser, allowing the relationship between the parties to be restored. On the other hand, some concern has been voiced that people might lose their rights if they engage in a legally-binding mediation process without knowing their actual legal position in the case.[133] More broadly, '[f]rom an equality law perspective, the main risk is that, in the process of negotiation, concessions have to be made in line with the essentials of the law.'[134] Furthermore, others underline that mediation is by definition not public and allows discriminatory practices to remain concealed. Equality bodies should, therefore, be aware of the fact that strategic enforcement may require emblematic cases of discrimination to

and for Equality (HALDE). See Moon, n 41 above, at 908–9. Note that in France, the HALDE is the only non-judicial institution with such a power.

128 Barry, 'Interventions and Amicus Curiae Applications', n 125 above, at 39–41; Moon, n 41 above, at 904.

129 *Igen Ltd & Others v Wong, Chamberlin and anor v Emokpae, Webster v Brunel University* [2005] EWCA Civ 142, reported in issue 2 of the *European Anti-Discrimination Law Review* (2005) at 77. See also Brown, Erskine, and LittleJohn, 'Review of Judgments in Race Discrimination Employment Tribunal Cases', in Employment Relations Research Series (2006) 64, at 33–5.

130 The Disability Rights Commission intervened because a key point of anti-discrimination law was at stake, although the cases did not concern the ground of disability as such.

131 On this issue, see n 119 above.

132 See also *Madarassy v Nomura International plc* [2007] EWCA Civ 33 (CA, petition to the HL refused on 17 May 2007).

133 PLS Ramboll Management A/S, n 72 above, at 78. This report refers especially to concern expressed by trade unions in Ireland.

134 Goldschmidt, 'Implementation of Equality Law: A Task for Specialists or for Human Rights Experts? Experiences and Developments in the Supervision of Equality Law in the Netherlands', 13 Maastricht Journal of European and Comparative Law (2006) 323 at 328.

be fought in courts. A fair number of equality bodies provide support to victims in seeking to facilitate the resolution of disputes out of court.[135] This approach of conciliation can be informal. For instance, the Belgian Centre for Equal Opportunities and Opposition to Racism has developed the practice of writing a complaint to the alleged perpetrator on behalf of the victim in order to try to reach a 'friendly settlement'.

In a typical case of an individual person asking the Centre to intervene in an instance of discrimination, the Centre will appraise the facts given, and in most cases where the allegation is not ill-founded it will seek to obtain an amicable settlement with the alleged discriminator. Because the discriminator may fear the bad publicity a suit for alleged discrimination would bring, he may be tempted to accept this, even in situations where it may be difficult to prove that discrimination has occurred. Where such an amicable settlement seems unsatisfactory, because the discrimination is flagrant or because the defendant does not cooperate, the Centre may propose to the victim to file a suit. If the victim consents, the Centre will proceed, as the law authorizes it to do.

The Centre for Equal Opportunites and Opposition to Racism has been particularly efficient in providing advice and legal assistance to victims of discrimination. It is particularly noteworthy for its practice of seeking to assist the victim in having the alleged perpetrator of the discrimination to agree to some form of amicable settlement in which the Centre, albeit in a discrete fashion, has developed significant expertise.[136]

In contrast, in Ireland, the Equality Tribunal offers a legally-binding mediation service[137] besides its quasi-judicial capacity. Providing that none of the parties object, every case is allocated for mediation by a trained Equality Mediation Officer who assists the parties to reach a mutually acceptable agreement. If the mediation succeeds, the agreement is signed by both parties and can be enforced through the civil courts. If the mediation fails, either of the parties can ask for a ruling. The case is then allocated to a different Investigating Equality Officer to insure impartiality.

In France, the High Authority against Discrimination and for Equality (HALDE) which began functioning in June 2005 was granted a new power in 2006: that of proposing a so-called '*transaction pénale*'—a form of negotiated criminal sanction—to perpetrators of direct discrimination. Accordingly, if an investigation of a complaint results in a finding of direct intentional discrimination, the HALDE may suggest a specific criminal sanction for the perpetrator. This could be a fine or a press release of the fact that discrimination has taken

[135] Jacobsen and Rosenberg Khawaja, n 72 above, at 21 fn 58.

[136] O De Schutter, *Belgium Country Report on Measures to Combat Discrimination* (2007) at 90. In Sweden, the DO (Ombudsman against Ethnic Discrimination) follows a similar procedure: see PLS Ramboll Management A/S, n 72 above, at 77.

[137] See the principles of the mediation process as reported in PLS Ramboll Management A/S, n 72 above, at 78.

place and, if relevant, an award of compensation to the victim. The perpetrator is not obliged to accept the 'transaction'. In case of rejection, the HALDE can initiate a criminal prosecution, in place of the public prosecutor, before the criminal court.[138]

3. Quasi-Judicial Functions

Several equality bodies have quasi-judicial functions. While some have the power to issue legally binding rulings, others issue opinions or advisory rulings. In the EU, the Irish Equality Tribunal has become a classical model of a body vested with the power to make binding legally reasoned decisions.[139] In the employment context, the Equality Tribunal may provide for a broad range of sanctions: compensation awards, arrears of payment, ordering employers to take specific courses of action (eg to fix a ramp for a disabled employee), re-instatement and re-engagement.[140] The Dutch Equal Treatment Commission is also a classical model within the EU, but of a body issuing non-binding opinions. The procedure is designed to facilitate access to victims of discrimination. The hearings are staged in a fairly informal setting and a large place is dedicated to informing the parties on the law and its implications.[141] This has proven to be of great value in ensuring a high degree of compliance[142] with the Commission's opinions as well as the substantial legal reasoning supporting them. After the Commission has rendered an opinion, a complaint may still be lodged before the relevant civil or administrative law courts to obtain a binding decision. In court, the Commission's opinion will constitute part of the evidence. Although the *Hoge Raad*, the Dutch Supreme Court, held that considerable weight must be attached to the Commission's opinions,[143] it appears that lower courts do not follow this guidance sufficiently.[144]

4. Investigations and Inquiries

An investigation usually requires a belief that discrimination has taken place and is directed towards a specific party. On the contrary, an inquiry is more general and can concern a whole sector (eg social housing). While the former could lead

[138] S Latraverse, *France Country Report on Measures to Combat Discrimination* (2007) at 67. Note that this system has much in common with the procedures followed by other administrative authorities, which have the power to propose on-the-spot fines for an infringement of criminal law, such as tax, customs, water, or woodland authorities.

[139] See the description in pt 3.B.5 above and in pt 4.B.2 above . In Hungary, the Equal Treatment Authority, established in 2005, also issues legally binding rulings and can impose severe sanctions (see A Kadar, *Hungary Country Report on Measures to Combat Discrimination* (2007) at 77).

[140] Quinlivan, n 68 above, at 73.

[141] For a description of how hearings are conducted, see PLS Ramboll Management A/S, n 72 above, at 86.

[142] Compliance with opinions of the Commission amounted to 84% in the first half of 2004. See Goldschmidt, n 133 above, at 327.

[143] *St Bavo v Gielen*, 13 November 1987, Nederlands Jurisprudentie (1989) 698.

[144] Moon, n 41 above, at 920.

to the issue of a finding of unlawful discrimination, the latter could only lead to recommendations.[145] Investigations and inquiries are valuable tools in situations where an equality body receives many complaints of a similar nature. More especially 'formal "belief" investigations are most effective in situations where the party under investigation is a repeat offender or in situations where prior litigation has been unsuccessful in instigating the desired cultural and organizational change, for example the [British] Commission for Racial Equality's investigation into the Prison Service in 2000'.[146]

As a matter of principle, the investigation ability requires, to be efficient, appropriate means of action to be given to the equality body. For instance, the French High Authority against Discrimination and for Equality may request explanations from any public or private person, including the communication of documents and the hearing of relevant witnesses. In the case of non-cooperation with the investigation services of the High Authority, a court order can be issued.[147]

To date, most experience and expertise has been within the UK (and mostly that of the Commission for Racial Equality[148]) where it appears that the mandate of the equality body in this respect is one of the broadest in the EU. Although investigations and inquiries provide an alternative way for individual complaints to be solved, they are expensive and resource-intensive. As a result, equality bodies use them sparingly and in situations where numerous complaints have been made.[149]

C. Surveys, Reports, Recommendations, and Promoting Good Equality Practices

Apart from providing guidance to victims of discrimination, investigating complaints, and dealing with legal case work more generally, equality bodies also have a duty to tackle situations beyond individual cases. These mainly relate to the role of government advisor and to various means of action to promote equality and raise awareness.

In order to put in place effective measures to counter discrimination and to define priorities, national authorities need to have a clear idea about where and

[145] White, 'Formal Investigations and Inquiries', in Report by Equinet Working Group 2 on Strategic Enforcement, *Strategic Enforcement: Powers and Competences of Equality Bodies* (2006) 25 at 27.

[146] Ibid at 28.

[147] See Latraverse, n 138 above, at 67. On the contrary, in Denmark, the Complaints Committee for Ethnic Equal Treatment 'has no power to demand information from the accused and it cannot hear witnesses'. As a result, many cases cannot be pursued (Holtmaat, *Catalysts for Change?*, n 101 above, at 54).

[148] For a comment on the experience of the Commission for Racial Equality, see Karim, 'A Legal Strategy to Combine and Coordinate Different Tools Available', in J Cormack (ed), Report of the sixth experts' meeting—Towards the Uniform and Dynamic Implementation of EU Anti-Discrimination Legislation: The Role of Specialised Bodies, *Strategic Enforcement and the EC Equal Treatment Directives* (2004) 26 at 33–5.

[149] Moon, n 41 above, at 929.

how discrimination is operating. Targeted research is therefore essential. The kinds of surveys and reports the equality bodies effectively carry out to fulfil the requirement of EU directives vary greatly. Some merely consist in analysing the results of their work (eg presenting statistics on complaints investigated according to the discrimination or the field concerned). Others are more ambitious and look into the impact of anti-discrimination legislation or study the prevalence and forms of discrimination. Universities, research institutes, or *ad hoc* institutions may be commissioned to undertake research or study. In Sweden, for instance, the 2005 survey consists of a general inquiry into the experience of discrimination on the grounds of disability, sexual orientation and/or ethnicity.[150] It was carried out by the Swedish Central Bureau of Statistics on behalf of the three Ombudsmen (HO, HomO, DO).[151] On the basis of reports assessing the existing anti-discrimination legislation, equality bodies are usually eager to make recommendations for new legal provisions and, most often, they issue comments on legislative proposals to promote equality of treatment.[152]

Recommendations are not limited to legislation. When it issues a 'deliberation',[153] the French High Authority against Discrimination and for Equality (HALDE) is concerned to address its recommendation to all relevant stakeholders. For instance, in 2007, HALDE received complaints from eight mothers of school pupils who were prevented from assisting, on a voluntary basis, teachers in school trips because they were wearing the *hidjab*. According to the school concerned, this was contrary to the principle of secularism in public education. On the basis of a legally reasoned examination of the complaints, HALDE considered that the decision of the school were discriminatory. It advised public school boards to revise their internal regulations on this matter. The schools were also asked to inform HALDE on their follow-up to the case within four months. At the same time, HALDE advised the Minister for Public Education on the need to ensure the implementation of the principle of equal treatment in this respect.[154] The wide publicity given to the deliberations of HALDE, their presentation similar to court rulings, and their easy access on-line all favour the building of jurisprudence and the promotion of good equality practices. The same is also true for the opinions of the Dutch Equal Treatment Commission and, to a certain extent, the rulings of the Irish Equality Tribunal.

In addition to standard ways of promoting equality, such as organizing workshops, awareness-raising campaigns, issuing leaflets, and setting up informative web sites, some equality bodies use other tools such as codes of practice, a manual of good practices, or even an assessment of the lawfulness of the practices of

[150] Holtmaat, *Catalysts for Change?*, n 101 above, at 51–3.
[151] See, pt 2.B.2 above.
[152] For examples, see Moon, n 41 above, at 930–2.
[153] On the legal status of the 'deliberations' of the HALDE, see D Borillo (dir), *HALDE: Actions, Limites et Enjeux* (2007) at 53–4.
[154] *Deliberation* No 2007/117, 14 May 2007.

specific organizations when asked to do so.[155] To give some examples, the Dutch Equal Treatment Commission advises hotels, restaurants, and discotheques on the practices that amount to unlawful discrimination against people of a non-Dutch ethnic background. In 2006, the British Commission for Racial Equality issued a statutory Code of Practice on Racial Equality in Housing.[156]

Finally, the application of a positive duty to promote equality is another promising tool that equality bodies are beginning to use. 'A positive duty is a requirement that organizations promote equality and diversity in all aspects of their work, in a manner that involves employees, employers and service-users alike. It is a proactive approach, with an emphasis on achieving results backed by enforcement mechanism and the measurement on outcomes.'[157] Positive duties aim at going beyond the breaking down of visible prejudices to tackle more deep-rooted patterns of exclusion and inequality.

Generally speaking, however, it should be kept in mind that many equality bodies lack social science competence to measure outcomes and they face a shortage of resources which prevent them from going far beyond their core duties of assisting victims of discrimination.[158]

D. ECRI Guidelines

As the EU requirement concerning the mandate of equality bodies is imprecise and leaves many questions open, especially in relation to the nature and the extent of assistance to be provided to victims, the ECRI General Policy Recommendation No 2 on Specialised Bodies to Combat Racism, Xenophobia, Antisemitism and Intolerance at National Level[159] provides a valuable benchmark to construe EU law. Although this recommendation is soft law and prior to the Racial Equality Directive, it codifies best practices in relation to equality bodies by pursuing the same path as this Directive: 'according the highest priority to measures aiming at the full implementation of legislation and policies intended to combat racism, xenophobia, antisemitism and intolerance'. In this way, ECRI, just as the European authorities, is '[c]onvinced that specialised

[155] Moon, n 41 above, at 933.

[156] The adjective 'statutory' refers to the fact that this Code of practice was approved by the Secretary of State and laid before Parliament. Although statutory codes of practice are non-legally binding documents, courts and tribunals are required to take them into account in deciding discrimination cases.

[157] Griffiths, 'Positive Duties to Promote Equality', in Report by Equinet Working Group 2 on Strategic Enforcement, *Strategic Enforcement: Powers and Competences of Equality Bodies* (2006) 43 at 44. The UK is a leading example of the development of positive duties. The Race Relations (Amendment) Act 2000 imposes a positive *general* duty on all authorities to 'have due regard to the need to eliminate unlawful discrimination and promote equality of opportunity and good relations in the carrying out of their functions'. A similar step was made with respect to disability (2006) and Gender (2007).

[158] Holtmaat, *Catalysts for Change?*, n 101 above, at 40.

[159] ECRI, Council of Europe, 13 June 1997, CRI (97) 36.

bodies . . . at national level can make a concrete contribution in a variety of ways to strengthening the effectiveness of the range of measures taken in this field and to providing advice and information to national authorities'.

In order to give equality bodies their full potential, it is therefore worth bearing in mind Principle 3 of ECRI Recommendation No 2 concerning the functions and responsibilities of specialized bodies:

Subject to national circumstances, law and practice, specialised bodies should possess as many as possible of the following functions and responsibilities:

a. to work towards the elimination of the various forms of discrimination set out in the preamble and to promote equality of opportunity and good relations between persons belonging to all the different groups in society;
b. to monitor the content and effect of legislation and executive acts with respect to their relevance to the aim of combating racism, xenophobia, antisemitism and intolerance and to make proposals, if necessary, for possible modifications to such legislation;
c. to advise the legislative and executive authorities with a view to improving regulations and practice in the relevant fields;
d. to provide aid and assistance to victims, including legal aid, in order to secure their rights before institutions and the courts;
e. subject to the legal framework of the country concerned, to have recourse to the courts or other judicial authorities as appropriate if and when necessary;
f. to hear and consider complaints and petitions concerning specific cases and to seek settlements either through amicable conciliation or, within the limits prescribed by the law, through binding and enforceable decisions;
g. to have appropriate powers to obtain evidence and information in pursuance of its functions under f. above;
h. to provide information and advice to relevant bodies and institutions, including State bodies and institutions;
i. to issue advice on standards of anti-discriminatory practice in specific areas which might either have the force of law or be voluntary in their application;
j. to promote and contribute to the training of certain key groups without prejudice to the primary training role of the professional organisations involved;
k. to promote the awareness of the general public to issues of discrimination and to produce and publish pertinent information and documents;
l. to support and encourage organisations with similar objectives to those of the specialised body;
m. to take account of and reflect as appropriate the concerns of such organisations.[160]

On this basis, it has been argued, for instance, that given that the *raison d'être* of national equality bodies in EU law is the promotion of equal treatment, they should have the competence to do things necessary to that end, including taking part in litigation concerning the directives in support of a party or to appear as *amicus curiae* in proceedings on the true meaning of EU equality law.[161]

[160] CRI (97) 36, (author's emphasis).

[161] Barry, 'Interventions and Amicus Curiae Applications', n 125 above, at 41.

5. Equality Bodies and Independence: A Key Question

The EU Directives do not require equality bodies to be independent as such but to work in an independent manner, ie free from governmental or other influence. The explicit use of the word 'independent' three times in the relevant EU provisions[162] highlights the paramount importance of this feature. There are, however, no guidelines or further clarification in the directives. Additional guidance should be found in traditional instruments addressing the issue,[163] chiefly the 'Paris Principles'[164] and their application in other soft law instruments, namely Recommendation No 17 of the UN Committee on the Elimination of Racial Discrimination[165] and General Policy Recommendation No 2 of the ECRI.[166]

The 'Paris Principles' define several main preconditions for the independent and effective operation of human rights bodies: the independence of the body should be guaranteed by a constitutional or legislative framework; the body should have autonomy from the government and be based on pluralism; the body should have a broad mandate, adequate powers of investigation, and sufficient resources.

On this basis, Janet Cormack and Jan Niessen identify three facets of independence: 'first, independence as the authority to implement its mandate free from state interference; second, independence as neutrality, enabling the body to act without being overtly influenced by any interest group; and third, independence in terms of competence and capacity to act.'[167]

A. Independence from Government

Independence from governmental interference requires a constitutional or statutory legal basis to prevent an unsympathetic government from abolishing or weakening the equality body without parliamentary debates. It also calls for detailed legal provisions on mandate, powers, composition, and appointment procedures so as to enable the equality body to act as a 'watchdog' for actions of public authorities and private actors alike. The legal status of the equality body should be independent from governmental structures so as to avoid any subordination to a particular minister. The equality body should have a distinct legal

[162] pt 2 above, nn 35 and 36.

[163] See Cormack and Niessen, 'The Independence of Equality Bodies', 1 European Anti-Discrimination Law Review (2005) 23 at 23–4; Holtmaat, *Catalysts for Change?*, n 101 above, at 33.

[164] n 33 above. See also, Murray, 'National Human Rights Institutions. Criteria and Factors for Assessing their Effectiveness', 25/2 Netherlands Quarterly of Human Rights (2007) 189–220.

[165] General Recommendation No 17, Establishment of National Institutions to Facilitate Implementation of Convention (42nd session, 25 March 1993), UN Doc A/48/18.

[166] n 32 above.

[167] Cormack and Niessen, 'The Independence of Equality Bodies', n 163 above, at 24. See also *Report on Gender Equality Bodies*, n 40 above, at 3–4. PLS Ramboll Management A/S, n 72 above, at 30–57.

personality and be accountable to Parliament. It should report periodically on its actions and favour periodical external evaluation to ensure full transparency.

These are only indicators however; independence is actually very difficult to measure. It should not only be guaranteed formally but also be operative in practice. From the 'influential models' of equality bodies described above in this chapter it appears, for instance, that many are accountable to Government, not to Parliament. And there are concrete issues concerning independence of equality bodies from governmental interference in member states. In Denmark, the Board for Ethnic Equality was closed in 2002 following the withdrawal of its funding.[168] In Italy, there has been severe criticism of the National Office against Racial Discrimination (UNAR) established in 2004, because it is physically located within the Ministry for Equal Opportunities (no adequate premises with a 'neutral face') and under the political responsibility of the Minister for Equal Opportunities. In addition, members of the Council that supervises the work of the Office are all part of the Government.[169] In 2006, there was a serious attack on the independence of the Dutch Equal Treatment Commission (CGB) by the Minister of Integration and Immigration at the time, Rita Verdonk. She publicly disagreed with one of the opinions issued by the Commission. It concerned the case of a Muslim teacher at a school for vocational education who had decided that she would no longer shake hands with men. The school board did not agree, stating that shaking hands was a basic requirement of respectful manners. Both the school and the teacher requested the CGB to investigate whether the school's decision was against the equal treatment law. According to the CGB, the requirement to shake hands with others, irrespective of sex, constitutes indirect discrimination on the ground of religion. It considered that the school's arguments failed to lead to an objective justification.[170] The Minister stated that children should learn what 'respect for both sexes' means and that in the Netherlands respect is shown by shaking hands. She called for the abolition of the CGB. The Minister got considerable support on this issue, both in public debate as well as from Members of Parliament.[171] In 2007, following federal elections in Belgium, the programme of the first coalition government suggested a very serious reduction of the mandate of the Centre for Equal Opportunities and Opposition to Racism.[172] And the French High Authority against Discrimination and for Equality, effective since 2005, had

[168] Cormack and Niessen, 'The Independence of Equality Bodies', n 163 above, at 24.

[169] Holtmaat, *Catalysts for Change?*, n 101 above, at 34–5. There are similar concerns for the Slovenian and Spanish equality bodies (see Bell, Chopin, and Palmer, n 25 above, at 69).

[170] CGB, Opinion 2006–220/221, 7 November 2006.

[171] R Holtmaat, *Netherlands Country Report on Measures to Combat Discrimination* (2007) at 63–4. Note that Rita Verdonk quit the VVD (Conservative Party) in 2007 and officially launched a populist movement, 'Proud of the Netherlands' (*Trots op Nederland*) in April 2008.

[172] The other coalition Government which was set up in the end abandoned this project. In this respect, on 7 March 2008, the Committee on the Elimination of Racial Discrimination 'expresses its satisfaction for the work of the Centre for Equal Opportunity and Action to Combat Racism, especially in bringing cases of racial discrimination to court, *as well as the assurances given by the delegation that there is no intention to narrow its mandate*' (n 64 above, CERD/C/BEL/CO/15, point 5, author's emphasis).

recently to face the process of the reform of the institutions that President Sarkozy is promoting and has potentially to adjust to the creation of a new Ombudsman (*Défenseur des droits*).[173] Serious concerns over the drawbacks of the reform were voiced as it is suspected to weaken the standard of protection previously offered.

B. Independence as Neutrality

This aspect of independence underlines the fact that equality bodies should also be independent from special interests.[174] This means that they should let representative organizations, trade unions, and NGOs act as the voice of their communities[175] and not appear to take sides or to be labelled as supporters of one interest. In practice, the right balance between equality bodies and NGOs is not an easy one to achieve.[176] On the one hand, too many links with NGOs may undermine the equality body's neutrality and objectivity. On the other hand, not enough links with NGOs puts in jeopardy a fruitful collaboration, on assisting victims of discrimination for instance, or a valuable source of information about the prevalence and forms of discrimination.

C. Effective Independence

The competence and capacity of equality bodies to act independently requires appropriate composition, appropriate powers, and sufficient resources.[177] As for *composition*, this particularly entails that the Board (or Commissioners) and the key staff should be chosen with a view to insure pluralism; appointment should be made through strict terms of reference laid down by law; and there should be appropriate safeguards against arbitrary dismissal and arbitrary non-renewal of appointment.[178] This also means that equality bodies should be entrusted with appropriate *powers*. They should not only be provided with sufficient powers to carry out their mandate effectively, but a clear focus should also be put on the need to avoid conflicts between powers that could lead to a confusion of roles.

This issue has been much debated in the Netherlands, where the Equal Treatment Commission has a quasi-judicial role in giving advisory rulings on

[173] In the process of the reform of the institutions in France, a Committee was set up in 2007 (*Comité de reflexion sur la modernisation et le rééquilibrage des institutions*). In its report, it recommends the establishment of an Ombudsman for Human Rights which should take over the mandate of several institutions. As part of a more inclusive Bill, this proposition was presented in Parliament on 23 April 2008 (*Projet de loi constitutionnelle de modernisation des institutions de la Vème République*, No 820) and adopted on 23 July 2008 (*Loi constitutionnelle No 2008–724* which inserts a Title XI *bis* in the Constitution dedicated to a new Ombudsman: the '*Défenseur des droits*').

[174] Cormack and Niessen, 'The Independence of Equality Bodies', n 161 above, at 26.

[175] O'Cinneide, 'The Racial Equality Directive', n 75 above, at 51.

[176] Holtmaat, *Catalysts for Change?*, n 101 above, at 36.

[177] Cormack and Niessen, 'The Independence of Equality Bodies', n 161 above, at 25–7.

[178] This seems not to be the case in Hungary, where the President's appointment of the Equal Treatment Authority may be withdrawn at any time without any justification. See Kadar, n 138 above, at 74.

equality cases and can also assist victims in bringing cases to court. The power to take legal action in court was given to the Dutch Commission to counterbalance the absence of enforceability of its rulings. Actually, since its establishment in 1994, the Commission has never taken any case to court, and does not assist victims, to avoid confusion between its missions.[179] As a matter of principle, '[d]oubts of a body's independence may be raised if, for example, it is acting as investigator of allegations of discrimination one minute, defending victims the next and adjudicating breaches of legislation after that.'[180] The Irish equality bodies avoid such criticism. There is a clear division of functions between the Equality Authority as a proactive body working to promote equality and to assist victims and the Equality Tribunal as a quasi-judicial body processing individual cases and issuing legally-binding decisions. The Dutch Equal Treatment Commission 'also has concerns around drafting codes of conduct or recommendations, and then being asked to interpret and apply these in a case, thereby acting as both judge and legislator (even if the codes of practice are not legally binding)'.[181] From a general point of view '[t]here are sometimes conflicts between the powers of a specialised body such as the roles of adjudicator, promoter of equal treatment and investigator and exercising those powers simultaneously. The competences should be clearly categorised and where necessary on the basis of the separation of powers, some competences should be undertaken externally.'[182]

Adequate financial *resources* are directly linked to staffing, as substantial resources are needed to appoint experienced and trained staff. The Government generally provides most of the budget. Staff shortage is a key difficulty that equality bodies are encountering in many member states. And the allocation of resources is a typical area in which the state may attempt to exert control. This was, for instance, the danger that the Hungarian Equal Treatment Authority was facing, where, at one point, its annual budget, although determined by Parliament, was actually in the hands of the Minister accountable for it who had the right to modify the Authority's budget during the year.[183]

6. Conclusion

Broad EU anti-discrimination law has only developed recently with the impulse of the Treaty of Amsterdam. From an institutional point of view, it has had a major impact,

[179] PLS Ramboll Management A/S, n 72 above, at 84. In the Netherlands, there are other institutions funded by the Government which assist victims, mainly the local Anti-Discrimination Bureaus (Holtmaat, *Netherlands Country Report*, n 169 above, at 63).

[180] Cormack and Niessen, 'The Independence of Equality Bodies', n 163 above, at 27.

[181] Ibid.

[182] J Cormack (ed), *Considerations for Establishing Single Equality Bodies and Integrated Equality Legislation*, n 78 above, at 32.

[183] Kadar, n 139 above, at 74.

being at the source of the setting up of many specialized bodies for the promotion of equal treatment and the reshaping of existent agencies. The spectrum of models of equality bodies found across Europe is large, but there are general trends beyond the differences and a high number of member states go further than EU law standards. First, more grounds of discrimination than race and gender often fall within the mandate of national equality bodies, thus filling the gap of the Employment Equality Directive. In this respect, the tendency is clearly not to multiply agencies, but rather to foster the establishment of a comprehensive equality body allowing a cross-grounds approach. Secondly, the powers granted to equality bodies to combat discrimination are not limited to assisting victims or making surveys, reports, and recommendations. Equality bodies develop alternative dispute resolution mechanisms; investigate complaints; go to court; issue opinions and recommendations; advise governments; assess the practices of public and private stakeholders; launch inquiries; enforce positive duties; highlight good practices; organize training; sustain education programmes; and initiate campaigns promoting equal opportunities.

The EU has undoubtedly given a strong boost to the flourishing and growth of specialized equality bodies across Europe. In some countries these bodies had roots in deep-seated national traditions which greatly influenced the Racial Equality Directive and its focus on enforcement bodies. During the stages of the implementation of EU law, these 'influential models' were of great help to other member states and the added value of the Equinet network was significant in this respect. On the other hand, it is striking to note that this process of cross-fertilization gave fresh impetus to most of these pre-existing models which joined in the momentum that the EU initiated. Following the implementation of the directives, such a process is still ongoing and will hopefully be reinforced by the new European Institute for Gender Equality[184] and the new EU Fundamental Rights Agency.[185]

Although impressive forward steps have been taken to enhance the implementation of the principle of equal treatment in Europe, the challenges that remain are significant. As regards the effectiveness of equality bodies, independence from governmental interference may prove delicate and should be carefully monitored. The issue of resources is also critical and one can only doubt the efficiency of equality bodies which only comprise a handful of staff members. In addition, equality bodies should pay particular attention to the dangers of becoming bogged down in the support of routine anti-discrimination cases. Their mission is not to replicate activities undertaken by individuals but to promote social changes by distinctive means. The focus should be on strategic enforcement and this calls for a definition of priorities and action plans that go far beyond individual litigation.

Brussels, May 2008

[184] n 97 above. [185] See ch 4 in this volume.

6

Minority Rights: Norms and Institutions

Gudmundur Alfredsson

1. Introduction

Persons belonging to minorities and minority groups are entitled to the equal enjoyment of all human rights and to non-discrimination in that enjoyment. This applies across the board to civil, cultural, economic, political, social, and solidarity rights. In addition to the fundamental rules of international human rights law on equal rights and non-discrimination, minority-specific provisions in a number of human rights instruments provide for special measures and special rights with the aim of eliminating discrimination and achieving equal rights and equal protection.[1]

Before the emergence of the United Nations, attempts at intergovernmental regulation of minority rights, notably peace treaties and other bilateral agreements, were not universal in scope. They concerned particular minorities and in most instances provided mere short-term relief, as was also the case for the texts negotiated and supervised by the League of Nations. Nevertheless, the substance of some of these arrangements and their supervisory mechanisms were in some ways ahead of our contemporary system, in particular as regards the role of the Permanent Court of International Justice.[2]

In the initial period after World War II, and with the advancement of international human rights instruments, governments under the auspices of intergovernmental organizations prescribed equal rights for all individuals and prohibited discrimination. However, more often than not, they shied away from special measures or affirmative action, leaving the achievement of equal rights for minorities in doubt. The same is true for group rights. References to preferential

[1] For collections of human rights instruments with minority-specific provisions, see H Hannum, *Documents on Autonomy and Minority Rights* (1993) and P Thornberry, 'Basic Documents on Minorities and Indigenous Peoples' in *World Directory of Minorities* (1997) 706–801. A useful survey of instruments and case law also appears on the website of the Minority Rights Group International at <http://www.minorityrights.org>.

[2] For a summary of these undertakings with extensive bibliographic references, see L B Sohn and T Buergenthal, *International Protection of Human Rights* (1973) 213–335.

treatment and group rights in the early human rights instruments and reports were few and far between; the monitoring mechanisms for existing rights and measures were rarely used effectively for minority causes, and complaints procedures were generally not available to the groups concerned.

The reasons for this neglect can be easily traced to outright opposition or delaying tactics by governments. A primary concern frequently voiced was and often still is the potential disruption or subversion which supposedly would result from an effective set of minority rights. It is often assumed in official circles that additional rights, in particular special arrangements delegating political, economic, and cultural functions to groups with eventual internal border lines, would fuel secessionist claims and thus threaten national unity and territorial integrity. Official objections and hesitations also relate to the perceived sharing of wealth and resources that would flow from the introduction of special measures in order to overcome discriminatory practices against minority persons and groups.

Numerous indications to the contrary have long been overlooked. Existing minority rights regimes have often succeeded in bringing about more harmonious relations between state and groups to the benefit of all parties. By upholding group dignity and preserving identities, the introduction of, and respect for, minority rights has eliminated or at least softened conflict situations; reduced other problems in fields such as education, social services, and health care; increased the productivity of groups and other contributions of theirs to society; and enhanced prosperity and cultural diversity at the national level.

Another reason for the slow progress of minority rights was and continues to be both the absence of effective minority lobbying and the infrequent use of existing international standards and monitoring procedures. It is as if minorities concluded in advance that they will not be any more successful in persuading governments at the international level than they have been at home. A major exception is indigenous peoples, who, by forging links among themselves and by crowding the corridors and conference rooms of the United Nations and the International Labour Organization, have significantly influenced standard-setting to their advantage; as they exist in fewer states and face even greater problems, it has also been easier for them to rally support.

The formulation and adoption of minority rights in international human rights law has therefore progressed at a slow pace. When, in 1948, the General Assembly adopted the Universal Declaration of Human Rights, minority-specific rights did not find their way into the text, but it was decided that the United Nations could not remain indifferent to the 'fate of minorities'.[3]

It was not until the 1980s and early 1990, when the end of the Cold War and a number of highly visible and violent ethnic conflicts and the potential for more violence gave cause for concern, that the United Nations and other international

[3] This was the title of pt C of General Assembly Res 217(III) of 10 December 1948. The Universal Declaration was adopted by the same resolution, in pt A.

organizations started to pay more serious attention to the fate of minorities. In the course of these developments, two human rights studies undertaken under the auspices of the United Nations by Special Rapporteurs Francesco Capotorti[4] and Asbjörn Eide,[5] facilitated and encouraged international attention to and understanding of minority rights.[6] There is now also substantial academic literature on minority rights both in specialized journals[7] and books.[8] The minorities themselves, and non-governmental organizations (NGOs) representing them, have also in the same period, albeit slowly, become more active in international fora.

Today, minority issues are addressed in some 60 international human rights instruments; specialized institutions and forums at regional and international levels have been set up, and the groups and their concerns have become more regular features on international human rights and peace agendas. Among the highlights of recent developments at the international and regional levels are quasi-judicial decisions of international treaty bodies, efforts to engage governments and groups in dialogue, judgments by regional human rights courts, and the strengthening of other monitoring instances. On the other hand, these standard-setting and monitoring undertakings are scattered, often incoherent, and certainly incomplete. States have not even been able or willing to agree on

[4] 'Study on the Rights of Persons belonging to Ethnic, Religious and Linguistic Minorities' (1977), report by Special Rapporteur Francesco Capotorti to the UN Sub-Commission for the Prevention of Discrimination and Protection of Minorities, E/CN4/Sub2/384/Rev1.

[5] 'Study on Constructive National Arrangements for Minorities, report by Special Rapporteur Asbjörn Eide to the UN Sub-Commission for the Prevention of Discrimination and Protection of Minorities, in documents E/CN4/Sub2/1993/34 and Add 1-4. His appointment was preceded by a working paper of Claire Palley, another expert member of the Sub-Commission, entitled 'Possible ways and means to facilitate the peaceful and constructive resolution of situations involving racial, national, religious and linguistic minorities' E/CN4/Sub2/1989/43. In the same spirit and in the same formative period, an expert report entitled 'The Status of Minorities and Ethnic Groups in the Member States of the Council of Europe', prepared by Etienne Grisel Council of Europe document AS/Jur (40) 7 of July 1988, presented an extensive factual and legal analysis of national undertakings.

[6] Another Special Rapporteur of the Sub-Commission, Jose R Martinez Cobo, prepared a report that was part of the evolution in thinking, namely the 'Study of the Problem of Discrimination against Indigenous Populations', E/CN4/Sub2/1986/7 and Add 1-4. Add 4 which includes the conclusions, proposals, and recommendations of the Rapporteur is also available as a UN publication.

[7] Both the International Journal on Minority and Group Rights and the European Yearbook of Minority Issues are published by Brill Academic Publishers. Journal on Ethnopolitics and Minority Issues in Europe is published electronically by the European Centre for Minority Issues and available at <http://www.ecmi.de>. A new bilingual journal, Europäisches Journal für Minderheitenfragen, is published by Springer and first appeared in 2008.

[8] See, eg P Thornberry, *International Law and the Rights of Minorities* (1991); H Hannum, *Autonomy, Sovereignty and Self Determination* (1996); A S Åkermark, *Justifications of Minority Protection in International Law* (1997); K Henrard, *Devising an Adequate System of Minority Protection. Individual Human Rights, Minority Rights and the Right to Self-Determination* (2000); P Thornberry and M A Martín Estíbanez, *Minority Rights in Europe* (2004); S Kay, *Democracy, Minorities and International Law* (2005); N Ghanea and A Xanthaki (eds) *Minorities, Peoples and Self-Determination* (2005); and M Weller, *Universal Minority Rights, A Commentary on the Jurisprudence of International Courts and Treaty Bodies* (2007).

the definition of the term 'minority', and group rights remain controversial. Furthermore, the ongoing reform of the United Nations human rights programme may undo accomplishments made, insofar as some bodies have been replaced with what seem to be weaker fora.[9] The interest of states in minority rights may have declined together with a perceived reduction in the risk of violent conflicts today compared to the 1990s.

After describing some of the human rights-related problems facing minorities and identifying the intergovernmental organizations involved in the promotion and protection of minority rights, this chapter sets forth elements for a definition of beneficiaries, outlines the availability of individual and group rights, and describes the main rules of human rights law concerning the equal enjoyment of all human rights, non-discrimination in that enjoyment, and the special measures for minorities considered necessary for achieving equal enjoyment in fact. The chapter then continues with a description of monitoring procedures and bodies, both those for human rights in general and minority rights in particular, as used by international organizations to ensure state compliance with the rights of minorities. Finally, the author attempts to evaluate the many pieces of the minority rights picture in order to establish whether one can talk about institutional trends as far as minority rights are concerned.

2. Human Rights and Security Problems

Notwithstanding the basic human rights standards as well as minority-specific provisions in the international human rights instruments, persons belonging to minorities and minority groups frequently face discrimination in the enjoyment of human rights. There is an abundance of evidence, in UN and NGO reports as well as national and international statistics, which shows that, albeit to varying degrees, such discrimination exists in practically all states in terms of, for example, access to and exercise of the rights to education, employment, political representation, and the administration of justice.

Compared with the rest of a state's population, again to varying degrees, persons belonging to minorities often receive less education, both in terms of quality and number of school years, and the proportion of minority graduates from universities or other institutions of higher learning is low. Minority persons are more likely to be unemployed and when they are employed, their average income is lower and they are less likely to be promoted to positions of management or influence. Minority persons are frequently underrepresented in political bodies, in the civil service, in the police, and in the military; they are often over-represented in prisons and, again compared with the majority population, they often find

[9] See pts 10 (International Monitoring) and 11 (Institutional Trends) below.

themselves, even in the middle of affluent societies, living in poor housing with inadequate availability and quality of health care and social services.

The frequent and consistent occurrence of these and other discriminatory practices makes them appear as patterns that often lead to or are combined with indignities and threats to identities and cultures. Even genocide and ethnic cleansing occur in this modern age. Some minorities, such as the Roma in several European countries,[10] frequently live in conditions of poverty and misery that one would not expect to see on a democratic and rich continent.

As minorities gain better knowledge of their rights, however, through education, training, and international exposure, they are raising their expectations and demands when it comes to equal opportunities and equal treatment at the national level, and thus are presenting more and more claims to international and regional organizations.

Much of the increased attention to minority rights in the last two decades has been security-oriented. Violent ethnic and religious conflicts have multiplied, and other potential crisis situations have seemed imminent. Human rights monitoring can constitute an excellent tool for early warning, and preventive action is certainly more desirable and less costly than reaction and reconstruction after violence has erupted. Respect for human rights, including minority rights, is considered one method of conflict prevention.

In 1992, in a report entitled *An Agenda for Peace*, the UN Secretary General observed, in relation to the prevention of ethnic conflicts: 'One requirement for solutions to these problems lies in commitment to human rights with a special sensitivity to those of minorities, whether ethnic, religious, social or linguistic.... [T]he increasingly effective machinery of the United Nations dealing with human rights, should enhance the situation of minorities as well as the stability of States.'[11] Many human rights instruments expressly acknowledge the link between conflict prevention and minority protection, and the establishment of an institution like the OSCE High Commissioner on National Minorities with a mandate to provide early warning and to seek to prevent violent conflicts is a model of what can and should be done.[12] Respect for minority rights can equally play a significant role in the management and resolution of violent conflicts and in the restoration of peace after conflicts.

The protection of cultural diversity is a further international concern that has a direct bearing on minority rights. Unfortunately, it seems that states in their national practice often appear to completely or partially forget this minority dimension or intentionally overlook it. Still, the relevant international instruments certainly acknowledge that minority cultures are a rich part of this diversity and that all cultures are valuable and are entitled to dignity. In 2005, UNESCO

[10] Jean-Pierre Liégeois, Roma in Europe, Council of Europe, 2008.
[11] A/47/277—S/24111, 17 June 1992, para 18.
[12] See pt 11 (Institutional Trends) below.

adopted the Convention on the Protection and Promotion of the Diversity of Cultural Expression. In Article 2, paragraph 3, the Convention spells out that the 'protection and promotion of the diversity of cultural expressions presuppose the recognition of equal dignity of and respect for all cultures, including the cultures of persons belonging to minorities and indigenous peoples'.[13]

The Human Rights Committee has also reminded states that the minority rights provision in Article 27 of the International Covenant on Civil and Political Rights imposes specific protection obligations on states parties.

> The protection of these rights is directed towards ensuring the survival and continued development of the cultural, religious and social identity of the minorities concerned, thus enriching the fabric of society as a whole. Accordingly, the Committee observes that these rights must be protected as such and should not be confused with other personal rights conferred on one and all under the Covenant. States parties, therefore, have an obligation to ensure that the exercise of these rights is fully protected and they should indicate in their reports the measures they have adopted to this end.[14]

Even those states which have positive human rights records react defensively to the full implementation of international standards on minority rights. This is so even if the minority-specific standards and the corresponding monitoring methods are still very cautious in their approach and are somewhat imperfect or insufficient when measured against the basic human rights norms concerning equal rights and non-discrimination. Furthermore, while democracy is integral to human rights, majority rule is not necessarily friendly to, or understanding of, minority needs. Experience at the national level shows that democratic countries need to enshrine minority rights, preferably at the constitutional level, with legislative guarantees and accessible remedies that are consistent with international standards.

3. The Organizations and the Instruments

Minority rights are part and parcel of human rights. All international human rights instruments, both treaties and declarations, are therefore applicable to persons belonging to minorities. In addition, several human rights instruments and a few specialized texts contain minority-specific language.

Several intergovernmental organizations are involved with minorities through standard-setting, monitoring and/or dialogue. For the UN system, consistent with the mainstreaming of human rights, minority rights are not only present in the human rights programme of the parent organization, but also in the work of other bodies such as United Nations Development Programme (UNDP)

[13] Entered into force 18 March 2007, for the full text see <http://www.unesco.org>.

[14] General Comment No 23, para 9, in UN document CCPR/C/21/Rev1/Add1.

(minorities in the development process), UNICEF (minority children), and UNHCR (the frequency of minority persons as asylum seekers, refugees, and internally displaced persons). This engagement with minorities is even stronger at some of the specialized agencies, such as the International Labour Organization (ILO) (non-discrimination in the work place), UNESCO (cultural diversity, non-discrimination, and special measures in education) and World Intellectual Property Organization (WIPO) (traditional knowledge), that have adopted relevant standards and/or undertaken monitoring and cooperative efforts.[15]

The best known and most used of the minority-specific provisions is Article 27 of the International Covenant on Civil and Political Rights: 'In those States in which ethnic, religious or linguistic minorities exist, persons belonging to such minorities shall not be denied the right, in community with the other members of their group, to enjoy their own culture, to profess and practice their own religion, or to use their own language.' Interpreting and in some respects expanding on Article 27, the Human Rights Committee has adopted the aforementioned General Comment No 23. Other instruments with minority-specific language are the International Convention on the Elimination of All Forms of Racial Discrimination,[16] the Convention on the Rights of the Child,[17] the Declaration on the Elimination of All Forms of Intolerance and of Discrimination Based on Religion or Belief,[18] and the UNESCO Convention against Discrimination in Education.[19]

In 1992 the General Assembly of the United Nations adopted a Declaration on the Rights of Persons belonging to National or Ethnic, Religious and Linguistic Minorities.[20] It was in a follow-up to this Declaration that the Working Group on Minorities (WGM) was established in 1995.[21] Ten years later the WGM adopted a detailed and influential commentary on a relatively short and weak Declaration.[22] After more than two decades of effort involving direct and active participation of indigenous organizations, the UN General Assembly in 2007 adopted a Declaration on the Rights of Indigenous Peoples.[23] In addition to recognizing the need for special protection of indigenous peoples, the Declaration also confirms their collective right to lands and natural resources.

[15] See <http://www.undp.org>, <http://www.unicef.org>, <http://www.unhcr.org>, <http://www.ilo.org>, <http://www.unesco.org>, and <http://www.wipo.int>. See also below in relation to standards and monitoring.

[16] 660 UNTS 195.

[17] 1577 UNTS 3.

[18] A/36/684 (1981).

[19] 429 UNTS 93.

[20] A/47/135 (1992).

[21] A subsidiary to the Sub-Commission on Prevention of Discrimination and Protection of Minorities, later the Sub-Commission on the Promotion and Protection of Human Rights. See T Hadden, 'The United Nations Working Group on Minorities', 14 *International Journal on Minority and Group Rights* (2007) 285–97. The Working Group had its last session in 2006 and was subsequently abolished. See also below on Institutional Trends.

[22] In UN Doc E/CN4/Sub2/AC5/2005/2. The chief author of the Commentary was Asbjörn Eide, the founding Chairman/Rapporteur of the WGM.

[23] A/61/295 (2007).

Regional organizations are also engaged in minority rights issues, especially in Europe. The Council of Europe has adopted the European Charter on Regional or Minority Languages[24] and the Framework Convention for the Protection of National Minorities (FCNM).[25] Among major texts originating from the Organization for Cooperation and Security in Europe (OSCE) with a minority rights focus are the Document from the 1990 Copenhagen Meeting of the OSCE Conference on the Human Dimension and the 1991 Report from an Expert Meeting in Geneva. A specialized institution, the OSCE High Commissioner on National Minorities, was established in 1992 with a mandate to identify and seek early resolution of ethnic tensions that might endanger peace, stability, or friendly relations between OSCE states.[26] In pursuing this role, several detailed minority rights instruments have been adopted under the auspices of the HCNM, such as the Hague, Oslo, and Lund recommendations on educational rights, linguistic rights, and political rights respectively.[27]

4. Definition of the Beneficiaries

Despite decades of work by international organizations, no universally accepted definition of the term 'minority' has been adopted. Many governments do not really want a definition so that they are able to label groups to their liking; lengthy definition debates have also served as a delaying tactic to avoid substantive issues.[28] Nevertheless, much of the time it is self-evident which groups constitute minorities. Most of the abundant definition proposals have common components. If one adds national and international practices, the necessary elements of a definition emerge quite clearly. The common components of the definition of a 'minority' are certain objective characteristics, self-identification, numbers, and long-term presence in the territory concerned.

On the basis of these four definition elements, this author estimates that worldwide there exist 12–14,000 minority groups amounting to a population of about 1.5 billion.[29] In other words, one is talking about very substantial numbers or some 25 percent of the world's population!

[24] ETS 148. [25] ETS 157.

[26] See pt 11 (Institutional Trends) below.

[27] For the texts of these and other recommendations adopted under the auspices of the High Commissioner, see the website of the HCNM at <http://www.osce.org/hcnm>.

[28] The UN Secretariat issued a lengthy compilation of definition proposals made over a 60-year period, E/CN4/1987/WG5/WP1. See also O Andrysek, 'Report on the Definition of Minorities', the Netherlands Institute of Human Rights, SIM Special No 8, 1989; and G Alfredsson, 'Minorities, Indigenous and Tribal Peoples, and Peoples: Definitions of Terms as a Matter of International Law', in N Ghanea and A Xantahi (eds), *Minorities, Peoples and Self-Determination. Essays in Honour of Patrick Thornberry* (2004) 163–72.

[29] For a demonstration of the sheer variety of groups see R Stavenhagen (ed), *World Guide of Ethnic Minorities and Indigenous Peoples* (1988). *A World Directory of Minorities* (1997) prepared by the Minority Rights Group International is now available at <http://www.minorityrights.org>.

1. Certain objective characteristics: The objective characteristics relate to joint affiliation or affinity of the members of a minority as far as national or ethnic origin, culture, language, and/or religion are concerned. This type of listing appears in some of the international instruments, even in the title of the above-mentioned UN Declaration on the Rights of Persons belonging to National or Ethnic, Religious and Linguistic Minorities from 1992. The reliance in European instruments on the term 'national minorities' does not change or limit this element; while different interpretations have been attached to the expression 'national minorities', it should be used by and large to cover the same groups as the international standards. National or ethnic origin, culture, language, and/or religion are presumably the only objective characteristics involved; political minorities and sexual minorities do not need the type of protection often offered by minority rights (from minority schools to land and autonomy) and are therefore not covered by the minority-specific standards described in this chapter. Blood lines are no longer a favoured component of the objective characteristics. Adopted children, spouses, and other members of a minority community, assuming that they have acquired the language, joined the religion, or otherwise picked up group characteristics, should not be excluded from the enjoyment of minority rights. This observation is of course closely related to the next element that has been steadily gaining in significance.
2. Self-identification: The subjective element, or self-identification is now acknowledged as part of the minority definition. This is the case for ILO Convention No 169 concerning Indigenous and Tribal Peoples in Independent Countries, (Article 1, paragraph 2), and UN Special Rapporteur Francesco Capotorti also recommended adherence to this element.[30] It presumably operates at two levels: an individual decides whether he/she is a member of a minority; and the group must accept the individual concerned on the basis of the characteristics. It must do so in a non-arbitrary fashion, and it must be possible to subject the group's decision to independent review.
3. Numbers: A minority group must constitute less than one half of the state population. This numerical element is inherent in the term and almost unnecessary for the purposes of the definition. Several countries are composed of minorities only. Provided none of the groups, assuming they meet the other criteria, makes up more than 50 per cent of the populations, all would be entitled to minority protection. If a minority group constitutes more than 50 per cent of the population, it is not in need of minority rights. An actual minority cannot designate and treat the majority as if it were a minority, as occurred in South Africa during the apartheid regime; in this type of situation the human

Neither listing comes close to being exhaustive; it is remarkable that the human rights profession has not as yet produced more comprehensive directories.

[30] n 4 above, paras 567–8.

rights solution rests on respect for human rights for all, including political representation.

4. Long-term presence in the territory concerned. The time element is perhaps the most difficult and at the same time controversial component of a minority definition, that is, the requirement that a minority must have a long-term, presence in the territory concerned. Refugees, migrant workers, immigrants, and other non-nationals are entitled to human rights, on an equal footing and without discrimination (with certain exceptions such as some political rights). Indeed, several separate instruments have been adopted to protect aliens, such as the 1951 UN Convention relating to the Status of Refugees,[31] the 1967 Protocol relating to the Status of Refugees,[32] and the Convention for the Protection of Migrant Workers and Members of their Families,[33] but these population groups do not immediately achieve minority status although many of the rights would be overlapping.[34] At some point in time, however, newcomers to a country become minorities. Some states would like to see four to five generations pass before minority status can be achieved (for example Hungary and Sweden), while other countries have been much more generous (for example the United Kingdom). In the opinion of this author, a reasonable turning point occurs when the individuals concerned identify more closely with the new territory or country (where they now live) than the old territory or country (where the parents or grandparents came from). We are talking about the time it takes for offspring to go through the school system, that is, one or two generations.

Other definitional elements have been proposed and some are even used by states at the national level, but they are not reflected in the international instruments or in case law. If groups in a given country meet the definition elements listed above (1 through 4), states should generally not have a discretion over the recognition or acceptance of groups as minorities. The existence of a minority is a question of fact, not of law or government recognition. This was stated by the Permanent Court of International Justice[35] and has been reiterated by the Human Rights Committee in General Comment No 23. Acceptance of minority status by governments can be a positive step, such as for example, in official lists of minority groups within a country. But these should not constitute exhaustive listings, since leaving this type of authority with states easily opens the door to abuse, and non-acceptance should not result in loss of minority status if the above-mentioned definition criteria are met.

[31] 189 UNTS 137. [32] 606 UNTS 267.

[33] GA Res 45/158, 18 December 1990, entered into force 1 July 2003.

[34] It is to be noted that the approach of the Human Rights Committee in General Comment No 23 on Art 27 of the ICCPR is more open-ended and inclusive, see n 14 above.

[35] Greco–Bulgarian 'Communities' Case , PCIJ, Ad Op of 31 July 1930 at 22.

Furthermore, a state should not be relieved of its minority rights responsibilities by denying citizenship to members of legitimate groups on an arbitrary or discriminatory basis.[36] According to the Human Rights Committee, the terms employed in Article 27 of the ICCPR:

> indicate that the individuals designed to be protected need not be citizens of the State party. In this regard, the obligations deriving from article 2.1 are also relevant, since a State party is required under that article to ensure that the rights protected under the Covenant are available to all individuals within its territory and subject to its jurisdiction, except rights which are expressly made to apply to citizens, for example, political rights under article 25. A State party may not, therefore, restrict the rights under article 27 to its citizens alone.[37]

Similarly calling groups by other names, such as cohabiting nations or nationalities, is insufficient to deprive them of minority protection. Vulnerability or non-dominance have also been suggested as definition elements, but they should not really be part thereof; instead they relate to the moment when minority rights become relevant or not. It goes without saying that minority groups are not homogenous;[38] some members face multiple discrimination due to sex, class, disability, or other factors.

Indigenous groups share the above-mentioned definition elements, but the time element refers to original settlements, from before the arrival of later settlers. In addition, the cultural elements stand in strong contrast, sharper than that of minorities, to those of the majority population and thus lead to greater vulnerability. Hence, indigenous peoples are entitled, not only to all minority rights, but also additional protection of, in particular, land and resources that form the cornerstone of their culture and way of life. The two main instruments are the ILO Convention No 169 concerning Indigenous and Tribal Peoples in Independent Countries and the UN Declaration on the Rights of Indigenous Peoples which, after some two decades of drafting, the General Assembly adopted in 2007.[39]

The terms 'minorities', 'indigenous peoples', and 'tribal peoples' are often used interchangeably when claims are set forth. Factual circumstances and applicable laws are subject to constant change. Indeed, it would seem that a sliding scale should apply rather than sharply drawn lines between the different groupings. To mention but one example, some of the Roma in Europe may qualify as both

[36] A Eide, 'Minority Rights of Non-Citizens' and G Alfredsson, 'Citizenship and the Definition of the Term "Minority"' in RF Jörgensen & K Slavensky (eds), *Implementing Human Rights. Essays in Honour of Morten Kjaerum* (2007) 372–86 and 363–71.

[37] General Comment No 23, para 5.1.

[38] As pointed out by the NGO, Minority Rights Group International on its website at <http://www.minorityrights.org>.

[39] n 23 above. The text has been referred to as the Daes Declaration in honour of the Chairman/Rapporteur of the UN Working Group on Indigenous Populations for much of the drafting period. For her recollections of this work, see Erica-Irene A Daes, *Indigenous Peoples. Keepers of Our Past—Custodians of Our Future* (IWGIA, Copenhagen, 2008).

minorities and tribal peoples.[40] The designation as tribal would raise the issue of land rights under ILO Convention No 169 to the degree that groups who are still nomadic rely on and have historically relied on campsites for their way of life. The land rights in question would be comparable to seasonal user rights, but the same conclusion could be reached with reference to the case law of the Human Rights Committee inasmuch as the term 'culture' in Article 27 of the ICCPR has been interpreted to cover the material base necessary for maintaining a minority culture.[41]

It is important to distinguish 'minorities' from 'peoples' or nations. As with the term 'minority', there is no universally accepted definition of the term 'a people'. The term appears in many human rights instruments and resolutions, notably those concerning external self-determination and political decolonization. In practice, the term 'people' has been applied to the populations of territorial or administrative entities, within some sort of acknowledged borders, more often than not without regard to the ethnic composition and cultural characteristics of the inhabitants. Minorities, on the other hand, are as a general rule not entitled to the right of self-determination, at least not its external dimension.[42]

Groups which are incorrectly reduced to minorities, or systematically denied political representation or otherwise subjected to massive rights violations, may exceptionally qualify for external self-determination.[43] However, in general it can be stated that the very idea of minority rights, as regulated and pursued by the international community, implies continued sovereignty and territorial integrity of states. In grey or disputed areas, delimitation of what groups constitute a minority will be left to state practice, as with the implementation of human rights in general. Such determinations must, however, be subject to supervision or monitoring by international organizations in accordance with existing standards and procedures.

5. Individual and Group Rights

In addition to the definition question, another area of divided opinion in the field of minority rights is that of individual and group rights. For good reasons: as individuals are usually the main victims, most international human rights

[40] The ILO and the World Bank employ the term 'tribal peoples' in their instruments and texts. Elsewhere, at the United Nations, depending on factual circumstances, a tribal people may constitute either a minority or an indigenous people.

[41] General Comment No 23, n 14 above.

[42] See pt 8 below—Special Measures in the Field of Political Rights.

[43] As indicated in the 1970 UN Declaration on Principles of International Law Concerning Friendly Relations and the 1993 Vienna Declaration and Programme of Action of the World Conference on Human Rights. See also the third preambular paragraph of the Universal Declaration of Human Rights. Kosovo may be such an example, but some of the recognitions granted so far may rely more on geopolitical considerations than minority rights.

instruments emphasize the rights of individuals or persons belonging to the minority group. Some texts declare that individuals enjoy minority rights in community with other members of their group, thus acknowledging a group element.

Article 27 of the ICCPR addresses 'persons belonging to minorities', but it goes beyond mere individual rights and recognizes the necessity of a group element by referring to these persons enjoying the rights 'in community with the other members of their group'. The Optional Protocol complaints procedure is open only to individuals, but in a 1990 case the Human Rights Committee may have opened the door for group leaders by entertaining their appeals on behalf of the group concerning group rights.[44] In General Comment No 23, the Committee stated: 'Although the rights protected under article 27 are individual rights, they depend in turn on the ability of the minority group to maintain its culture, language or religion.'[45]

A number of instruments provide for group rights and group access in order to ensure equal rights and effectiveness. Some instruments are straightforward in their establishment of rights or measures for groups, such as the International Convention on the Elimination of All Forms of Racial Discrimination, including its Article 14 which empowers groups to submit complaints to the monitoring committee body. The UNESCO Declaration on Race and Racial Prejudice contains a well-known phrase: 'All individuals and groups have the right to be different, to consider themselves as different and to be regarded as such.'[46]

In their monitoring work and dialogue functions at the United Nations, the WGM and now the new Minorities Forum,[47] the Independent Expert on Minority Issues and the Special Rapporteurs on Racism and Racial Discrimination, on Religious Intolerance, and on the Rights of Indigenous Peoples, work with group representatives as well as individual group members. In terms of preventing violent ethnic or religious conflicts, contact with the group is unavoidable.

Group rights for minorities are necessary to guarantee a number of rights, including those to identity, culture, language, education, land, and political participation, not least self-government, to approximate circumstances enjoyed by the majority, to allow individuals to draw on the strength of their groups, and to facilitate interaction of groups with the states in which they live and with international organizations. It is particularly important in the security context that, for the prevention and resolution of violent conflicts, international standards concerning both individual and group rights be respected. The group is a necessary and inevitable partner. If group rights are rejected and preferential treatment denied, discriminatory patterns will persist and the equal enjoyment of human rights by minorities will never be realized.

44 See *Bernard Ominayak, Chief of the Lubicon Lake Band v Canada* HRC No 167/1984.

45 n 14 above, para 6.2.

46 E/CN4/Sub2/1982/2/Add1, Annex V, 27 November 1982.

47 For further elaboration of these institutions, see pt 11 (Institutional Trends) below.

6. Equal Enjoyment and Non-Discrimination

International human rights law establishes equal enjoyment for everyone of all human rights and prohibits discrimination in that enjoyment. Article 1 of the Universal Declaration of Human Rights, provides that 'We are all born free and equal in dignity and rights.' Repeated stipulations in the UN Charter (Articles 1 and 55), the Universal Declaration (in addition to Article 1, see Articles 2, 7, 10, 16, 21, 23, and 26), in the two International Human Rights Covenants, in a large number of other treaties and declarations, in general comments by the treaty bodies, and in case law and monitoring reports demonstrate clearly that the rules on equal enjoyment and non-discrimination are fundamental to international and regional human rights law. Some of these widely ratified treaties are of a general character; others focus on particular grounds, such as racial or sex discrimination, discrimination on grounds of disability, or in employment and education.

The Human Rights Committee observed in its General Comment No 18 on non-discrimination:

> that the term 'discrimination' as used in the Covenant should be understood to imply any distinction, exclusion, restriction or preference which is based on any ground such as race, colour, sex, language, religion, political or other opinion, national or social origin, property, birth or other status, and which has the purpose or effect of nullifying or impairing the recognition, enjoyment or exercise by all persons, on an equal footing, of all rights and freedoms.[48]

The Committee added that 'equality' does not necessarily mean identical treatment. In certain instances, groups may be treated differently for purposes legitimate under the Covenant, such as achieving equal rights, if the action is reasonable and objective.[49]

The grounds on which discrimination is prohibited may differ from one instrument to another, but the repeated references to race, culture, colour, language, religion, and national and ethnic origins clearly cover the objective characteristics of the minority definition as well as situations normally faced by minorities. The non-discrimination clauses, and the equal enjoyment rule on which they rest, extend to every sphere of human rights including, obviously, education, language, labour law, democracy, and the administration of justice. The stipulation of equal rights and non-discrimination in law, even constitutional law, alone is not enough for states to fulfil international standards; the law must be effectively implemented and equal rights and non-discrimination must exist both in law and in fact.

In addition, all members of minorities are guaranteed equality before the law and equal protection of the law, equality before the courts, and equal access to

[48] CCPR General Comment No 18 para 7.

[49] Ibid, paras 7, 8, and 13.

public services. These equal rights clauses extend equally to civil and political rights and economic, social, and cultural rights, although electoral rights may be restricted to citizens.

In its General Comment No 23 on Article 27 of the ICCPR, the Human Rights Committee thus made a clear distinction between:

> the rights protected under article 27 from the guarantees under articles 2.1 and 26. The entitlement, under article 2.1, to enjoy the rights under the Covenant without discrimination applies to all individuals within the territory or under the jurisdiction of the State whether or not those persons belong to a minority. In addition, there is a distinct right provided under article 26 for equality before the law, equal protection of the law, and non-discrimination in respect of rights granted and obligations imposed by the States. It governs the exercise of all rights, whether protected under the Covenant or not, which the State party confers by law on individuals within its territory or under its jurisdiction, irrespective of whether they belong to the minorities specified in article 27 or not.[50]

As a result of the provisions of the UN Charter and the Universal Declaration and on the basis of international custom (with ample evidence of long-standing state practice accepted as law), all countries are without a doubt bound by the equal rights and non-discrimination provisions of international law. States must ensure the equal enjoyment of all human rights by minorities living within their borders and by persons belonging to these minorities, and they must prohibit and eliminate discrimination against them. It is evident, however, that equal rights and non-discrimination are slow in bringing about the desired results; that is, where special measures and special rights enter the picture.

7. Special Measures and Special Rights

In the face of historical and modern-day discrimination against minorities, the rules in the international human rights instruments on equal enjoyment and non-discrimination have frequently been complemented by what UN and European human rights instruments variously call special, positive, and/or concrete measures.[51] In the literature and in state practice, the measures may be referred to as preferential treatment, positive or reverse discrimination, or affirmative action, but they serve the same or similar functions.

Special measures and special rights are intended to accelerate the realization of equal enjoyment and the elimination of discrimination, by placing minorities as well as their members in a position equal to or comparable with the rest of the state's population or at least in approximate circumstances which the majority often takes for granted. By instituting special measures and special rights, the

[50] n 14 above, para 4.

[51] K Myntti, 'The Prevention of Discrimination v. Protection of Minorities—With Particular Reference to 'Special Measures', 2 *Baltic Yearbook of International Law* (2002), 199–226.

international instruments recognize that equal enjoyment under the law and the prohibition of discrimination are not enough; equal enjoyment in fact must also be achieved.

Special measures and special rights do not constitute privileges; like non-discrimination they are rooted in the rule of equal enjoyment of all human rights. A group and its members cannot be really equal to the majority population unless and until equal conditions prevail; even then the group may continue to be disadvantaged because of the majority's dominance in national life.

The state usually has choices in terms of which special measures should be introduced. The measures may involve setting targets, establishing quotas, providing financial or other incentives, engaging the groups in consultation, and/or obtaining group consent. Whatever the choice(s) made with respect to special measures, the state should not only allow but also fund and otherwise facilitate and support such approaches on a basis equal and proportional to the services provided to the rest of the population. The test is whether equal enjoyment of the rights concerned, to the degree possible, has been achieved in actual fact (aim and result).

Special measures and special rights extend to civil, cultural, economic, political, and social rights in matters that are particularly relevant to the identity and existence of a minority group. They include allowing minority persons and/or groups to use their own languages, to identify themselves with their own personal and group names and to have these recognized, to run their own schools, to access and benefit from other cultural and religious institutions set up and services provided by the group for the group, and to participate in the political and economic affairs of states. The prohibition of hate speech and of incitement to discrimination and violence are also included.

Article 27 of the ICCPR is the best known of the minority-specific provisions. Notwithstanding the negative formulation of Article 27, 'persons belonging to minorities shall not be denied the rights . . .', it should nowadays be read to positively imply the obligation of states to provide special measures of protection.[52] In the words of the Human Rights Committee:

> Although article 27 is expressed in negative terms, that article, nevertheless, does recognize the existence of a 'right' and requires that it shall not be denied. Consequently, a State party is under an obligation to ensure that the existence and the exercise of this right are protected against their denial or violation. Positive measures of protection are, therefore, required not only against the acts of the State party itself, whether through its legislative, judicial or administrative authorities, but also against the acts of other persons within the State party.[53]

In protecting minority characteristics and cultural, religious, and linguistic activities, Article 27 reaffirms, strengthens, and adds to the equal enjoyment of the

[52] To this effect, see General Comment No 23 of the Human Rights Committee, paras 6.1, 6.2, 7, and 9, n 14 above.

[53] Ibid, para 6.1.

rights enumerated in the other articles of the two Covenants, such as the rights of individuals to take part in cultural life and to profess and practice a religion. According to the Human Rights Committee, in order to maintain the ability of a minority group to maintain its culture, language or religion, positive measures by states may be:

> necessary to protect the identity of a minority and the rights of its members to enjoy and develop their culture and language and to practice their religion,...it has to be observed that such positive measures must respect the provisions of articles 2.1 and 26 of the Covenant both as regards the treatment between different minorities and the treatment between the persons belonging to them and the remaining part of the population. However, as long as those measures are aimed at correcting conditions which prevent or impair the enjoyment of the rights guaranteed under article 27, they may constitute a legitimate differentiation under the Covenant, provided that they are based on reasonable and objective criteria.[54]

The ICCPR and its first Optional Protocol are of particular importance because the Human Rights Committee, composed of independent experts who monitor compliance with the Covenant, has made significant contributions to the jurisprudence on minority rights. The Human Rights Committee has adopted some 20[55] Optional Protocol cases concerning the rights of minorities, including several on indigenous peoples.[56] Its jurisprudence is reinforced by General Comment No 23 that the Committee has adopted on Article 27.[57]

The case law is noteworthy for the progressive interpretation of the term 'culture' in Article 27. The Committee has found that traditional economic activities[58] and land rights,[59] if they are essential for the cultural life of an ethnic community, may fall under Article 27. While these cases on land and traditional economic activities have dealt with the rights of indigenous peoples, it is entirely possible that certain minorities could benefit in the same manner. As already suggested above, this could have application to the Roma in connection with their traditional way of life and historical camp sites, as far as seasonal users' rights are concerned.[60]

The UNESCO Convention against Discrimination in Education provides in Article 2(b) that the 'establishment or maintenance, for religious or linguistic

[54] Ibid, para 6.2.

[55] That is a strikingly low number considering the number of ratifications of both the Covenant and its first Optional Protocol.

[56] For surveys of international case law, see G Pentassuglia, 'Inside and Outside the European Convention: The Cases of Minorities Compared', 6 *Baltic Yearbook of International Law* (2006), 263–91; A Moucheboeuf, *Minority Rights Jurisprudence Digest* (2006); and M Weller (ed), Universal Minority Rights, n 8 above .

[57] See General Comment No 23 of the Human Rights Committee, paras 3.2 and 7 and the cases quoted there, n 14 above.

[58] See, eg *Ivan Kitok v Sweden* HRC No 197/1985.

[59] *Bernard Ominayak, Chief of the Lubicon Lake Band v Canada* HRC No 167/1984.

[60] See pt 4 (Definition of the Beneficiaries) above.

reasons, of separate educational systems or institutions' shall not be deemed to constitute discrimination.[61] The logical corollary of this position is set out in Article 5(c), 'It is essential to recognize the right of members of national minorities to carry on their own educational activities, including the maintenance of schools and, depending on the educational policy of each State, the use or the teaching of their own language...'

Special measures relating to minority education are widely accepted but, as in the UNESCO Convention, they are as a rule qualified by references to the best interests of the child, the quality of the education offered, the necessity of learning the majority language, and awareness of majority cultures so as to avoid isolation of the groups concerned. As to the funding of minority schools, this author would argue that states should carry the costs, and as a minimum contribute the same amount per student as they provide for public schools; anything less would amount to discrimination. The argument should probably be extended to the provision of additional funding if such contributions from states are necessary for achieving equal enjoyment of the right to education.

The International Convention on the Elimination of All Forms of Racial Discrimination provides in clear language (in Article 2(b)) that, when necessary, states shall take 'special and concrete measures to ensure the adequate development and protection of certain racial groups or individuals belonging to them' in order to guarantee the full and equal enjoyment of all human rights. The Convention also states (in Article 1.4) that such measures are not to be considered discriminatory.

Generally, special measures for the groups and their members are thought of as temporary; they should no longer be necessary when discrimination has been eliminated and equal rights have been realized. Some special measures, however, such as those relating to minority languages, cultures, schools, political participation at the national and local levels, will require prolonged or even semi-permanent measures in the face of dominant national or religious majorities.

In addition to special measures, the international instruments also contain some special rights for minorities and the persons belonging to them. The human rights instruments and case law provide for the right to physical existence as evidenced by the prohibition of genocide that is now also covered by international criminal law; the right to self-government (see below on autonomy); the right to communicate and maintain contact with fellow kin across state borders; and the right to own land that has historically been in the possession of the minority and that has been and continues to be linked to the group's culture.

Minority issues often prevail in interaction with other human rights. Building on general human rights standards, minorities thus benefit from the preservation of identity, the freedom of speech and association, language guarantees in the administration of criminal justice, and property rights, where the minority rights

[61] 429 UNTS 93 entered into force 24 October 1962.

standards alone would have been insufficient. As explained by the Human Rights Committee:

The right of individuals belonging to a linguistic minority to use their language among themselves, in private or in public, is distinct from other language rights protected under the Covenant. In particular, it should be distinguished from the general right to freedom of expression protected under article 19. The latter right is available to all persons, irrespective of whether they belong to minorities or not. Further, the right protected under article 27 should be distinguished from the particular right which article 14.3 (f) of the Covenant confers on accused persons to interpretation where they cannot understand or speak the language used in the courts. Article 14.3 (f) does not, in any other circumstances, confer on accused persons the right to use or speak the language of their choice in court proceedings.[62]

Conflicts may arise between human rights and minority rights claims. This is nothing unfamiliar; clashes arise between a variety of rights, such as between freedom of expression and privacy. In particular this may occur in connection with cultural practices of minorities, such as the equal rights of men and women, dress codes, religious practices, including the slaughtering of animals, other food traditions, traditional medicine or the abstention from medicine, and so on. As a general rule, persons belonging to minorities should respect human rights, but each case involving these types of conflict should be examined by the courts or other impartial tribunals. The best interests of the child and essential safety regulations are among the considerations that may prevail over minority cultures.

Regional human rights instruments of a general character usually provide for equal enjoyment of human rights and non-discrimination. While the regional human rights conventions do not specifically address minority-specific measures of rights, the monitoring institutions have at least been flirting with special measures.

The European Convention of Human Rights does not contain minority-specific standards, except for providing in Article 14 that membership of a national minority is one of the prohibited non-discrimination grounds. As a result, the European Court of Human Rights (ECHR) has been seized with relatively few minority rights cases. Minority issues may thus prevail in Strasbourg in interaction with other human rights. This is likely to come up in connection with the right to family life and privacy, the freedom of speech and association, due process, and the right to property. A recent judgment, *D.H. & Others v Czech Republic*, about so-called segregation in education concerning the placement of Roma children in special schools, could be indicative for the future. Here the ECHR found, relying mainly and interestingly so on statistics, that the Roma plaintiffs had been victims of discrimination under Article 14 in conjunction with Article 2 of Protocol 1.[63] It seems that the question of positive measures

[62] Para 5.3 General Comment No 23, n 14 above.

[63] Case of *D H and ors v The Czech Republic*, Application No 57325/00, judgment European Court of Human Rights, Grand Chamber, 13 November 2007.

did not arise in this particular case as the attorneys for the complainants did not make that sort of demand.

Examining the case law and other developments in Europe, one author has wondered what role the ECHR will play in the future and the possible expansion of that role.[64] With Protocol 12 to the European Convention on Human Rights, introducing a general prohibition on discrimination, in force since 2005,[65] and as the number of ratifying states grows, it is possible that the Court will increasingly have the opportunity to speak out on minority rights and employ special measures that are addressed in the explanatory report to Protocol 12. In the meantime, except for discrimination cases, the chances are that appeals to Geneva (the Human Rights Committee and the Committee on the Elimination of Racial Discrimination) are more likely to meet the demands of minorities and minority persons than going to Strasbourg (the ECHR). In addition, it is worth noting that several cases, again largely relying on non-discrimination clauses, have recently been decided by the Social Affairs Committee under the collective complaints procedure related to the European Social Charter.[66]

The two regional conventions for Africa and the Americas similarly lack minority-specific standards.[67] It does not come as a surprise therefore that the main implementation bodies, the African Commission on Human and Peoples' Rights and the Inter-American Commission and Court of Human Rights, have only sporadically addressed minority rights. There has been a debate as to whether the peoples' rights provisions of the African Charter on Human and Peoples' Rights could be interpreted and applied to indigenous and tribal peoples, but the answers are hardly conclusive yet.[68]

As far as minority-specific standards are concerned, regional organizations in Europe, both the Council of Europe and the Organization for Security and Co-operation in Europe (OSCE), have adopted instruments expressly calling for special measures in order for minority persons to achieve equal enjoyment in law and in fact.

As mentioned above, the Council of Europe has adopted the European Charter on Regional or Minority Languages and the Framework Convention for the Protection of National Minorities (FCNM). These two treaties have nevertheless been seen as something of a disappointment.[69] One would have expected

[64] G Pentassuglia, 'Inside and Outside the European Convention: The Cases of Minorities Compared', 6 *Baltic Yearbook of International Law* (2006) 263.

[65] ETS No 177. [66] n 82 below.

[67] The African Charter on Human and Peoples Rights 1981, and the American Convention on Human Rights 1969.

[68] F Ouguergouz, *The African Charter on Human and Peoples' Rights. A Comprehensive Agenda for Human Dignity and Sustainable Democracy in Africa* (2003) 209–11.

[69] G Alfredsson, 'A Frame with an Incomplete Painting: Comparison of the Framework Convention for the Protection of National Minorities with International Standards and Monitoring Procedures', 7 *International Journal on Minority and Group Rights* (2000) 4, 291–304. For a response, see F Stekete, 'The Framework Convention: A Piece of Art or a Tool for Action', 8 *International Journal on Minority and Group Rights* (2001) 1, 1–15.

more from an organization with democratic member states, a first class human rights record, a strong emphasis on the rule of law, and an advanced system of monitoring institutions. Instead, the Council of Europe minority-specific texts focus on state actions and state choices rather than the rights of minorities and their members. The Advisory Committee in charge of monitoring compliance with the FCNM has to rely on state reports and is not authorized to receive complaints, but fortunately the Committee has demonstrated willingness and ability to come forward with a series of meaningful recommendations.[70]

Likewise, as mentioned above and below, the OSCE has adopted several relevant reports and documents of a minority-specific character where, also in line with the security purpose of the Organization, minority rights figure as one of the tools available for preventing violent conflicts.

8. Special Measures in the Field of Political Rights

The political rights of minorities, both representation and participation, constitute an essential aspect relevant to all of their other rights. Political and legislative processes, both national and local, have a crucial bearing on the realization of human and minority rights, including and perhaps especially those relating to initiative and control over identity, culture, language, and education. These areas are also often the subject of delegation to minority autonomies.

Special measures are often necessary to guarantee minority participation in national politics, particularly when policies and decisions may affect the destiny of the group. States have a choice between a variety of measures, but the aim and result must be equal enjoyment of political rights. The measures may include giving groups power disproportionate to their size, in order to ensure at least fair influence and consultation on political issues.

Special political measures can include the requirement that governments obtain consent from or engage in meaningful consultations with minority groups about matters affecting them; constitutional or legislative recognition of minority laws and customs and their application by the groups; guaranteed seats or observer status for minorities in legislative assemblies and municipal and other public institutions; and the appointment of officials chosen by the group to either specific positions or to a fixed, proportional percentage of positions in general. Solutions must also be found for small groups that do not have the necessary numbers for representation; this can be accomplished through, for example, observer status or access to parliamentary and municipal committees. One must

[70] For an analysis of the accumulated observations and recommendations of the Advisory Committee, see M Weller (ed), *The Rights of Minorities. A Commentary on the European Framework Convention for the Protection of National Minorities* (2005). See also the website of the Council of Europe at <http://www.coe.int/T/E/human_rights/minorities>.

remember that the state is there for its entire population, that is the people, and not just for the national or ethnic majority.

Paragraph 35 of Part IV of the Document from the 1990 Copenhagen Meeting of the OSCE Conference on the Human Dimension provides that the participating states must give persons belonging to minorities sufficient opportunity to participate in public affairs and to protect and promote their identity. Furthermore, the same paragraph notes:

> the efforts undertaken to protect and create conditions for the promotion of the ethnic, cultural, linguistic and religious identity of certain national minorities by establishing, as one of the possible means to achieve these aims, appropriate local or autonomous administrations corresponding to the specific historical and territorial circumstances of such minorities in accordance with the policies of the State concerned.[71]

Autonomy is one of the best guarantees a minority can wish for.[72] It has been successfully implemented in many states, by this author's estimate in about 100 states, albeit with many variations in form and content. The reference may be to autonomy, self-government, self-governance, tribal or traditional government, self-management, home rule, the delegation of powers to a municipal authority with an expanded set of functions, or even internal self-determination (as distinct from the external dimension). The label ought not to matter as long as central governments agree to share power in a meaningful way and to leave local matters in the hands of group representatives. Other countries continue to resist this type of arrangement for either the usual reasons of discrimination or for fear of secession, or both.

On the basis of the Copenhagen Document convened under the auspices of the OSCE High Commissioner on National Minorities, an expert group adopted in 1999, after a series of meetings, the Lund Recommendations on the Effective Participation of National Minorities in Public Life.[73] A shorter title would have been recommendations on the political rights of minorities. In Chapter III on self-governance, the Lund Recommendations outline the minimum functions and institutions foreseen for such governance.

The real delegation of power and allowing a group to control its own local and internal affairs, including those affected by special measures, is an effective way of protecting group dignity, identity, and diverse customs and thus places minorities on an equal footing with other parts of society. State practice varies considerably when it comes to the autonomous institutions and the delegated functions. The institutions would usually involve an elected assembly and an executive but

71 For the text of the Copenhagen Document see <http://www.osce.org/odihr/documents.html>.

72 L B Sohn, 'The Concept of Autonomy in International Law and the Practice of the United Nations', 15 Israel Law Review (1980) 180–90; and M Suksi (ed) *Autonomy: Applications and Implications* (1998).

73 For the text, see <http://www.osce.org/documents/hcnm/1999/09/2698_en.pdf>. See also K Myntti, *A Commentary to the Lund Recommendations on the Effective Participation of National Minorities in Public Life* (2001).

rarely a judiciary. Paragraphs 18 and 20 of the Lund Recommendations list some of the minimum functions foreseen. It is also pointed out, in paragraph 15, that the central authorities will generally be in charge of 'defence, foreign affairs, immigration and customs, macro-economic policy and monetary matters'.

Under the Lund Recommendations and in the practice of states, self-governance can be both non-territorial and territorial. If a minority group's members are spread over a large area and/or are intermixed with other population groups, non-territorial or personal autonomy, meaning membership of and participation in the group's political institutions regardless of residence, is a legitimate and workable solution that will benefit all the parties. This avenue, which is intentionally listed first in the Lund Recommendations, is likely to reduce the fear of secession, as an internal border is not necessary. If a group is concentrated in one area, a territorial arrangement becomes a feasible option. In addressing autonomy, the Lund Recommendations employ the term self-governance; the use of the term self-determination never appears.

Autonomy is by its very nature a group right (see above on individual and group rights). The collective minority entity claims the right, enjoys it and through its institutions runs the local administration. In exercising its powers, the minority group regime must respect democratic principles and other universally recognized human rights. The group should thus protect not only the rights of its own members but also those of other population groups. Cultural practices may have to give way to human rights on issues like representative leadership and equality of the sexes. Autonomy must also be exercised in a manner consistent with other principles of international law relating to, for example, the sovereignty, territorial integrity and national unity of states and the maintenance of international peace and security.

9. National Implementation

As is the case with human rights, states carry the primary responsibility for implementing the minority rights standards to which they have subscribed. When it comes to minority rights, not least because of the groups' vulnerabilities, constitutional law provisions would seem the most desirable approach, otherwise legislation and administrative decrees. Remedies through access to courts and other national institutions must be available to both persons belonging to minorities and the minority groups in pursuit of their rights, as is the case with other human rights. The minority rights practice of states should, of course, be subject to international monitoring.

One should also keep in mind, just as dialogues with minority groups have become a welcome additional tool for the international organizations, that talking together should also take place at the national level. At the request of the former Working Group on Minorities, the OHCHR prepared a draft pamphlet for guiding minorities in their dealings with national human rights institutions.[74] The model foreseen in Article 14, paragraph 2, of the International Convention on the Elimination of All Forms of Racial Discrimination could also work well in minority situations.[75] The fora could be presidential roundtables, parliamentary committees, or bodies under the executive branch, but they need to include serious and independent minority representation and to be guided by a sense of justice, fairness, and professionalism.

An essential tool for the realization of minority rights is education for majorities and other minorities about each population group and about minority rights. Such education is so important that it could be seen as a pre-condition for overcoming the ignorance and arrogance that often characterize official reactions to minority rights, and thus lead to the successful implementation of those rights. The international human rights instruments call for such education, but it is sorely lacking in most states.

International and regional standards with accompanying monitoring procedures are helpful only if people know about them. States are obligated to educate the public about human rights.[76] According to Article 26 of the Universal Declaration, Article 13 of the Covenant on Economic, Social and Cultural Rights, and many other instruments, education and particularly human rights education shall promote understanding, tolerance, and friendship among nations and racial, ethnic, and religious groups and further UN activities for the maintenance of peace. In 1995, the United Nations proclaimed a Decade of Human Rights Education for promotional purposes, followed by yet another world-wide programme to the same end.[77] A lot more concrete work is essential because lack of knowledge and understanding often leads to inter-communal distrust, prejudices, and tensions.

10. International Monitoring

Persuasion is often needed for pushing states towards compliance with international human rights and minority rights standards, and international and

[74] Minorities and National Institutions for the Promotion and Protection of Human Rights, in UN Doc E/CN4/Sub2/AC5/2005/3. See also pt 11 (Institutional Trends) below.

[75] Art 14.2: 'Any State Party which makes a declaration as provided for in paragraph 1 of this article may establish or indicate a body within its national legal order which shall be competent to receive and consider petitions from individuals and groups of individuals within its jurisdiction who claim to be victims of a violation of any of the rights set forth in this Convention and who have exhausted other available local remedies.'

[76] G Alfredsson, 'The Right to Human Rights Education', in A Eide and ors (eds), *Economic, Social and Cultural Rights. A Textbook* (2001) 273–88.

[77] The United Nations Decade for Human Rights Education (1995–2004), GA Res 49/184 of 23 December 1994; World Programme for Human Rights Education (2005–ongoing), GA Res 59/113 of 10 December 2004.

regional organizations employ a variety of institutions and procedures. The methods for monitoring compliance range from confrontation and embarrassment to dialogue and cooperation, including complaints procedures under both treaties and resolutions, investigative and fact-finding mandates, state reporting obligations, and public debates with the consequent political and diplomatic pressure. These rely on the embarrassment factor through the naming and shaming of countries if their behaviour does not live up to the international standards. On the softer side, dialogue functions,[78] good offices undertaken by high officials of international organizations, and technical assistance and advisory services are less controversial and more cooperative in their execution.

All of these procedures have been used on behalf of minorities, but the focus below is on (a) those human rights monitoring instances which have been or are likely to be used by minorities and (b) monitoring instances that have been created specifically to address with minority rights.

Having said that, in light of the frequency of minority problems, it must also be stated that human rights monitoring bodies and political organs have paid scant attention to many minorities in trouble, and when they do pay attention, they are at best inefficient. Situations facing Basques, Berbers, Kurds, Roma, Tamils, and West-Irians, just to mention a few, have gone largely unnoticed and have not been effectively addressed by intergovernmental organizations. Several exceptions relate to situations where states, for reasons of domestic or international politics, aggressively follow up on given situations, often abroad, but unfortunately such efforts do not always build or rely on minority rights and when they purport to do so, may give them a bad name. Still, monitoring and dialogue institutions have increasingly become available and relevant.

A. Monitoring Compliance with Human Rights

Some expert committees created by human rights treaties can receive complaints concerning alleged violations of minority rights. The Human Rights Committee has delivered a few significant decisions, as mentioned above, that have given additional meaning to the right to culture in Article 27 of the ICCPR. Under one petition procedure, the under-utilized Article 14 of the International Convention on the Elimination of All Forms of Racial Discrimination, both groups and individuals can file complaints for consideration by the Committee on the Elimination of Racial Discrimination (CERD).

A complaints procedure under the UN Human Rights Council (formerly known as the 1503-procedure governed by Economic and Social Council Resolution 1503 (XLVIII) as subsequently amended) allows individuals and groups to submit complaints demonstrating a consistent pattern of gross human

[78] On dialogue, see pt 11 (Institutional Trends) below.

rights violations.[79] The resolution is universally applicable and does not require separate ratification or acceptance of instruments. In addition, complaints procedures under human rights instruments set up by the ILO, UNESCO, the World Bank, and several regional organizations offer possible avenues for complaints by minority persons and/or minority groups.[80]

Special Rapporteurs, Special Representatives, and Independent Experts often address minority concerns in their country-specific and thematic reports to the UN Human Rights Council. The country reports have included, Guatemala, Iran, Iraq, Myanmar, Romania, Rwanda, and the former Yugoslavia, and the thematic reports include minority rights (see below), religious intolerance, racism, racial discrimination, xenophobia, and related intolerance around the world. Minority groups have easy access to the Rapporteurs, and some of the reports have included excellent suggestions.

A new monitoring procedure, the Universal Periodic Review (UPR), has commenced under the Human Rights Council.[81] The purpose is to look at and scrutinize the performance of all states, not just a select few, and thus overcome selectiveness and politicization. With diplomats in charge of carrying out much of the scrutiny, drawing the conclusions and making the recommendations, it remains to be seen how effective this new approach will be and whether or to what degree minority rights will be covered.

Committees of expert members set up under several international human rights treaties routinely question government representatives about minority rights when they present state reports. This is true for the Human Rights Committee, the Committee on the Elimination of Racial Discrimination, the Committee on the Elimination of Discrimination against Women, the Committee on Economic, Social and Cultural Rights, and the Committee on the Rights of the Child. These committees and other treaty bodies scrutinize the reports and the replies of governments and make recommendations if discrepancies are found between the human rights obligations and performances of the states concerned. Observations and recommendations made by the committees quite regularly touch upon minority rights. Minorities often supply relevant information to the treaty bodies or to their individual members in anticipation of the examination of relevant state reports.

The UN Secretary General, the UN High Commissioner for Human Rights, and director-generals of specialized agencies and regional organizations have undertaken good offices, that is, the pursuit of quiet (non-public) diplomacy for the sake of groups in distress. This action can be requested by both governments and groups, but it is unlikely to be used unless the monitoring procedures are deemed to be inadequate or too slow in the face of urgent or peace-threatening situations.

[79] A/HRC/RES/5/1 paras 85–109 and see ch 1.

[80] For accounts of these procedures see H Hannum (ed) *Guide to International Human Rights Practice* (2004).

[81] See chs 1–3.

Apart from the more formal procedures, public debates in intergovernmental fora about human rights standards and violations can attract attention and improve compliance. Governments do not welcome institutional pressure and criticism and would rather avoid the embarrassment, as has become so evident in the debate on reforms in the UN human rights programme. Discussions about minority rights in the UN Human Rights Council, the former Commission on Human Rights, and its Sub-Commission for the Promotion and Protection of Human Rights have often embarrassed governments whose records are under examination. The debates in these and other fora and under various agenda items, thus put political, diplomatic, and public pressure on governments to address minority rights issues.

References have already been made in this chapter to regional standards and mechanisms. A notable newcomer to minority rights is the European Committee on Social Rights which, under its collective complaints procedure, has in recent years decided a number of cases.[82]

B. Monitoring Compliance with Minority Rights

As minority rights are part of human rights, obviously persons belonging to minorities and occasionally the groups as such have access to and can make use of the monitoring institutions and procedures set up for human rights in general. Some of the best monitoring results have been achieved in this manner, as is evidenced by the case law of the Human Rights Committee. In addition, in a few instances, monitoring institutions and procedures have been created for minority rights in particular.

In 2005, the UN Commission on Human Rights requested the High Commissioner for Human Rights to appoint an Independent Expert on Minority Issues (IEMI).[83] The Expert reports to the Human Rights Council under the umbrella of the special procedures, but the general state reluctance over minority rights is notable in her mandate (research rather than investigation) and title (issues rather than rights and Expert rather than Rapporteur). The Expert's mandate is to promote the implementation of the 1992 Declaration, to identify best practices, and to explore technical cooperation. Her early reports are promising.[84] In 2004, drawing on Security Council Resolution 1366/2001, the former Secretary General appointed a Special Adviser on the Prevention of Genocide, a position which has a direct and obvious bearing on respect for minority rights. The present Secretary General, Ban Ki-moon, made the position full-time in 2007.[85]

[82] See <http://www.coe.int> under Human Rights and Monitoring.

[83] Res 2005/79, 21 April 2005. The Expert appointed is Gay McDougall.

[84] Available on the website of the UN High Commissioner for Human Rights at <http://www2.ohchr.org/english/issues/minorities/expert/index.htm>.

[85] For additional information, see the website of the Special Adviser at <http://www.un.org/depts/dpa/prev_genocide>. In May 2007, Francis Deng succeeded Juan Mendes as Special Adviser.

11. Institutional Trends

This survey of minority rights in international human rights law leaves a picture of fragmented and scattered standards and monitoring procedures. The standards are set forth in multiple instruments, where both overlaps and gaps (eg, the definition of terms) and inconsistencies (eg, the question of individual and group rights) occur. Likewise, the several monitoring institutions are thinly spread; they have in recent years brought about few new developments and overall they produce remarkably few cases. In other words, there are few trends, just more of the same, with perhaps a few exceptions. Promising if limited institutional trends relate to dialogue functions as well as other cooperative approaches, and increased case law from two treaty bodies. Less promising is the cancelling of the UN Working Group on Minorities and its replacement with what looks like a weaker forum.

Documents adopted at OSCE gatherings, for the purpose of confidence-building and prevention, contain far-reaching minority rights provisions building upon the principles of non-discrimination and special measures set forth in order to keep the peace. They favour an approach to minority rights that centres on dialogue between the parties and institutions for encouraging and facilitating the same. The OSCE High Commissioner on National Minorities (HCNM) has such a substantive mandate to involve both groups and governments in dialogue in order to prevent violent conflicts.[86]

The HCNM has been quite successful in conducting dialogues in a number of countries thanks primarily to the first High Commissioner, Max van der Stoel of the Netherlands. His successors, Rolf Ekeus of Sweden and Knut Vollebaek of Norway, have held up the banner in more difficult and less understanding political circumstances. The discussions constitute quiet diplomacy so it is not always known what dialogues are underway or how successful they are or have been; suffice it to say that there is enough evidence to indicate that they have made a significant difference in several situations of tension and potential conflict. Furthermore, the HCNM has elaborated and promoted standards through a series of recommendations and documents that have been drafted and adopted by expert meetings rather than by governmental gatherings. This approach has enabled standards to be more detailed and suggest larger steps forward than some of the other international instruments.

The dialogue approach was for a while increasingly influential at the United Nations. Article 9 of the 1992 Declaration on the Rights of Persons belonging to

The title of the position was changed to Special Representative of the Secretary General on the Prevention of Genocide and Mass Atrocities, see Letter dated 31 August 2007 from the Secretary General addressed to the President of the Security Council, S/2007/721.

[86] See J Packer, 'The OSCE High Commissioner on National Minorities: Pyrometer, Prophylactic, Pyrosvestis' in N Ghanea and A Xanthaki (eds), n 8 above, at 249–68.

National or Ethnic, Religious and Linguistic Minorities,[87] declared that organizations of the UN system have a role to play in 'the full realization of the rights and principles' set forth in the Declaration, and it expressly ties minority rights together with the 'development of society as a whole and within a democratic framework based on the rule of law'.

In a report to the former Sub-Commission on Prevention of Discrimination and Protection of Minorities, Special Rapporteur Asbjörn Eide of Norway dealt with constructive national arrangements for minorities based on human rights.[88] Such arrangements would improve the relations between majorities and minorities and inspire legislators, judges, and other national leaders to achieve equal rights, particularly equal political representation, and to avoid ethnic conflicts.

In 1995, as a result of Eide's report, the Commission on Human Rights authorized the establishment of a Working Group on Minorities (WGM). It reviewed compliance with the 1992 Declaration, considered solutions to problems, promoted mutual understanding between groups and governments, and recommended measures for the protection of minority rights. At its 12 sessions, the WGM considered ideas such as the facilitation of national conciliation machineries and the establishment and promotion of dialogues between the parties involved, both with a view to providing early warning and preventing conflicts. Minorities and their representatives had free access to the WGM and could freely speak and submit documents at its meetings. The WGM met annually in Geneva and reported to the Sub-Commission, but in 2006, having come under review by the UN Human Rights Council in connection with the ongoing reform of the UN human rights programme, it was abolished along with its parent body, the Sub-Commission.

By Resolution 6/15, the UN Human Rights Council established a Forum on Minority Issues.[89] Its purpose is to provide a platform for promoting dialogue and cooperation on issues pertaining to persons belonging to national or ethnic, religious, and linguistic minorities, to identify and analyse best practices, challenges, opportunities, and initiatives for the further implementation of the 1992 Declaration, to contribute to dialogue and the promotion of inclusive and stable societies at the national level, and to provide thematic contributions and expertise to the work of the Independent Expert on Minority Issues (IEMI) who is in charge of forwarding any recommendations of the Forum to the Council.

This Forum on Minority Issues will convene for the first time in December 2008. While the Forum is open to minority participation and while the mandate looks impressive, it will meet only for two to three days a year; it does not have regular expert or other members from the five regions so in that respect continuity will be lacking, and it will channel ideas and suggestions to the IEMI, not directly to the parent body as was the case with the WGM. One must wait for

[87] GA Res 47/135 of 18 December 1992. [88] n 5 above.
[89] See Hadden, n 21 above.

some years before determining how successful the new arrangement will be in terms of dialogue functions or thematic recommendations. There would seem to be little doubt that both the Working Group on Minorities, and together with it the Working Group on Indigenous Populations, were abolished as they generated too much trouble and embarrassment to governments.[90]

Minority rights are from time to time included in international and bilateral technical cooperation programmes in the field of human rights. Mainly upon requests by governments, assistance is available for minority rights training and teaching, for the review of existing legislation or the drafting of bills of rights and other laws which conform to international standards, and for the creation of national infrastructures which safeguard minority rights. Ideally, technical assistance should be made available not only to states, but also to minority groups in cooperation or with the consent of national governments. In particular, for the prevention and resolution of violent conflicts, all parties need to be involved if the technical assistance is to bring the desired results.

Also encouraging as an institutional trend is the case law from the Human Rights Committee under the International Covenant on Civil and Political Rights and the European Committee on Social Rights. The two treaty bodies, under their respective complaints procedures, have decided several cases that constitute progress and advancement for minority rights. There is every reason to encourage minority persons, minorities, and organizations representing them to make more active use of these bodies. The same is true for other treaty bodies such as the Committee on the Elimination of Racial Discrimination and the Committee on the Elimination of Discrimination against Women, that operate under human rights treaties with substantive provisions and complaints avenues that could benefit minorities.

In all of these endeavours, the role of non-governmental organizations is critical for the promotion and protection of minority rights. NGOs perform a wide variety of relevant functions, including carrying out research and fact-finding activities, informing and educating the public, generating public support, contributing to policy-making and legislative debates at all levels, pressuring governments to live up to their obligations, speaking up and speaking out on violations and abuses when governments and international organizations are ineffective or even silent, and bringing such issues to the attention of international and regional monitoring bodies, in particular their complaints and investigative procedures.

Since minorities and their representatives often have limited opportunities to access intergovernmental fora, NGOs serve a crucial role in bringing minority issues to the attention of the international organizations and their monitoring instances. Well-known international NGOs are actively involved in minority

[90] Under Human Rights Council Res 6/36 of 14 December 2007, an Expert Mechanism on the Rights of Indigenous Peoples was established. This new forum replaces the Working Group on Indigenous Populations that was established by ECOSOC Res 1982/34. The WGIP was also a subsidiary body of the Sub-Commission on the Promotion and Protection of Human Rights.

rights, in particular Minority Rights Group International (MRG),[91] as well as Amnesty International, Article 19, Human Rights Watch, and the International Helsinki Federation for Human Rights. All regularly report on issues concerning minority rights. The accumulation of NGO information, together with views expressed by intergovernmental fact-finders and observers, strongly indicates that many states in all parts of the world are experiencing difficulties in fulfilling their commitments on minority rights.

12. Conclusion

Loyalty is a two-way street; states must be loyal to all persons within their jurisdictions, including persons belonging to minorities, who in turn should be loyal to the state in which they live. The initiative should rest with the state as the stronger party. Nationalism and the drive to preserve identities are strong forces and they apply in equal measure to nation-states and to minorities. States cannot, in the long run, ignore or suppress minority sentiments as oppression breeds violence.

With thousands of distinct minority groups, the idea of one state for every group is far from the political reality. Groups without states are vulnerable in a community of nation-states, they resent and resist assimilation through nation-building, and situations involving them are a frequent source of friction within, and even between, states. The consequences of discriminatory practices are evidenced by the large number of ethnic conflicts of a violent nature, or the threat of the same, and by continued secession movements in many countries with ethnic, linguistic, or religious undertones.

Interestingly, the sum total of international standard-setting, monitoring, and conciliatory efforts may surpass that of most national legal systems. Many states are reluctant partners in this work. Despite commitments to minority rights in international and regional instruments, government policies and practices are still heavily influenced by the ideas of sovereignty and national unity. Outdated 'nation-state' concepts often reduce minorities to second class members of society. And states have so far not shared the benefits of globalization and integration with their minority populations.

Minority rights aim to achieve equal enjoyment of all human rights and non-discrimination in that enjoyment, with the support of special measures and special rights. The measures and rights have been further developed by reports by governments to international organizations, studies and reports by Special Rapporteurs, views of other monitoring organs, the work of NGOs, and academic literature. National practices in a handful of countries also provide sources

[91] For information about the multiple activities of MRG, see the organization's website at <http://www.minorityrights.org>.

of inspiration. Special measures and various methods of conflict prevention and resolution may need better elaboration and more detailed standards, but much could be accomplished under currently available instruments if they were applied, as intended, on the basis of the rule of law, objectivity, impartiality, judicial or quasi-judicial review, and international scrutiny.

As stated above, the very idea of minority rights in international law is the continued sovereignty and territorial integrity of states. By guaranteeing equal rights to everyone within states, and by prohibiting discrimination and providing special measures and special rights as tools for realizing equal rights, the intention is to improve the quality of life and to keep minorities content within the states, thus avoiding separatist claims and tensions that may lead to violent conflicts.

Much work remains to be done. Governments must learn to recognize the benefits of tolerance and pluralism. The will of the people is not only the will of the majority; for governments to be representative, they must also respect the rights of minorities. It is important to bear in mind, and it is too often forgotten, that the realization of minority rights is intended to benefit all parties. This will be the case provided geo-political interests like those of kin-states or large powers do not enter the picture. States gain political and social stability and economic prosperity; the groups preserve their identities and improve the quality of life for individual members; and the international organizations maintain peace and stability which, after all, is the major reason for their existence.

Index

Lightning Source UK Ltd.
Milton Keynes UK
UKOW030624140313

207621UK00013B/335/P

9 780199 570546